S0-BKW-149

BETTER WINES
FOR
LESS MONEY

WINE INSTITUTE LIBRARY

BETTER WINES
FOR
LESS MONEY

Nathaniel Korshin

STEIN AND DAY/*Publishers*/New York

663.2
K84

First published in 1974
Copyright © 1974 by Nathaniel.Korshin
Library of Congress Catalog Card No. 73-02191
Designed by David Miller
Printed in the United States of America
Stein and Day/*Publishers*/Scarborough House, Briarcliff Manor, New York 10510
ISBN 0-8128-1692-7

2907

8/19/74 — Edelman Agency -
Gift (7.95)

To Carolyn

My warmest thanks go to

Mrs. Marguerite L. Bodycombe, who knows
better than anyone else how invaluable her help
has been

Mr. Richard W. Hoag, of the Berenson Liquor
Mart, whose guidance has been so unstintingly
and generously given

Mr. Joey Ullmann, of Leonard Kreusch, Inc., for
so freely making available to me whatever I
required of his professional knowledge and

those of my family and friends who encouraged
me when in doubt and who shared my wine
tasting and bore my enthusiasms with fortitude

Contents

... Credo che molto felicità sia agli homini che nascono dove si trovano i vini buoni. (... I believe that much happiness awaits those who are born where good wines are found.)

—Leonardo da Vinci

Introduction

WINE HAS BECOME BIG BUSINESS IN THE UNITED STATES. EVERY DAY advertisements appear in the daily press and in magazines for the sale of wines. More than one magazine devotes itself entirely to wine. Articles on the subject appear, for example, in such widely different publications as the first issue of *Oui*, a "girlie" magazine, *New York*, a consumer-oriented magazine, *Barron's*, a highly respected financial and stock market publication, and *Time* magazine.

The public reads of fabulous prices paid for single bottles of wine, up to $4,000 and $5,000 per bottle. Almost everybody knows by now the name of Château Lafite Rothschild and the prices it fetches. A single bottle of the 1961 vintage can be bought nowadays at the trifling cost of $160 or so.

The reader is flooded with vintages: good years, poor years, miraculous years; wonderful in Burgundy but only ordinary in Bordeaux, different for the Loire Valley than for the Rhône Valley, for Germany than for its neighbor, Alsace—and so on, to utter confusion.

How does the serious or would-be serious wine drinker of limited means cut through this maze? It does him no good to learn that many wealthy Texans drink only Château Lafite

Rothschild. It does him no good to study the article in the "girlie" magazine, which suggests a wine cellar of 100 bottles of wine, which sold for an average of $7.50 to $8 per bottle in the fall of 1972, but go for much, much more now. True, there is a two-page spread picturing the actual 100 bottles, almost as eye-catching as the more numerous spreads depicting naked women. The cost of the wines listed, however, remains the same—too high for the average drinker.

He will get no help from the *Barron's* article, which deals with wine purely as a speculation and ignores the fact that it is illegal for the consumer to resell wine without a license. Certainly, enormous profits can and will undoubtedly be made from wine, but by the dealers, not the consumer. Only dealers have the financing, the storage facilities, and the resale license to enable them to speculate and thus make profits. For the drinker, this means no more than a continual round of higher prices.

The reader will get a good amount of guidance from some of the articles in *New York* magazine. But even those that deal quite directly with where to buy specific lower-priced wines usually assume a body of basic knowledge that many, perhaps most, wine drinkers do not have and that the novice certainly lacks. And there are many novices, more and more all the time, who would really like to know.

Actually, wine is nothing new or recent in America. Benjamin Franklin had a wine cellar of almost 1,000 bottles. Mark Twain enjoyed champagne parties in the 1860s—in Carson City, Nevada, not in a big Eastern city.

Somehow, partly because of Prohibition, America was sidetracked away from wine and led on to hard liquor. Now the pendulum has begun to swing back. Nor is this new thirst at all restricted to the East Coast and California, as some from those areas like to believe. Everywhere in the United States, more and more people are beginning to experience the delights of wine.

The Wine Institute reports that per capita consumption of

all wines in the United States in 1972 was about 1.6 gallons. Industry estimates for 1980 are 1.79 gallons per person, and for 1990, 2.4 gallons. (Some professionals estimate much higher, as high as almost 3 gallons per capita, 650 million gallons, as early as 1980.) This may not sound very impressive, especially if compared with per capita consumption in France and Italy, where the figure is roughly 30 gallons per person annually. Still, it amounts to some 337 million gallons in 1972 and would come to about 650 million in 1990, if not much sooner.

Today's wine drinkers will no doubt drink more. Many new drinkers are coming and will come onstage. They know little or nothing about wine and certainly want to know such things as what wines to buy at prices they can afford, the comparative merits of imported and domestic wines, how to go about selecting, how to store and handle bottles, and how much of the extensive tradition (and pseudo-lore) of wine they need to know or whether it should be disregarded altogether.

This book is devoted to answering these and many other questions with the aim of helping the reader to learn how better to enjoy wine. There is much to enjoy. Buying can be fun. Collecting is a hobby. Serving can add pleasure. Even drinking is not the culmination. Pleasant recollections and comparing notes with other wine buffs is part of the delightful process.

Despite the constant emphasis on "vintage" wines at higher prices, there is available in great quantity good, comparatively inexpensive wine from many countries. This book concerns itself, on the whole, with those that can be bought at up to about $4 a bottle, with most emphasis on those in the price range of $2.50 to $3.50. Occasionally, a wine costing up to $5 will be mentioned.

The reader should not suppose that he is thus limited to mediocre, run-of-the-mill wines. A good many quite excellent wines can be bought for about $3, and at under and just over $4, a few of the great wines of the world can still be found. A distinction is made between inexpensive and cheap. A cheap wine is not worth drinking at any price. An inexpensive one is always good value and it is frequently exceptional.

A further distinction is necessary. By wine is meant table, aperitif, dessert, and sparkling wine, and in all cases, grape wine. Fruit wines, "mod" and "pop" wines, and the various weird concoctions advertised under names more suitable for automobiles and tourist attractions are not included, any more than is Coke or 7-Up.

There are many aspects of the story of wine that this work is not intended to cover. There will be no detailed geographical descriptions of winemaking areas nor topographical details of vineyards, no mention of which hillside faces in what direction, and no eulogistic travelogs about ancient tree-lined towns in the wine country. The reader will not learn from this volume on which hillside an angel shed a tear, thus causing the vine to grow, or who said about which wine that it should be drunk kneeling, with the head bared. At the prices this wine fetches today, it would be more appropriate, anyhow, for all but the rich to drink it groveling, with empty pockets turned inside out.

The history of wine goes back to pre-biblical times. The tale of the wines and vineyards of the world is fascinating. Many excellent volumes have been written on all aspects of the subject. This book concerns itself only with limited discussions of wine regions, types, and characteristics necessary to equip the reader to begin to find his way through the intricacies of a complex subject. For those who wish to learn more, a Bibliography appears at the end of this volume. In fact, it is strongly recommended that the subject be pursued further. More knowledge will always mean more pleasure.

Some twenty years ago, I was virtually ignorant about wine. I knew almost nothing besides the difference between red and white. Once in a while, I happened on a wine that was really enjoyable instead of hardly bearable. For many reasons I became interested in knowing more. I began to buy and try a variety of wines chosen more or less at random, with an eye mostly on price. I started to keep a few bottles in my basement. After a time I would actually buy a whole case now and then. I read books on wine, I studied, I learned.

I am still learning today. Nobody knows all there is to know about wine. But my knowledge has become substantial, I believe, and the few bottles have long since grown into a cellar of hundreds of bottles with considerable variety. Looking back on this long educational process, I realize how much I would have appreciated and profited from the guidance of someone more knowledgeable.

It is the feeling that this painstakingly acquired body of information can prove of value to many other beginners or near-beginners that prompted me to write this volume. The approach has been to consider the reader a complete neophyte. Some of what is contained herein may therefore prove somewhat elementary to the more sophisticated, but I believe that they, too, will find much that is worthwhile.

I have listed herein a goodly number of the best wine shops in the country, but I make no claim to knowing all of them in every community. Anyone who is, or wishes to be, a serious wine drinker, however, will be able to ferret out the various good shops in his area after reading this book. The classified telephone directory, plus some attention to advertising in the local press, coupled with the guidance given herein as to how to choose a wine shop, should suffice.

In recommending specific wines I have included many that have broad regional or national distribution. There is no single shop anywhere in the country, not even any single city, where every one of these will be available, but every reader will find enough recommended ones in his own area to provide him with far more choices than he actually needs.

Whitestone, New York
October, 1973

PART I

Economics and Attitudes

WINE IS A COMMODITY, BOUGHT AND SOLD LIKE ANY OTHER, AND SUB-
ject to the same economic influences that affect everything else
we buy. The three most potent factors in the past three years or
so have been dollar devaluations, inflation, and product scarcity.

Two devaluations of the dollar have had no effect on
domestically produced wines but have increased the cost of
imported wines, simply because they have decreased the buying power of the dollar abroad.

Inflation is by now a familiar, if unwelcome, part of American life, and its effect on prices needs no comment here. It
should not be forgotten, however, that the higher cost of
imported wine results from inflation both here and abroad, a
sort of double-barreled attack on prices.

Product scarcity has for a long time been a prime factor in
the high cost of the great wines. Greater affluence in many
countries as well as the increase of wine drinking all over the
world is now having a distinct effect also on wines of good and
fine quality.

And let us not forget another factor—greed. It is not exactly
unknown in human history, nor in business in general, nor in

the wine business in particular. I have been made aware of a few shocking instances of greed during 1973, and I am in no way involved in the wine business so I know very little of all that occurs within the industry. Whatever I have noticed has occurred in Europe and here in the distributing end. The American retail wine establishment is singularly free of it. I know of many real, cut-price sales in the midst of the price spiral, of more than one dealer who has not raised given prices until long after the distributor has done so. The wine buyer can take much comfort from this. But the wine shops' forbearance merely helps a little, and temporarily. It solves nothing.

The industry has been trying to alleviate the pinch in more ways than one. It has hunted out and promoted some wines that were "sleepers," excellent but somewhat overlooked. They are "sleepers" no longer. It has been importing French "country" wines and other lesser wines. (Many not all, seem to be lesser because they deserve to be and some are not even low cost.) It has been emphasizing wines of some countries whose wines have been little known here.

The wine dealers can be relied on to bring in more moderate-priced wines. The retailer knows the customer's gripes at first hand. He is all too familiar with the gasps of those who ask the prices of the more expensive wines. He knows the danger of tying up large blocs of cash in a few cases of wines that may move slowly at today's prices. He prefers low and medium prices because they make happy customers, and he likes happy customers.

What is the outlook for the future? To be able to forecast with any certainty would require far better economists than the best available nationally, considering how they have done with (or "to") our economy. But it does not require more than some informed common sense to look intelligently into the near future.

For all I know, the present pace of worldwide inflation could end in another worldwide depression. If that were lamentably to happen, good wine could be bought for pennies, if you had the pennies. Let us not contemplate calamities.

As this is being written, the dollar has been strengthening since midsummer of 1973 in relation to European currencies. As a result, existing prices of imported wines may hold steady for some months. It would be a welcome change. Depending on the performance of the dollar, some prices might, just might, conceivably move down a bit. What a luxury to contemplate.

But beyond such a brief respite, there is every reason to believe that inflation will continue here and abroad and that the trend in wine prices will be upward, albeit perhaps slowly. One thing is certain in my mind. The era of low wine prices, for they were low, is over as surely as, we are told, the era of low food prices.

Perhaps the present $20 wine that sold for $5 as recently as 1971 may come down to, let us say, $15 to $16 if demand for it decreases enough, but that is as much as I think can be hoped for—and it is of no help to the buyer of modest means. Perhaps the whole crazy structure of $50 to $150 or more per bottle for the great wines will come tumbling down soon, as it certainly should and sometime will. It depends only on how long people can be found who are foolish enough to pay such prices. When that does happen, it will not benefit the modest buyer either.

The American consumer of wine needs a complete rethinking of his entire attitude toward wine drinking. Until recently, the average drinker was a person of at least moderate means. The best wines of the entire world were arrayed before him at prices that suddenly seem ridiculously low, and were, indeed, low. In December, 1972, one of the great Bordeaux of the 1967 vintage sold at $6.50 per bottle. Today it is just under $20. A case of a great 1970 Bordeaux cost $46 in September, 1971 (less than $4 per bottle), and is now selling for $19 per bottle. Yes, low indeed!

Of course you or I can decide not to compromise with quality and insist on buying only the best. I can't be sure of you, but I know that, in that case, what I can afford to spend on wine would only buy me bottles, not cases, and very few bottles, at that. I have little doubt that I'd choke on each sip.

The realistic alternative is to recognize finally, and firmly, that we've been badly spoiled, that the halcyon days are over, and that we'd better start buying wine intelligently. Nor do I mean by this that we merely declare poor to be good, good to be fine, and fine, great. That kind of thinking belongs in Gilbert and Sullivan. I mean that we recognize that there is a simply enormous variety of wines other than the mere handful of French and German ones that are accepted as great, and that many among these are actually good and fine, and even, occasionally, great, and yet within our means. Only a snob turns up his nose at the excellent wines of countries other than France and Germany.

Most of us have no trouble living our entire lifetimes without owning, or hoping to own, a Rolls-Royce or even a Cadillac or Continental. We manage very well with lower-priced cars that afford us adequate prestige, to say nothing of less costly transportation. An enormous number of women manage to be extremely well dressed without ever buying a couturier gown at $1,000 or so.

It should be the same way with wine. Almost always it has been so with me and I have derived tremendous pleasure from it. There is no reason why every American wine drinker should not follow the same philosophy, with resulting great enjoyment while staying within his means. Learn, and follow a few basics and leave the outrageously expensive wines to the millionaires.

A great wine at $20 is not five times as good as a fine one at $4. Perhaps it is twice as good, perhaps not. The law of diminishing returns says that a reasonable person of modest means does not pay the extra $16 for possibly only $4 more in value. Instead, he buys five bottles of the very enjoyable $4 wine and multiplies his pleasure by five.

And suppose, for that same $4, give or take a few cents, you could buy a wine virtually, perhaps literally, as good as our

$20 great. Would you buy it? That's a silly question. Such wine exists, and is not hard to find.

Of course, some definitions are required. To the wine drinker who has heretofore been able to afford the best and can perhaps still do so now, only the greats are worth drinking and all else is beneath his notice. This is snobbery of the worst kind. To me, the greats are necessarily outside my notice, but any other wine of good to excellent quality deserves my attention, if it does not cost too much.

It is worth considering how wine is drunk in the European wine-producing countries. Even the well-to-do drink the wine of the region or other modest wines for everyday consumption and finer wines only for quite special occasions. They serve the ordinary wine to guests without apology. The less-than-well-to-do drink what they can afford, which is often far less good than the poorer wines on the American market.

We do not have to emulate the European exactly. It is still only the rare American wine lover who has wine with meals, and before as well as after, virtually or literally every day. Even then he does not drink wine all day long as well, at home or at a café table, actually to quench thirst, as the Europeans do.

Very few, if any, Americans have need of an everyday wine at so low a price as to require compromise with quality. For that very reason, this volume concentrates on better-quality rather than lowest-quality wines, but at affordable prices. Here and there a fairly good wine can be found at a price that justifies its use as an everyday wine. I do not know of many, but the few that are described are my own everyday wines, for in my household wine is drunk literally every day.

Remember this: There is no need to feel diffident about buying less expensive wines. The wine industry wants and encourages it. They are worried about the high cost of wine. And for you, the wine drinker, it is plain common sense.

Which countries are likely to provide us with the best buys?

The worst offender in terms of sharp price increases has

been France. Possibly most of the rise is over, though I would not count on it. There are still a number of French wines of good to excellent quality within our price range.

It is at least probable that the price spiral on German wines has not yet ended. At any rate, as of the time of this writing, a fair number of good wines and even estate-bottled wines still fall within our range.

Italian wines have gone up much less than most others in price during the past two or three years. It has been suggested to me that this is because the Italians just aren't very good merchandisers. Could the consumer interpret merchandising to mean greed? I believe it is due in part, at least, to the fact that the lira is the weakest of West European currencies and has not risen at all in relation to the dollar since the last dollar devaluation in early 1973. In any case, Italian wines are one of the fine values on the American market today, if you know which ones to buy.

American wine prices have been, and will be, affected only by inflation in the United States, not by foreign inflation or dollar devaluation. Some very fine wines indeed are made in the United States and these, you will find, represent some of the best values available to us.

Spanish wines of various qualities, from everyday to really great, are the best value on the American market today. Prices began to rise in early 1973 and undoubtedly will rise more, but since they all started from so low a price base I believe they will remain superb buys for years to come.

There are wines of other countries that also represent best buys. To go into any detail now would be anticipating. All in due time.

PART II

How to "Use" Wine

IT MIGHT SEEM MORE LOGICAL TO START WITH WHICH WINES TO BUY. I
don't think so. Knowing what to drink is meaningless without
first being certain of what to drink it with and how to handle it
so that it will give a maximum of pleasure and enjoyment.

Wine is a highly complicated subject, not nearly so easy as
opening a bottle and pouring. It is also shrouded in a mystique
of tradition, some of it pure nonsense, but some very important to maximum enjoyment. Common sense, and an understanding both of the advantages and the limitations that modern urban life offer, are the keys to drinking pleasure that are
dealt with in this section.

Which Wines Go with What Foods?

Tradition specifies quite rigidly what to drink with what.
Books on the subject generally do the same thing. Some
catalogs of wine issued by retail wine shops have such listings
as well.

However, after giving exhaustive descriptions of wines
that match foods, it has become fashionable to end by saying

25

that this should all be ignored because the correct wine for any occasion is the one that you, the consumer, like best.

I disagree. In the final analysis, you will drink what you like best. It's your money. But what a pity if you end up drinking nothing but German white wines, or nothing but rosés. What a wealth of taste, of variety, of pleasure you will miss.

The tradition has grown out of centuries of knowledge and experience and is basically correct. Delicate foods require lighter wines. Hearty dishes call for a more robust accompaniment.

Any red wine, no matter how delicate, is too big for such dishes as omelets, seafood, or broiled fish. The wine would overpower the food and rob it of its delicate goodness.

Almost any white wine is inadequate to cope with the hearty, mouth-filling flavor of beef, a cassoulet, or such dark-meat fowl as duck and goose. The wine would be over-shadowed by the food and would taste thin and watery.

There are exceptions among white wines. They are very few. Hungarian white wines, and one or two French ones, are big enough to cope with rich foods. They will be dealt with later. In general, the relationships, the matching of wine to food, have been accurately described.

Many seek to solve the problem by drinking rosés. Rosés are widely drunk in such wine-producing countries as France, Italy, and Portugal, as well as here. But in the European countries they are drunk almost exclusively in the summertime in place of reds, during a season when the heaviest, heartiest dishes are generally avoided. They are almost never drunk during the balance of the year.

Here, however, rosés are drunk at all times on the theory that they go with everything. The obverse of the coin is that they go with nothing.

To discuss rosés properly it is necessary to understand just a little about how wines are made. Red wine is made by bruising red or purple grapes just enough to burst the skins so that the juice will flow out freely, then placing the grapes in vats, where the juice begins to ferment. The skins and pits, which finally form a rather solid mass known as must, are removed after varying periods of time, usually about three weeks. During those weeks, the must imparts the red color and many subtleties of flavor to the wine.

For white wine, the juice is pressed out of white or red grapes (with rare exceptions, the juice of all grapes, white, red, or purple, is pale in color, varying from a greenish to a golden yellow) and allowed to ferment in the vats. The resulting wine may lack some of the subtlety of the reds, but has, as a rule, the delicacy and lightness that are the outstanding characteristics of whites.

Rosé wine is made by allowing the skins of the grapes to remain in the vats just long enough to impart the characteristic pink color, a period varying from about one to three days. At the point of removal, the wine is no longer a white, free to develop its own delicacies, nor is it a red, able to grow in subtlety. It is a bastard red, if you will, a wine with arrested development.

Rosés can be perfectly pleasant to drink. They lack character. They are just as unable as white wines to cope with hearty foods, and hence are no substitute for reds. Dollar for dollar, they are almost never as good a buy as whites. They are merely the way out for those who don't wish to take the trouble to inform themselves.

Only the broad outlines of what goes with what can be established with definiteness. There is no doubt that only drier white wines go with seafood and broiled, boiled, or fried fish. But what of a spicy stew of fish, or seafood, or both, such as bouillabaisse or many Italian fish stews, especially in a tomatoey sauce? A white wine could be inadequate. It would be entirely proper to serve a light red such as Beaujolais or one of the lighter red Bordeaux. There, individual taste must take precedence over rigid rules.

Similarly, a white is clearly called for with boiled, broiled, or fried chicken. But as soon as we come to the area of roast chicken, if roasted brown, succulent, and juicy, as it can be, the light red wine becomes at least as appropriate as a white. And an arroz con pollo in the Caribbean manner, with the chicken flavor enriched, almost overpowered by the spicy chorizos, requires a light-to-medium-bodied red wine. On the other hand, a paella, because of its admixture of seafood and fish with the chicken, should have a white despite the presence of some chorizos.

Smoked ham, roast pork, veal, and turkey all fall in the indeterminate area where either a more robust white or a lighter red wine might do equally well. At the other end of the spectrum, there can be no doubt that only robust, full-flavored reds are suitable to accompany beef, duck, goose, pasta served with rich sauces, and game, if you can afford it or shoot it yourself.

Some common sense is necessary. For example, pasta with a meat sauce or tomato sauce calls for red wine only. But what of linguine or spaghetti served with clam sauce? It may be pasta, but the clams require a dry white wine. For that matter, what about spaghetti served simply with butter sauce and grated Parmesan cheese? (Some finely chopped parsley goes well with this. This is no cookbook, but a hint on cooking here and there won't hurt the reader's enjoyment of wine.) White though it may be in color, and mild in flavor, it is surprising how good a red Chianti is with it.

A bit of caution must be exercised, too. There are some foods with which wine just does not go. Foods heavily flavored with vinegar or citrus juices will make the wine taste sour. It would be a waste to serve it.

I have found, though, that a modest light red or white wine is enjoyable with a salad containing, besides greens, such foods as sardines, anchovies, tuna fish, ham, or cheese, and seasoned with a dressing containing some, not too much, vinegar. Nor does a dash of lemon on oysters or clams on the half shell appear to detract from the pleasure of a well-chilled dry white wine.

Indian food, even when not hot, is so highly spiced that the subtleties of a finer wine would be lost and, at best, only an ordinary red should be served. Cold beer would be better and is by all means the best drink with the hot curries. Copious mouthfuls of ice-cold beer help to cool the mouth and, with the hotter dishes, the mouth can use some cooling. The same applies to all hot, as distinguished from spicy, cuisine, such as Mexican.

Russian shchi or borscht (both are forms of cabbage soup), being sweet and sour in flavor, don't go well with any wine. The same would be true of Hungarian stuffed cabbage, which is usually noticeably sweet and sometimes sweet and sour. It would apply equally to German sauerbraten or Cantonese sweet-and-sour pork.

There is no reason why a company dinner cannot be dressed up by serving different wines with different courses. Obviously, a single wine will not do for a first course of seafood or shellfish and a main course of beef. Where more than one wine is served, a simple and good rule is to go from white to red, from lighter-bodied to bigger and fuller-bodied, from lesser to better quality.

In summation, then, white wines with delicately flavored foods, red wines with more robust dishes. In between, personal taste may reasonably select either. Do not be afraid to experiment. You may find, as I have, that you like reds and whites, both, with a given dish and will select your wine to suit your mood or your desire for a change.

Only one plea is made. Do not insist on sticking to one wine for all foods just because you know you like that one. Do not deny yourself the opportunity to test and enjoy new sensations.

If you get to the point of having a collection of several different wines and finally begin to think, at times, of which dish would go with which wine, rather than which wine to serve with what dish, then you're hooked. You will no longer be a wine drinker, but a wine buff. You will have become a wine collector, a wine hobbyist, and a whole new dimension of enjoyment will have opened up for you.

Storing Wine

It is here, more than anywhere else, that the greatest part of the "written tradition" exists. There is a tendency to consider the traditionalist a snob and, in the process, to disregard the very sound reasons that exist for much of wine lore. The snobbery certainly exists. Is it really necessary to drink only out of the thinnest of goblets in order to enjoy wine? If you can afford, or care to spend, $9 or $10 for a single Baccarat goblet, perhaps yes; otherwise, certainly not. But that is not to say that the knowledge acquired over centuries of wine drinking should be thrown away.

Wine, to begin with, is a living thing. It is usually matured in casks over a period of time, sometimes for many years, before being bottled. It continues to change in the bottle, growing and maturing, finally fading and dying. The greater the wine, the longer every part of this process is likely to take. Even the simplest of wines, however, is subject to this cycle.

All that happens in the bottle is the result of that great invention of comparatively recent times, the cork. It is the cork that, while preserving the wine from open contact with the air, still allows entry of the tiny quantity of air needed to assist maturation. Hence the very practical reason for laying bottles on their sides—to keep the cork moist and tight in the neck. Should the cork loosen, the wine will spoil.

It should also be understood that some wines will throw sediment. This is more likely to occur with finer, older wines, primarily with reds, but it can happen with others of the kind dealt with most here. Sediment does not mean spoiled wine. It is harmless but not likely to taste good, so it must be kept out of the glass and out of the mouth.

With these facts in mind, it is now possible to discuss storage intelligently. Bottles should be laid on their sides, preferably at a very slight backward slant to avoid any possibility of falling out and breaking, but not so slanted that the wine fails to touch the cork. They should be laid labels upward and should not be turned periodically. This makes it possible to easily identify the bottle and also assures that the sediment, if any, will always accumulate along the side opposite the label.

Where to store becomes a problem, especially for the city dweller. Roomy, vaulted stone wine cellars are mostly a product of Hollywood. The apartment dweller may have no more room available than a closet, or part of one. The homeowner can usually fare much better. To whatever extent a choice is available, the darkest, coolest spot, least subject to vibration from outside traffic or any other cause, should be selected.

Temperature, too, is important. Wine should never be stored or even kept for the shortest time near a stove, a furnace, or any other source of heat. Heat is not kind to wine and will ruin its balance quickly. Much has been said about the ideal temperature. Wine warehouses are often kept at controlled temperatures of 55 degrees. This is quite impossible for the average householder.

Actually, wine will stand quite substantial temperature variations without being seriously affected. Of course it will freeze at below about 24 degrees, although even this will not literally spoil it, and it certainly will not prosper at above about 80 degrees. The secret is that *gradual* changes in temperature are not damaging. The variations that might occur in the unheated basement of a private home from perhaps 50 degrees in the wintertime to possibly 80 degrees in the summer will not hurt wine, particularly the less than great ones. As a matter of fact, there is one national distributor in the New York area who allows his storage warehouse to fluctuate between exactly that, 50 and 80 degrees.

To store wine requires a wine rack or a reasonable substitute for one. The term immediately brings to the mind's eye the handsome polished wood racks in a diamond pattern so often seen in wine stores. Those are for display. The stores keep the bulk of their wine in more prosaic surroundings.

A specialty store in New York sells a wine jail, a wrought-iron cage with a padlocked door. A 50-bottle jail is $55 which, with sales tax, comes to well over $1 per bottle. The 300-bottle jail costs $150, considerably less per bottle but still costly. Many department stores nowadays offer cheap, flimsy racks at what appear to be low prices, but really are not. I do not think that a 9-bottle, shaky plastic rack is cheap at $5. My advice is, save the money and buy wine.

A homeowning do-it-yourselfer can easily build an adequate rack out of any kind of wood, as I have done. Shelves should be slightly tilted and there should be enough space between shelves to allow two layers of bottles per shelf. A horizontal top will provide space for aperitif and dessert wines, which may safely be kept standing up.

An old bookcase, or a cheap, unpainted one, will serve the same purpose. Here again it would be wise to provide a slight backward tilt, easily done by laying a strip of wood under the bookcase at the appropriate point. Even an empty corrugated wine case with the cubbyholes intact, when laid on its side, makes a perfectly adequate wine rack. This can be especially practical for the drinker who has only part of a closet to give to the cause of wine. I know a young wine buff who has some hundreds of bottles stored in the basement of his home, every one of them in corrugated cartons. He spends his money on wine, not trimmings.

Because wine is a living thing, movement disturbs it. A bottle should be allowed to rest quietly, ideally for as long as a week, at a minimum for a day or two, before being opened and drunk. Once the wine has had this period of rest, all handling should be gentle and gradual. Of course, a bottle may lie untouched for months, even years, without any harm to the wine. If the wine has sediment, four or five days may be a minimum to allow it to settle.

A simple way to determine whether a bottle contains sediment is to hold it up to a ceiling fixture so that the light shines through the bottom, and gently rotate it, if necessary. Remember that if it has been laid down properly, all the sediment will have gathered on the side opposite the label. It is wise to set a sedimented bottle upright for a few hours, even for a day, before opening, to allow all of the sediment to settle from the side to the bottom.

An interesting and important fact, the explanation for which I do not know, is that wine will not spoil and will retain its full taste for a month or more after opening, in half-gallon and larger bottles. I have found this to be so over a period of many weeks even in the middle of summer when my wine cellar reaches temperatures in the upper 70s. Great economy can be effected by buying in half-gallons and gallons and consuming the wine gradually.

As for wine left over in ordinary-sized bottles, it can be stored successfully for a few days in the refrigerator. Whites appear to retain their full flavor unimpaired while reds do not do quite so well, but well enough to make it worth saving them. Even a white so stored will be colder than it ought to be, and should be removed and allowed to stand at room temperature for a half hour. Reds should have at least two hours. This, of course, is a "heresy." It goes without saying that it is best to consume a bottle completely at one sitting, but this is frequently not possible and, with today's inflation, who can afford to throw out undrunk wine?

Opening and Serving

We have now gotten to actually opening a bottle and, therefore, to the subject of the corkscrew. Never use the kind that is part of a composite tool that includes a can opener, a pry, and one or two other assorted instruments. It is doubtful whether any of the parts of a composite tool ever work properly. Anyone who is or will be a frequent user of a corkscrew deserves a good one.

Pulling a cork is not easy and, with a long cork of good quality, may be impossible. It is essential to have a corkscrew that works by exerting mechanical pressure. One of the most effective corkscrews is an Italian-made one purchasable almost everywhere, which has two winglike levers that rise as the corkscrew sinks into the cork, and which are then pressed downward, effectively lifting the cork. Its cost is something under $2. Unfortunately, the more recent versions, instead of ending in a hooked point that enters the cork easily and holds securely, have a straight point like the end of a drill bit. This tends to drill away at the cork instead of entering it. If one of the old type can be found, it is the best buy.

A zigzag cork puller that works on much the same principle sells for about $5. There is also the type used by waiters, with a sort of flange that fits over the rim of the bottle neck, used as a lever to raise the cork. It is not as easy to use as some others but is effective and can be bought for about $2. A more effective one is made of boxwood with two handles, one of which drives in the corkscrew and the other, turned in the opposite direction, draws the cork up. It can be found at about $2.50.

It is advisable, however, to have at home a simple pull-type corkscrew as well. It should never be used for extraction as such but can be very useful when a crumbly cork is encountered or the cork breaks off, leaving a part still in the bottle neck.

A type frequently advertised is a needlelike contraption which, after insertion through the cork, releases compressed air that pops the cork out, or so the ads say. Such a device should never be used. After carefully allowing wine to rest for many days, why disturb it with compressed air?

Care should be taken to prevent any bits of cork from

falling into the wine. The corkscrew should not be inserted through the length of the cork and beyond. A bit of practice makes this quite simple. In the case of a crumbly or otherwise recalcitrant cork, it may not be possible to avoid dropping some bits in the wine. If it does happen, remember that it does not spoil the wine. After all, wine and cork had been lying in happy juxtaposition for a long time before opening. Just remove the bits from the glass with a spoon or, if they are too powdery, drink them. They won't have a noticeable taste and are in no way harmful. The ceremony of pouring a few drops first for the host is not just so that he can judge excellence before the wine is served to others but also so that he may be sure that he, and not the guests, gets the cork, if any.

The cork and the top of the bottle are covered with a metal foil, occasionally replaced by plastic nowadays. Depending on the conditions in which the wine has been kept, before as well as after purchase, the bottle top beneath the cap may be dry and clean, moldy, or damp and dirty. None of this has the remotest effect on the wine in the bottle. If the cork itself is firm and not dried out, the wine will be unspoiled. Before uncorking, the mold or dirt or moisture should be wiped away from the top of the cork and the rim of the bottle with a paper towel, moistened if necessary. Cleaning the rim is most important to insure that no dirt is poured out with the wine.

Red wines should be opened about one hour, or at least half an hour, before being drunk and should be allowed to breathe, that is, to stand open. It is amazing how contact with the air will improve the flavor and bouquet of the wine. Don't take anyone's word for it. Open a bottle of red wine and at once smell it and taste it. One hour later smell it and taste it again, being sure to use a duplicate of the first glass since, as you will learn shortly, the glass can affect the flavor. Unquestionably you will notice much more bouquet and a much richer taste on the second occasion.

Letting a wine breathe is not merely a rite worth observing with great wines. If the wine is good enough to drink, it is good enough to be so treated as to bring out its qualities to the fullest.

I have a prejudice, however, against allowing wines to breathe in the kitchen while cooking is in progress. I have no way of proving that wine will absorb cooking odors, only an uneasy feeling that it does, so why take chances? Set down the opened bottle in the dining room, the living room, anywhere away from the cooking odors.

It is commonly said that red wines should be served at room temperature. What is room temperature? Is it the suffocating 85 degrees at which some apartments are kept? Wine cannot even be stored properly at above 80 degrees maximum. Actually, room temperature once meant the temperature of rooms in European houses, often quite cool in summer and unheated in winter, conditions for the most part not likely to be duplicated in the room of an American home. It has come to be accepted in this age of thermometers as meaning 65 degrees.

I can almost hear you asking, "Am I supposed to carry a thermometer around with me, too?" Hardly! A bit of common sense is needed. If a wine cellar in the basement of a private home is 50 degrees or so in wintertime, the bottle might well be brought up about two hours before drinking and opened one hour before. Or, if the storage place is a closet in an overheated apartment, the bottle might well be opened an hour and a half before drinking, allowed to breathe for an hour, and then recorked and placed in the refrigerator for half an hour.

White wines should be served fairly well chilled, somewhat less so perhaps in the wintertime, more thoroughly in hot weather. They do not profit much from breathing before being drunk, especially the lesser whites. A good rule of thumb is to cool white wine in the refrigerator for about two hours before opening, and then open and drink.

Battles have raged between the traditionalists, who frown on refrigerators, and the moderns, who are winning out. As a matter of ordinary common sense, it is plain stupid not to take advantage of refrigerators, which the wine drinkers of yesteryear simply did not have available. On the other hand, a wine cooler has certain positive virtues and no serious wine drinker should be without one. A bottle can be adequately cooled in fifteen or twenty minutes in a cooler, whereas the use of the refrigerator requires some two hours of advance planning. It is also true that using a cooler keeps the wine at the same cold temperature throughout a meal, whereas the refrigerated bottle slowly warms up at the table as it is being consumed.

The reader who sets out to buy a cooler will find pitfalls. He is likely to go through store after store and find nothing but champagne coolers, which look, in profile, something like oversized flowers and which are simply not deep enough for the purpose. What is needed, as a practical matter, is a bucket-shaped cooler, deep enough so that an ordinary bottle can be pretty well covered while standing upright. They can be found, although not with ease, in handsome and expensive Sheffield, expensive but not necessarily handsome glass, and also, recently, in a stainless steel imitation of the Sheffield bucket, quite handsome and costing only $6 or $7.

To use a wine bucket properly, open the wine (to avoid having to do so later, when the bottle is dripping wet), reinsert the cork part-way (to avoid any accidental spilling), stand the bottle in the empty cooler, dump in two trays of ice cubes and add cold tap water to within an inch or two of the top. Do not fill the bucket with ice and water first and then stand the bottle in it. You may have a minor flood on your hands if you do.

If the wine has a sediment, it should be decanted. A moment's thought will explain why. Much care has been taken for many days to insure that the sediment has all dropped to the bottom. If the wine is then served out of the bottle in the ordinary way, the pourings, the setting down of the bottle, and the pourings again will cause the sediment to swirl up and negate the care previously taken. The secret of decanting is to pour slowly and, above all, steadily, to the point where the sediment is about to, but has not quite yet, reached the lip of the bottle, and then to cease pouring. It may as well be done as soon as the bottle is opened.

The suggestion is often made that a lighted candle be placed under the bottle to help in seeing its contents. Many households in urban America do not possess a candle. In most cases, if the process is carried out in a brightly lighted room, as a kitchen is likely to be, there is quite enough light without adding any more under the bottle. If it is needed, a flashlight serves very well.

To decant means literally to pour into a decanter. Wine decanters, especially if they bear such a label as Waterford, can be as costly as $75. If a decanter is used, it should be left unstoppered. A much less expensive, and perhaps more convenient receptacle, is a carafe. One-liter carafes, made in Italy, can be purchased at the Pottery Barn in New York City for a little over $2 and can be found readily at somewhat higher prices elsewhere. Such carafes, ranging in size from a quarter liter to two liters, are indispensable for serving wine bought in half-gallon or gallon containers.

When the residue after decanting amounts to only a few drops, of course it should be thrown out. Sometimes, however, because of the character of the sediment, an ounce or two or even more of wine will be left in the bottle. My parsimonious soul rebels at throwing away so much wine. I always filter it out, using the same type of paper filter employed in making filtered coffee, and serve it after the carafe or decanter has been consumed. Neither I nor any of my guests have ever noticed any difference between the decanted and the filtered wine. In terms of the "tradition" this is downright sacrilege. Nevertheless it is recommended to those who have such filters available. Four thicknesses of a linen handkerchief will pretty well serve the same purpose but this method tends to be messy and to inflate the laundry bill.

Then there is something known as a wine cradle. It is

usually made of a woven fiber, so built that a bottle will lie on its side at a slant, and it comes with a handle for easy carrying. Nowadays, ads are seen occasionally for lucite cradles at rather fancy prices, to say nothing of silver cradles at very fancy prices indeed. A restaurant now and then will serve wine at table in a cradle.

The original purpose of a wine cradle was to enable the wine to be laid on its side as it had been stored, without disturbing the sediment, to carry it in this position from cellar to table, and to allow the butler or sommelier (wine steward) to draw the cork while it lay on its side, an operation requiring a fair amount of skill. It was not intended as a wine server. To use one for serving is ostentatious, a phony part of the "tradition," and an unnecessary expense.

Wineglasses

Having gotten our wine now to the point of drinking, into what should it be poured? Just any glass? It can be drunk out of a tumbler, and often is. There has been a tendency in the United States, happily disappearing now, to place on the market not-quite-thimble-sized wineglasses. Some that I have seen and, alas, drunk from, are really not much more than big enough for serving liqueurs.

At the other end of the spectrum, a whole variety of sizes and shapes of wineglasses are advertised. There are glasses, literally, for red Bordeaux, white Bordeaux, red Burgundy, white Burgundy, Rhine and Moselle wines, sherry, port, champagne, and a few others. Many ads appearing in the daily press and in magazines depict as many as nine different glasses.

Are all or most of these really necessary for the proper enjoyment of wine? Absolutely not! The fact is that, over centuries, a particular shape and size of glass has become traditional in each of the wine-producing areas of the world.

Just because the American wine drinker has available to him all of the traditional wines of the world, and some others, does not mean that he must adopt all the glasses as well. There is every reason, on the contrary, for using a bit of intelligence and making the traditional wineglass of America the all-purpose glass. This is a term, and a conception, that is becoming increasingly popular here.

Wine is tasted with the nose as much as with the tongue. A radical statement? Not at all! It is equally true of food. The sense of smell is an integral part of tasting. Whoever has had a head cold with stuffed-up nostrils knows how completely the sense of taste disappears when that of smell goes. Therefore a proper wineglass should be wide enough at the mouth so that the nose is inside the rim while sipping. It should also be large enough so that an adequate serving fills the glass not more than half full, preferably even less, and allows the rest of the glass to act as a funnel for bringing the bouquet of the wine to the nose.

Again, do not take anybody's word for it. Try it for yourself. Pour a little wine into a 4- or 5-ounce, straight-sided glass, such as is commonly used for orange juice. Pour a little of the same wine, at the same time, into the bottom of a large water goblet. Taste each in turn. You will discover for yourself that what has been said here is correct. You'll never afterward drink wine from a juice glass.

Wine is a lovely thing to look at. In all its many tones of red and purple and yellow and almost green, it adds beauty to the most simply served meal, but not if it is poured into smoked or colored glasses. Wine should always be served in colorless glasses so that the fullest visual pleasure can add to that of taste. Also, there are many, including me, who believe that a smooth glass, rather than cut glass, will show off the clarity and intensity of color best.

Thus, from examining what a glass can and should do for the wine, it is easy to arrive at what the all-purpose glass should be. A 10-ounce, tulip-shaped, stemmed glass is ideal.

Some are available in 12 ounces. There are also some monstrosities that hold as much as 20 or 30 ounces. They might make good conversation pieces but are not for serious wine drinkers. The 10-ounce glass allows of a 2-, 3-, or 5-ounce serving with enough of a "funnel" left to give maximum play to the sense of smell.

Wineglasses of the kinds described are readily available in department and other stores in most larger cities. They can often be found at a cost not exceeding $2.50 per glass. They are not as lovely as such fine stemware as Baccarat, Val St. Louis, and Waterford, but are quite handsome enough to serve their purpose well. Let us remember that, in terms of what is being presented in this volume, the purpose of a wineglass is not merely to serve the wine to its absolutely best advantage, but to do so at prices that the average wine lover can afford.

The tulip-shaped glass has the additional advantage of serving admirably as a champagne glass. More accurately, the term sparkling wine should be used, since champagne is, for the most part, too expensive to fall within the price limits set here. But more of that later. Suffice it to say now that, fortunately, the lamentable tendency to serve sparkling wine in a wide, shallow glass is disappearing. No better way could be found to allow the bubbles to dissipate as quickly as possible and, without its bubbles, sparkling wine is a sad drink indeed. Sparkling wines require a deeper glass of almost exactly the tulip shape.

While we are concerned here only with wine, it is not inappropriate to point out that the same tulip glass makes a very satisfactory brandy server as well, even though it is undoubtedly more elegant to serve brandy in a genuine snifter.

All of what has been said so far applies only to table, or dinner, wines. Aperitif and after-dinner wines require something a little bit different. The drinker does not profit from inhaling their bouquet, although the aroma of such wines is always pleasant. Hence, a deep glass is not only unnecessary, it is too large and almost clumsy for the purpose. Here, too, different shapes and sizes of glass proliferate. An ideal glass for serving all aperitif and dessert wines is what is known as a sherry glass. It is almost always tulip-shaped and should hold about 5 ounces.

With the two kinds of glasses recommended, all wines can be served properly and the most meticulous host need not fear being inadequately equipped.

A word about plastic glasses. No wine should ever be drunk from paper cups or styrene-type plastic. A noticeable and unpleasant flavor will be imparted and the simplest wine is too elegant a thing ever to be disgraced by paper or thick white plastic. For outdoor eating in warmer weather, good or fine stemware is impractical and, therefore, it makes sense to use the thin, colorless plastic glasses that have become common and are, in fact, reusable. Even clear plastic stemware can now be found and can add an elegance out of doors to equal that of wine itself.

PART III

How to Select Wines

BY TASTING! IT'S AS SIMPLE—AND AS COMPLICATED—AS THAT.

Even in the case of the great wines, with centuries of acceptance as the best, any given individual will not drink them if they happen not to suit his taste. How much truer this is of lesser wines.

To build up a "wine cellar," whether of half a dozen wines or considerably more, you will have to try and taste, try and taste, eliminating many that do not suit you and re-ordering those that do. This will mean time and effort as well as knowledge. If the time and effort spell work rather than the pleasure that any collector experiences, then learning about wines may not be for you.

I estimate that, for each wine of which I keep a supply and drink regularly, I have tasted and eliminated at least ten that I liked less or not at all. What will be presented here is not a blueprint to make wine selection as easy as simple arithmetic but rather many guides to provide at least the basic knowledge needed for selecting intelligently and more effectively than one in ten. After all, it is not difficult to pick the fine wines. An ample purse and a reliable wine shop are enough. It is precisely in the area of good, lower-priced wines that some knowledge and effort become essential.

Reading Wine Labels

Bottle labels can be very revealing and it is worth learning how to read them. They frequently tell a good deal about the wine inside, such as the country and region of origin, the maker or shipper or both, where bottled, the bottle size, alcoholic content, and vintage year. All of these can be significant. None is unimportant.

The easiest way to illustrate is by reading a label or two. I have two bottles before me as I write. The label on the first says:

1970

CHÂTEAU ROLLAND

Appellation Bordeaux Contrôlée

Mise en Bouteilles au Château

A further, small label on the bottle's shoulder says:

SELECTED BY G. C. SUMNER

Product of France   ¾ quart table wine

The two labels together tell us that the wine is of the 1970 vintage, that its name is Château Rolland, that it is a Bordeaux wine meeting the quite stringent requirements of the French law known as the *Appellation Contrôlée*, and the fact that the wine was put in bottle at the château. We learn further that it is a French wine, that the bottle size is three-fourths of a quart or 24 ounces, and that George C. Sumner selected it.

How to interpret this information? The 1970 vintage in Bordeaux was a great one. Even minor wines, like this one, will be better in that year's vintage. The wine meets the standards that the French law sets for the best of its wines. The fact that the wine was bottled at the château is important. It indicates that it was made only of grapes grown at that château, not from a mixture of grapes grown in many vineyards in the region and, consequently, that it is likely to be a better wine.

Lastly, if your experience has told you that G. C. Sumner's selections tend to be good, his name means a good deal on the label. It happens to have been a delightful wine. Unfortunately, very little, if any, can still be found.

Now let us look at the other bottle. Starting this time at the top, the label at the shoulder reads:

Frank Schoonmaker Selection

Product of France   Table Wine—¾ Quart

The main label is as follows:

Alcohol 13% by volume   Mise en bouteilles par
Récolte 1970   les propriétaires

Blanc de Blancs
Pinot Chardonnay
Mâcon Clessé

Appellation Mâcon Contrôlée
Caves Coopérative de Clessé   France

Some of this needs no explaining. What does, tells that the wine is of the 1970 vintage, was bottled by the proprietors, is made of white grapes only (Blanc de Blancs), is a Pinot Chardonnay from the village of Clessé in Mâcon, is a Mâcon wine that has met the standards of the Appellation Contrôlée, and that the proprietors are the Clessé cooperative.

How do we interpret this? Mâcon is a part of the Burgundy region. The 1970 vintage in Burgundy was excellent. The Pinot Chardonnay grape is used in making the famous white wines of Burgundy, considered to be among the greatest in the world. The fact that the wine was bottled by the proprietors is, by itself, meaningless. The proprietors, being a cooperative, collect grapes from an area, so that the wine is as good—or as poor—as the care of the cooperative in selecting the grapes and making the wine. Most important in the case of this wine is that Frank Schoonmaker selected it. It happens to be a lovely wine.

It is obvious that the label is a mine of information. It is equally obvious that some knowledge is needed to understand properly all that the label has to tell. Some familiarity with French, Italian, German, and Spanish can be helpful, even a bit of Hungarian and Portuguese might come in handy, but this is really far from important. The serious student of wine will quickly come to recognize and understand the relevant phrases, even if he does not know how to pronounce them.

What is stressed here is to make it a point to read the label thoroughly before buying. Your dealer will wait or will serve another customer in the meantime. If he is at all dedicated to wine as an idea and a source of pleasure, not merely as an item for sale, he is likely to know enough to help you interpret it if you are confused. But try puzzling it out for yourself first. It is fun and is part of learning your own way about.

Bottles–Sizes and Shapes

The bottle itself can often be revealing. Certain shapes and colors of glass are traditional for certain wines. Mainly, these are wines of particular regions in France, Italy, and Germany. There is no point in describing them here at length, as they often are elsewhere. The wine student will become familiar with them quickly enough as he goes about buying wine and will eventually almost automatically identify the wine by the shape of the bottle.

The wines of most other countries usually come in bottles approximating these traditional shapes. There is no significance to these shapes. Some bottles, notably of Portuguese and Chilean wines, are unusual and will be described specifically later.

However, there is a general rule that should be learned and followed: Be suspicious of unusual bottle shapes. Stay away from them. They are frequently a method for concealing, or diverting attention from, the inferior wine contained in them. Furthermore, bottles of peculiar shape may be comparatively expensive. Too much of what you pay goes for the bottle, too little for the wine.

A few examples:

A gallon of red Chianti, an Italian wine, in a squat *fiasco* (flask) with a neck about 3.5 feet—feet, not inches—long. The cost, $10.47. A gallon of very satisfactory Chianti in an ordinary fiasco can be bought for just over half that price. Of course, if the buyer wants a curiosity to stand somewhere in his home, the cost may be worth it, but a good general rule for wine drinkers is that wine dollars are to buy wine, not bottles.

Italian wines, red Chianti as well as others, that come in something called an ice decanter. This is a rather weird contraption that has a separate, sealed space surrounded by the wine bottle. The space is intended for the insertion of ice cubes to chill the surrounding wine but it is doubtful that this procedure would ever chill the wine properly. It is certain that red Chianti, at any rate, should not be chilled. It is also certain that no serious wine drinker ought ever to contemplate buying such a contraption.

An Italian wine, the name of which is Bianco della Costa Toscana, also known as the "fish-bottle" wine because it comes in a bottle shaped like a fish standing on its tail. The cost, $3.35 for a 23.5-ounce bottle, is a high price for all except a few exceptional white Tuscan wines.

A Portuguese wine, very well known in the United States, Lancers Rosé, comes in a fake brown earthenware bottle really made of glass. Perhaps only the bottlers and those in the glass business have any idea of what part of the inordinate cost of this wine goes to pay for the bottle. The wine inside the bottle certainly doesn't begin to repay the cost.

Sizes of bottles should be watched carefully as well. They vary, and anyone seeking the best value must keep this in mind. Generally speaking, European table wines come in 24-ounce bottles. Among European wines there are a fair number of exceptions, however. Chianti usually comes in the traditional and well-known straw-covered fiasco, in a 1-quart size. Orvieto, a superior Italian white wine, is found in what appears to be a somewhat smaller version of the Chianti fiasco. Actually, the Orvieto fiasco contains only 22 ounces. Most Hungarian wines are shipped in 23-ounce bottles but the best known, Tokay, comes in 16-ounce bottles. French wines, notably Beaujolais, occasionally appear in a bottle called a *pot*, which contains 17 ounces. There is a growing tendency, unfortunately not yet widespread, to bottle wines in liters as well. (One liter equals about 33.5 ounces.) American wines usually come in four-fifths-quart bottles, equal to 25.6 ounces.

There is no reason to suppose that the wine makers do this to confuse you, but it can confuse just the same. It is certainly important to read labels in order to be sure of the quantity of wine you are buying. (Sometimes the contents appear not on the label, but in raised letters around the foot of the bottle.) Simple arithmetic tells why. A 24-ounce bottle at a price of $2.40 is no cheaper than four-fifths of a quart at $2.56. The cost is exactly the same.

It can be argued validly that an ounce or two more or less will still be sufficient for one meal and that the quality of the wine you drink is far more important than whether you have a bit more or a bit less. This is true but actual cost comparisons are still worth making. Furthermore, where a four-fifths-quart bottle of American wine has previously proved sufficient for a given number of people at a meal, a 23-ounce bottle of Hungarian wine may be literally inadequate and perhaps embarrassing to a host. Certainly this could not fail to be true in the case of a 22-ounce fiasco of Orvieto, by comparison with a 1-quart fiasco of white Chianti.

Many American wines, a fair number of Spanish wines, and a few Italian ones can commonly be found also in half-gallon and gallon bottles. These are never the best wines of the particular countries, but they can be quite good. They are usually better buys than the ordinary-sized bottles and, as has already been indicated, they will keep after opening. Once you have determined that you like a particular wine and want to have a supply of it on hand, by all means consider buying the larger bottles where available.

Just as there has been a tendency to put up wine in liters, larger bottles of lower-priced European wines are beginning to appear. These range in size from a magnum (two-fifths of a gallon) to 2 liters (about 67 ounces) or more than half a gallon. Some Italian wines are sold in 59-ounce bottles! It is obvious that anyone who wishes reasonably good value for his money had best watch these bottle sizes carefully.

A word of comfort—for some time, work has been in progress to have the United States join the metric system, at least as far as wine is concerned. In the industry it is believed that, within two years, all American wines will come in liter bottles or proportions thereof. This has, of course, always been true of European wines. It will naturally require some mental adjustment, but will eventually make life much easier.

In the meantime, remember—buy wine, not bottles, and be sure you know what quantity you are getting for your money.

Corks and Bottle Caps

Most wine bottles are corked. Some have metal screw-on caps, or heavy foil screw-off caps of the type always used on bottles of vermouth, which is not a dinner wine and needs no corking.

Occasional bottles of Italian wine may be found with a metal cover. Most, if not all, of the larger bottles of European wines are corked. American "jug wines"·are generally pasteurized, then capped. Corking would not help a pasteurized wine in any way.

As has already been pointed out, the cork serves a maturing function from which even the most modest wine, if not pasteurized, can profit at least a little. Wine in a capped bottle loses that advantage. It may be said accurately that a metal cap on a bottle of table wine is a mark of the wine maker's low opinion of his wine's quality. Capped rather than corked wines should be avoided, except to the extent that the purchaser recognizes that the wine, while it may be reasonably decent and a good buy because of price, is one that will never electrify the world of wine.

Corks can often carry a message, though one that cannot be discovered without opening the bottle. Hence it is one that can be of no help in buying a wine for the first time, but can be a guide to future purchases. Very simply, the length and quality of the cork, as well as what is printed on it, if anything, tell something about the wine. A long cork of firm texture almost automatically denotes a better wine. Conversely, a short, porous, almost crumbly one is some indication of the bottler's own opinion of the quality of his wine. The fine wines of Bordeaux and Burgundy are bottled with corks fully two inches long, sometimes even a bit longer.

One outstanding exception to this is the wine of Spain, which is, after all, the home of cork. Spanish wines of even the most modest kind tend to have quite long corks of good quality.

Corks quite frequently bear a legend along the sides. In French wines, it is likely to be *Mise au Château* or *Mise au Domaine* or *Mise au Propriété*. These all mean "bottled on the property." All are meant to indicate that the wine was bottled where it was grown and made, and when true (as it usually is) it can be expected to be of at least fairly good quality. The legend might read *Mise dans nos Caves*, meaning "bottled in our cellars." In that case, the quality of the wine depends on the ability and integrity of the bottler and shipper. These legends often merely repeat what also appears on the label and is therefore visible before a bottle is bought and opened. Sometimes they appear only on the cork.

Wines of other countries frequently bear legends of similar meaning on their corks. The language may be unfamiliar but the meanings of these simple phrases are unmistakable. For example, it takes no linguist to understand that *Embotellado en la Propiedad* on a bottle of Spanish wine means "bottled on the property."

Get into the habit of examining corks, noting their length and quality, and reading what is printed on them. They are another guidepost to quality in wine.

A "tip"—sherry and sometimes other aperitif and dessert wines have corks that are attached to a flat top of cork or plastic. A few should be saved. They are easy to handle and may be of much use when a partially consumed bottle of wine needs recorking.

Vintners, Shippers, and Selectors

In this area, the force of advertising is considerable and, as in other phases of merchandising, each advertiser makes or distributes the best for the least. Actually, in the case of wine, the best buy (not necessarily the very best wine) is seldom, if ever, the best advertised wine, or an advertised wine at all.

American wines are always strongly associated with the names of the vintners, those who actually make the wine. They may also grow the grapes, though they often do not, or, at any rate, not all the grapes used in the winemaking process. They also frequently distribute the wine to retailers, who will be dealt with in detail later.

In the case of European wines, the *négociants*, or shippers, are frequently of importance. There are many hundreds, perhaps thousands, of them and there is no intention here of making any comprehensive list. It would be most boring and

WINE INSTITUTE LIBRARY

useless. Nevertheless, it is appropriate to discuss a few of those whose names tend to bear weight when appearing on a label.

Some, like JOSEPH DROUHIN and HENRI GOUGE et FILS, are synonymous with the finest Burgundies but are, alas, of little significance to the purchaser of lower-cost wines. Others, like BARTON & GUESTIER with the well known B&G monogram, CHANSON, CHAUVENET, and CRUSE are advertised extensively in the United States and present a cross section of wines from the various regions of France. To a great extent, their wines are priced too high for us. Their prices also reflect the costs of advertising and the snob appeal of an established name. Their wines are likely to be good but will never be the best buys that can be found with some effort mixed with enthusiasm.

Others that fall pretty much into the same category are SICHEL et FILS for both German and French wines, DEINHARD for German wines, and both BOLLA and RUFFINO for Italian wines. All of these have a number of wines that are priced within our limits but they are rarely best buys.

Several names are well worth remembering, however. A. DE LUZE et FILS are known nationally for quality and ship French wines of all the best regions. There is a bit of representation of good, medium-priced wines. FREDERICK WILDMAN et FILS are both French shippers and American distributors. The firm has been owned by Hiram Walker since 1971 and I do not know whether any Wildman is still associated with it, but I find that their wines can be counted on for quality. There is adequate choice of reasonably priced wines from most parts of France and from Italy.

ALEXIS LICHINE is one of the best known figures in the wine business, an author and vineyard owner. He sold his shipping business to BASS, CHARRINGTON, a British wine giant, in 1965 and has had no connection with it since. Bass, Charrington has a fine reputation and has continued to use the Lichine name and carried on the tradition established by Lichine for quality. A fair number of Lichine's wines, including selections from most areas of France, are still within our price range and may be bought with assurance.

CAVES de CHARNAY-BELLEVUE are wine merchants at Mâcon in Burgundy. Their wines are frequently selections of George C. Sumner. They are never great, occasionally distinguished, but always good for their price and an honest value. They may safely be bought wherever they can be found.

J. THORIN is a *négociant* in Burgundy, shipping mostly Beaujolais. His wines are excellent for their respective prices and should be bought freely.

PIERRE OLIVIER is one of the fine shippers of Burgundy. His wines range in price from far above our limits to some, fortunately, well within it. His name on a label is an assurance of fine quality.

Finally, there is a very small, very special group who, for want of a better name, I call "selectors." Their choices of wine can be very important to wine drinkers.

FRANK SCHOONMAKER. He has been in the wine business for close to four decades, as retail store operator, author, consultant, and selector of wines. The small label, like a collar around the neck of a bottle, reading "Frank Schoonmaker Selection" indicates that he has tasted and knows the wine and recommends it. His selections range through the wines of the major producing areas of Europe. They are rarely other than good to excellent.

Unfortunately for the purposes of this volume, most of Mr. Schoonmaker's selections have priced themselves beyond the limits being adhered to here. A fair number are still within those limits, as will be seen later and, where the dollar price is not too high, the reader should, in most cases, buy his selections with enthusiasm.

GEORGE C. SUMNER. He is not so well known but has been at the business of selecting wines possibly longer than Mr. Schoonmaker. He is much better known in England than here. There is a fairly large number of his selections available in lower-priced wines. They are almost always excellent buys and should be bought eagerly by the wine drinker who can find them.

There are a couple of other "wine selectors" who should be mentioned. One is ANDRÉ SIMON. Mr. Simon was one of the great deans of the wine industry. He died three or four years ago. Wines can still be found labeled as his selections. Obviously, they aren't. Whose selections they may be it is impossible to say. They are on the whole decent, but in no way unusual, and overpriced for their quality. They should be avoided.

The second is MONSIEUR HENRI. A good many bottles will be found with the legend "A Monsieur Henri Selection." A more thorough reading of the label will reveal in all cases that the wine has been imported by Monsieur Henri Wines, one of the giants of the industry and, incidentally, owned by Pepsi-Cola since 1972. There is no such "selector" as Monsieur Henri. Wines so labeled are good or poor, depending purely on what quality of wine the importer has chosen. As a guide to the wine drinker, the label "A Monsieur Henri Selection" means exactly nothing.

Making use of the seasoned judgment of Frank Schoonmaker and George C. Sumner can prove an invaluable aid to proper selection of good wines. The learner and, for that matter, the more knowledgeable drinker, should accept such guidance freely.

Vintages

This is undoubtedly the single most discussed subject relating to wine, and the subject about which least is known by the most people. Here, as elsewhere attitudes range from the belief that any emphasis on vintages is a form of snobbery to the certainty that vintage charts are the absolute and final guide. The truth lies somewhere in between, as common sense usually lies between two extremes.

The difficulties of clarifying this area are epitomized by an article on best buys in wine written not too long ago by the owner of one of the great wine shops of this country. He indicates that he considers emphasis on vintages a kind of snobbishness, says point-blank that they are of no significance in wines priced under $5, and then proceeds to specify in much detail which vintage years to favor and which to avoid in selecting wines of moderate price.

The fact is that a knowledge of vintage years is very important indeed in buying the costlier wines. Although that phase of wine buying does not concern us here, some knowledge of vintage years is useful in purchasing moderate-priced wines as well. However, the less sophisticated drinker should not burden himself with overly detailed vintage facts. A general knowledge of better and worse years will suffice for buying the less expensive wines.

First and foremost, it should be recognized that vintage years have significance mainly for French and German wines. Second, it must be understood that, French wines dominating all of wine as they do, the vintage years so glibly mentioned by many people always refer to French wines. Not only have they no significance for wines of other countries, but the quality of French wines within a given year almost always varies materially from region to region and, very often, even among sub-regions within a given region.

Complicated? Unbelievably so. Yet, a few criteria are useful and can be established. For our purposes, for example, it is unimportant that, let us say, the Médoc in 1970 was greater than the Graves or vice versa. It is sufficient that, in Bordeaux generally, embracing both these sub-regions and others, 1970 was a great year. Equally, it is quite enough to know that 1965 was a disaster in both Bordeaux and Burgundy and that 1968 ranged from poor to very bad. It must be understood further that, so far as the lesser wines are concerned, information as to vintages earlier than 1966 or 1967 is altogether unimportant since, in general, only the greater and costlier wines of earlier years are still available. Many of them, in fact, are still far from mature.

Vintage years in Italy have no significance except for a few of its finest wines. Frequently, quite improbable vintage years appear on the label. I drank with pleasure a red Chianti labeled Vintage 1964 until about 1971. It is most doubtful that this very enjoyable wine could have lasted for six or seven years. The 1969 of the same wine has been available since 1971 and is not perceptibly different from the 1964. Both are undoubtedly labels intended merely to cater to the American belief in vintages and mean nothing as to the year in which the wine was actually made. Growing conditions in Italy tend to be rather stable (1972, a disaster, is a notable exception) and the wines produced there tend to be much the same from year to year.

Vintages usually have no more significance in Spain—with one notable exception, namely the Reservas, the finest among their red wines. Spanish wine starts off in life big and harsh and the Reservas require many years of aging in cask and bottle to attain their full stature. Hence, a truly mature and great wine must be an old wine and the vintage year becomes a genuine guide to the maturity and drinkability of the wine.

The same may be said of the wines of Portugal. Their main exception is Dão, which will profit from aging as do the great Spanish wines. Here, therefore, a vintage-year label is of importance too, but not with most of the other Portuguese table wines available here.

Vintages are, for the most part, unimportant with American wines also. The lesser ones are quite uniform in quality from year to year. The more expensive ones may show noticeable variation from one year to the next, but, with the highly modern and mechanized methods of American wine production and with a generally even climate for each region on a year-to-year basis, differences in vintages are not great. There is also a lamentable tendency for the American wine industry to sell its better wines too young and not yet mature, which also tends to negate the significance of vintage years.

For that matter, the increasing use of modern scientific methods in France is tending to even out year-to-year differences and to develop more good to great vintages and fewer disasters. It was once uncommon to experience two very good French vintage years in a row. Yet, in the past dozen years, there have been two such occurrences, 1961 and '62 and 1966 and '67, and, what is more, an almost unheard-of series of three excellent vintages, 1969, '70, and '71. Vintage years may become less important, even for French wines.

For the various regions of France, and for Germany, numerous charts exist. Many are in the form of cards that can be carried in pocket or purse. They are frequently prepared by the larger importer-wholesalers and are generally available free of charge at better wine shops. Some simply rate the wines of the various regions on a scale of 1 to 10 or 1 to 20. A few also indicate those that need further maturing, those that are ready for drinking (as of the time the chart was prepared, of course), and those that are likely to be past their prime. Others use such ratings as "poor," "good," "excellent," "great," etc., instead of a numerical system.

The serious wine drinker should arm himself with such a chart. He should also get a new one each year, since obviously a new vintage each year means an updating of the chart. For the lesser wines, only the most recent four or five years will have any relevance.

Some common sense should be exercised in using a chart. For a lesser Côtes du Rhône it matters little to the buyer whether the year is marked excellent or great. It matters only that his wine should come out of a better vintage year, rather than a poor or truly disastrous one.

Frank Schoonmaker produces annually a pocket-sized booklet that is more than a chart. It contains a quite comprehensive description of each vintage of the previous ten years, as well as his ratings. It is thoroughly enjoyable reading, as well as an excellent source of information applicable largely, but not entirely, to costlier wines. It is also available free of charge now and then at better wine shops. If the reader can obtain one, he should.

To recapitulate—be aware of the few areas where vintage years can be of some importance, pay no attention to them elsewhere, learn enough to enable you to buy intelligently those wines that you want, and, above all, don't let vintages worry you.

Wherever vintage years are of particular significance, they will be discussed as specific wines, and those of particular regions are described.

How to Select and Use a Wine Shop

In such states as Pennsylvania, New Hampshire, Vermont, Utah, and Idaho, where all wine and liquor stores are run by the state, there is, alas, no problem. The selection is quite standardized and, at least in the case of wine, rather minimal. The same is true in Wyoming, where the state buys at wholesale and resells to private retailers. A similar effect results from somewhat different causes in Arizona, Kansas, and Oklahoma. No amount of shopping in these states will produce any bargains or exceptional buys and the wine drinker can only apply what he has learned from this volume or elsewhere, as much as possible within the existing limitations, or travel to other states to buy.

Elsewhere, and especially in big metropolitan centers, the choice is bewildering to a beginner, both among shops and as to the merchandise available in them. The big cities, particularly, almost teem with wine stores, many of which advertise extensively, and the wines available come in enormous variety from almost every corner of the world. To a novice, the display in a well-stocked shop must be overwhelming.

It would be comforting if we had here what once existed widely in England and still does to a considerable extent. There the wine merchant selected his wines on the continent, imported them in cask, and bottled them himself. His integrity and judgment were his greatest stock in trade. His clientele relied on him, bought what he recommended, and presumably were seldom disappointed. Needless to say, this system existed only for the wealthy and well-to-do, but then it was principally they who drank wine. It is disappearing there and never existed here, at least in modern times.

We do not have wine merchants in that sense here. We have wholesalers, who import bottled wines from other countries or elsewhere in this country and who distribute to retailers; and we have retailers whose mission in life it is to make money by selling to the consumer. What they know about their products varies from zero to a great deal. How they may use, or fail to use, their knowledge to make sales is another question.

A few simple preliminary rules are obvious. Avoid buying where the retailer's knowledge is clearly nil or nearly so. Seek out the wine dealer who is likely to be knowledgeable about his merchandise.

In such states as New Jersey or California, where wine may be sold in grocery stores and all sorts of other shops as well as in large, well-stocked stores selling only alcoholic beverages, it is perfectly clear that the proprietor of the corner grocery is most unlikely to know anything at all about the wine he sells. It is much more likely that some real guidance may be found, if needed, in the large wine shop, which specializes. Certainly, that is where real selection will be found.

In New York State and New York City, alcoholic beverages for home consumption may be sold only in retail liquor stores. These can and do vary from the small neighborhood shop to the giants of Manhattan. The neighborhood dealer will logically carry the merchandise in demand in his area. There are some areas in and around all of the bigger cities where there are many wine drinkers, usually because of a concentration of population of European background, or those in better income brackets, or both. In such communities there will always be found well-stocked wine shops that are worth patronizing.

Elsewhere, the local dealer is likely to have a very sad

representation of wines and his knowledge usually consists of recommending some wine, which he will do very readily, because "I sell a lot of it." There can be no better reason for avoiding a wine than such a recommendation. Such shops should also be avoided. It is worthwhile traveling, or carrying wine home from the center of the city, rather than patronizing such stores.

Where, then, to start? For the neophyte, with the large wine shops in the center of the city. It is best to try two or three. Loyalty to only one shop, if it ever comes at all, should come only slowly, over a period of time, as the buyer becomes sure that that one shop affords him the good buys and service that he wants. If a wine drinker's tastes develop to much variety, no one shop will ever be able to service him completely.

Some wine shops have unostentatious wine lists that they will freely furnish to anyone. A few of the big ones prepare quite elaborate catalogs that, as a rule, are also readily available. The serious wine buyer should obtain several.

It then becomes possible to study these lists at leisure and to use reference volumes, whether this one or many other books, and so to determine what wine or wines should be tried next. Upon revisiting the shop, the buyer will find that the bewilderment of the first visit is largely gone. He knows what he wants to buy on this trip, and neither the enormous array of wines nor the self-assured salesmen hold any terrors for him. As a matter of fact, the array soon becomes fascinating.

The question arises, How far can the beginner trust the large store? Certainly it is true that, in the aggregate, among owners and salesmen, a great deal of knowledge exists. It is equally true that the store is a business, it is profit-oriented, and the salesman will try to sell you something. In a fine shop (not all large shops are fine shops) the salesman's knowledge and respect for, if not love of, wine, will prevent his misleading you. But the more you know yourself, the less you need to rely on him.

A look at a few advertisements, all of which appeared in the

New York papers in the fall of 1972, will illustrate how important it is for the buyer to be armed with some knowledge.

D. Sokolin Company offers a listing of ordinary Beaujolais (that is, not labeled as superior to just Beaujolais) and white Mâcons of Monsieur Bocuse at not at all ordinary prices. A case of 1971 Beaujolais at $36 was then quite a price, considering that, only a week earlier, I had bought a case of 1971 Beaujolais Tête de Cuvée ("best of the barrel") for $23.50. This seems to be trading a good deal on M. Bocuse's name, he being described quite correctly as owner of a three-star restaurant near Lyons.

There were then only twelve (now sixteen) three-star restaurants in all France and surely M. Bocuse is very selective about the wine he serves, but, no matter how good this Beaujolais might be, its price had to include some profit to him for the use of his name. But D. Sokolin hardly tells you that.

In the same paper on the same day, the same retailer advertises a sizable list of 1967 red Bordeaux wines under the heading "The now amazing 1967 Château-bottled Red Bordeaux." While the '67 vintage in Bordeaux was, on the whole, very good, and was excellent in one or two regions, the term "amazing" ought to apply to great vintages, which '67 was not. The prices thereafter listed are commensurate with the actual quality of the '67s. They would be dirt cheap for a great vintage.

These are the advertising methods of a businessman, not a devotee of wine. A neophyte would be wrong to trust them blindly.

Another advertisement, this time of Sixty-Seven Liquor Shop, Inc., lists no fewer than four different Château Lascombes, a red Bordeaux, in four different vintage years, a '66 at $6.58 per bottle, a '67 at $5.89, a '68 at $2.69, and a '70 at $5.84. Theoretically, the older years should cost more because they are closer to maturity and the expense of storing them is a justifiable addition to the cost. Why, then, the low '68 price and the '70 price, which seems to be higher than it ought to be in relation to the '66 and '67? Because '68 was a disastrous year and '70 was far greater than '66 or '67. There is no reason to suppose this explanation would not have been given by the dealer if asked. They are thoroughly reputable. There is every reason for the buyer to have enough knowledge himself not to leap at the $2.69 apparent bargain.

Leland's, a fairly large wine shop on Fourteenth Street in Manhattan, naturally caters to the clientele of that shopping area by emphasizing lowest-priced wines. In the fall of 1972 a large sign in the window announced: Beaujolais, Pouilly-Fuissé, Pinot Chardonnay—$1 per bottle. The price of Beaujolais has just been mentioned above. Can it be expected to be purchasable at $12 per case? It is commonly believed among wine people that more than twice as much wine is shipped out of the Beaujolais in a year as is made there, the rest being cheap Algerian and Côtes du Rhône wines and who knows what else. For $1 per bottle you could not then buy Beaujolais, no matter how poor the quality was. Pouilly-Fuissé, for several reasons, is expensive beyond its worth and the cheapest could not then be bought here for much under $3.89. Genuine Pinot Chardonnay might have been purchasable then at $1 but it would have been awful stuff.

These few instances show clearly enough that the more facts the buyer is armed with, the more intelligent his buying will be. And the more he knows, the more he can trust the salesman. This is not paradoxical. The more he knows, the less he has to rely on the salesman. And the more he knows, the more the salesman will respect him as a customer.

And finally, when he simply does not know, he should not hesitate to admit it and ask the salesman. Many know a great deal and will share their knowledge. Much can and will be learned in this way over a period of time, over and above the inevitable disappointments.

The wine buyer should seek to deal regularly with the same salesman of a large shop, for obvious reasons. He should not hesitate to assert his right to browse for as long as he likes before buying, or not to buy at all on a particular visit. It also makes sense, if at all possible, to visit the shop outside of the busiest hours which, for a centrally located shop, would be between 11:00 A.M. and 2:00 P.M. and at the end of the working day. When the salesmen are less busy they will be much readier to talk and discuss. Need it be said that no one in his right mind should seek to browse in a liquor shop between about December 15 and New Year's Day?

The buyer should expect to have the right to return bad bottles of wine. With today's excellent corking, a bad bottle is seldom found, but it does sometimes happen. Any reputable wine shop will take back such a bottle. But the customer, too, must play fair. If the wine is not spoiled, but the buyer simply finds that he does not like it, he has no right to return it. The store should not be expected to pay for his education. Similarly, if the buyer has stored the wine for many months or even years, no matter how carefully, before opening it, the shop can hardly be expected to take back a spoiled bottle.

No more than one bottle of any new and previously untried wine should ever be bought, for obvious reasons. On the other hand, purchases should be made in quantity as soon as, and whenever, possible. There are some clear advantages in doing so.

There is always some discount on a case of wine. (A case is twelve ordinary bottles, twenty-four half-bottles, six half-gallons, or four gallons.) In most parts of the country the discount was once regularly 10 percent. With the sharp price rises of recent years there has been a tendency to reduce the case-lot discount, but it still exists and is worth having. The wine buyer who is disposed to try to bargain may do better at the neighborhood dealer, though probably never in the larger shops. Although the discount ordinarily applies only to full cases of the same wine, it is sometimes possible to obtain it for twelve or more bottles of different wines bought at the same time.

Most or all of the large central shops make delivery to

surrounding areas of the city and such delivery is free for a certain minimum purchase. Some neighborhood shops will also make free delivery. The advantages are obvious. Once the wine drinker has reached the stage of ordering specific wines in some quantity, he can shop very easily by phone or mail. The big stores encourage it.

On the other hand, alcoholic beverages sold at the retail level may not, by law, be shipped across state lines. Hence New Jersey and Connecticut residents must transport New York purchases themselves, as must also Virginia and Maryland residents who buy in the District of Columbia.

Some Fine Wine Shops of America

It is not my purpose to list here every good or decent wine shop in the country. This is not, after all, the classified directory. On the other hand, I would be remiss if I did not list some that I know of.

Every one of those appearing here is an exceptionally fine shop, among the very best wine stores in the country. In most, if not all cases, the owners know wine well and travel to Europe yearly to make their selections of foreign wines. They choose some of the less well known American wines with equal care. Their sales staffs are trained and knowledgeable and can generally be relied upon to give some straigtforward guidance when needed.

The list is alphabetical by states and cities. It is not, nor is it intended to be, all-inclusive. There are a number of other excellent wine shops in the country, though not as many as the average citizen might think.

CALIFORNIA

All Californians know, or think they know, wine. The state is proud of its wine industry. Wine is sold everywhere. Actually, a great many Californians appear to be no better informed than people elsewhere, especially about the imported wines that can be found in their state.

VENDOME
327 North Beverly Drive, Beverly Hills

This is a chain of some two dozen stores in the Los Angeles area. They are located in different income areas, and the stock ranges from modest variety in working-class neighborhoods to only the great wines of the world in the shop in the Century Plaza Hotel. Most of these shops have a wide selection of imported and domestic wines in all price categories, particularly the eight most recent ones, known as Vendome Party Centers. These are all large, well stocked, attractive stores, primarily self-service, but a knowledgeable staff is available. Store personnel attend wine tastings at least twice monthly, and tend to know about the wines they sell. Vendome operates on the basis of selecting types of wine via blind tastings so that any wine type or region represented in its stock can be pretty well depended upon to be authentic and of good quality. Vendome advertises rather extensively in the local press. Watch for its ads and consult the 'phone directory for location of the various stores.

JURGENSEN'S
601 South Lake, Pasadena

This is a supermarket chain with twenty outlets; each store has one of the best wine shops in the state, with a very complete collection of imported wines in all price ranges. Much of the stock is acquired by personal visits to the European vineyards. Jurgensen's wine shops are in no sense like the ordinary California supermarket wine sections, which are so often limited to the popular California brands, and readers in the communities served by Jurgensen's should seek out its stores. They are located in Beverly Hills (one Jurgensen and one Gourmet), Burlingame, Encino, Laguna Beach, La Jolla (one Jurgensen and one Fancy Pantry), Los Angeles, Palm Springs, Pasadena (one Jurgensen and one Linda Vista), Rancho Mirage, San Diego (one Jurgensen and one Gourmet), San

Francisco, San Marino, Santa Ana, Santa Barbara, and West-wood Village. Jurgensen's wine shops advertise regularly in the local press. Look for their ads.

MACY'S WINE & LIQUOR SHOP
Macy's, San Francisco
A very fine wine shop with the same selections of imported wines as Macy's, New York. For details, please see comments regarding Macy's under New York City.

COLORADO

HARRY HOFFMAN, INC.
511 18th Street, Denver
This is the largest single retail wine and liquor shop west of Chicago and the third or fourth largest in the United States. Wine is treated here with care and affection. It is stored in large air-conditioned cellars, with display bottles on shelves in the store proper. Salespeople are trained and knowledgeable. The store sends out a quarterly wine newsletter that is interesting and instructive to the serious wine drinker. It advertises regularly in the local press.

Hoffman's serves an exceptionally wide area. In addition to much of Colorado, it has considerable patronage in Arizona, Idaho, Kansas, western Nebraska, South Dakota, Utah, and Wyoming—all states where the state liquor control systems result in poor variety and meager choice. Hoffman's selection of imported wines is exceptional. It also has exclusive regional rights to the wines of some good, smaller California vintners such as San Martin and Concannon. It stocks over 1,000 different wines, an unusually large selection.

CONNECTICUT

MACY'S WINE & LIQUOR SHOP
Macy's, New Haven
A fine wine shop with the same selections of imported

wines as Macy's, New York. For details, please see comments regarding Macy's under New York City.

ILLINOIS

ARMANETTI LIQUORS
7324 North Western Avenue, Chicago

This is a chain of eighteen stores serving Chicago and most of its surrounding suburbs. The selection of imported wines, not merely European but from other parts of the world, is very complete and ranges from the great down to the good but affordable. Many wines recommended in this book will be found at the Armanetti stores, which advertise extensively in the local press. Wine buffs in the Chicago area should watch for the ads and consult the local telephone directories for location of the various Armanetti shops.

MASSACHUSETTS

BERENSON'S
70 Summer Street, Boston

Boston and the New England area are indeed fortunate in having Berenson's. This is the best wine dealer in New England and certainly one of the best in the country. It has a remarkable selection of wine, including many of excellence not available everywhere else. Its wine people are thoroughly knowledgeable and entirely to be trusted. They do not sell liquor and the liquor salesmen will not sell wine. Frequent visits are made to Europe by the owner and two of the staff, and good and still inexpensive wines are often found. This is of course true, as well, of all of the fine shops mentioned in this book.

There are two branch stores, at 242 Prudential Plaza and at 1024 Beacon Street in Brookline. Berenson's has wide patronage among residents of nearby states with state-operated liquor stores, as well as a devoted clientele, including me, from elsewhere.

MICHIGAN

LONDON CHOP HOUSE
155 West Congress, Detroit

This is one of the excellent restaurants of the United States and probably the best in Detroit. In addition to serving fine wines, the London Chop House also sells its wines by the bottle and case. The bottle price is 40 percent off the price appearing on the restaurant's wine list, and there is an additional 10 percent reduction for case lots. The wines are expensive, even at the reduced prices. Few will be found within our price range, but those that are will be excellent. What is perhaps more important to the buyer of moderate-priced wines is the fact that the same partner of the London Chop House who is responsible for their excellent cellar also serves as wine consultant to the wine shops of J. L. Hudson Company.

J. L. HUDSON COMPANY
1206 Woodward Avenue, Detroit

This is the biggest wine retailer in the state, with a wide selection of wines in all price categories. Wines are stored properly in temperature-controlled stockrooms. Hudson's has a wine shop in each of the seven shopping centers in the Detroit area, plus one in Flint, Michigan, and one in Toledo, Ohio. A new store is to open in 1974 in Ann Arbor. Personnel are trained, knowledgeable, and helpful. Like most better wine shops, they offer free delivery within the areas of their shops. Hudson's does not advertise, but their store locations will be found in the local 'phone books.

J. L. HUDSON COMPANY
Flint

A branch of the Detroit store. Please see comments immediately above.

MINNESOTA

HASKELL'S LIQUORS
23 South Seventh Street, Minneapolis

As this is being written, Haskell's is a single store, but three branches are being planned and all may be in operation in suburban locations by the time this appears in print. The store has a very complete selection of imported and domestic wines, including many recommended here. Like all of the better dealers today, Haskell's has been emphasizing a selection of good but less expensive wines and makes many available to the residents of the area. Haskell's advertises regularly in the local press. Watch for the ads, and consult the local directory, or inquire at the main store for information as to the branch stores now being planned.

MISSOURI

BERBIGLIA'S
110 East 9th Avenue, Kansas City

The owner visits Europe each year and has had much success in selecting good, modestly priced wines. While the selection of imported wines is very complete, there is particular emphasis on German, Spanish, and Portuguese wines, which are best sellers in that area. Berbiglia's advertises extensively in the local press. There are quite a few branch stores serving all of the Kansas City area, including Raytown, Lees, Summit, and Independence. The local directory or a call to the main store will give their locations.

9-0-5 STORES
Pet Plaza, 400 South Fourth Street, St. Louis

This chain has a fine and complete selection of imported wines, some not generally available. There are quite a few modestly priced wines of good quality, including many recommended here. The local press carries the chain's ads regularly. There are thirty-seven branch stores, which cover the surrounding area thoroughly. The 'phone book will give you the location within your community.

NEW JERSEY

CALDWELL LIQUORS
3301 Atlantic Avenue, Atlantic City
Caldwell's has a very complete selection of imported and domestic wines. Among the less expensive bottlings of the kind that are of interest to us, many are their private labels. The quality of the store is such that there should be no hesitation in trying them. At least some of those recommended here will also be found. There is one branch store. Caldwell's advertises regularly in the local press.

BAMBERGER'S WINE & LIQUOR SHOP
Bamberger's, Newark
Bamberger's is part of the Macy's chain and has a fine wine shop with the same selections of imported wines as Macy's, New York. For details, please see comments regarding Macy's under New York City.

PACKARD LIQUOR AND FINE WINE SHOPS
This is a chain of eighteen wine shops in many areas of New Jersey, owned by Frank W. Packard, who also owns Vendôme Liquor Inc., in New York City. For details as to these shops, please see the comments regarding Vendôme under New York City. Shopping for good wine is strongly recommended at any of these shops within your reach.

NEW YORK

There is a simply enormous number of wine and liquor stores in New York City and its surrounding suburbs. The variety of wines available in this city is greater than that offered anywhere else in the world, with the possible exception of London. Outside of the very poorly stocked neighborhood store, almost any wine and liquor shop in the area will have some of the wines recommended here. I confine myself to listing the few shops with which I have done some business.

ASTOR WINES & SPIRITS
12 Astor Place

This is a large and well stocked wine shop that seeks to emphasize low cost and economy. The owners make their annual pilgrimages to Europe like those of all the fine shops. They carry some imported and domestic labels exclusively. Such labels are usually good value and good quality. They advertise occasionally. They publish a wine list (it becomes increasingly hard to do so, for all stores, because of the constant and frequent increase in prices) and also update those on their mailing list with sales catalogs two or three times each year. The sales, by the way, are genuine.

MACY'S WINE & LIQUOR SHOP
Seventh Avenue between 34th and 35th Streets

This is part of Macy's department store, with its own separate entrance. It is one of the fine shops of the city, with a wide selection of imported and domestic wines. It is one of the oldest, perhaps the oldest, of all wine stores in New York, having been in existence long before Prohibition, and is rather proud of having New York State Liquor License 1. It carries some wines that are excellent values under its own private labels. Marceau, its label for many French wines, still includes some pre-Prohibition shippers. York House is the private label for ports and sherries. Several of the department stores in the Macy chain in other cities also have wine shops. All of these stock the same imported wines, while their selection of domestic wines might vary with local market conditions.

MORRELL & CO.
307 East 53rd Street

A very fine shop with an exceptional selection of wines. They are usually, though not always, somewhat higher priced than the same wines elsewhere, but convenience of location to some buyers and the assurance of careful selection for which Morrell's is noted makes it worthwhile to try some of their less expensive and lesser known wines, many of which cannot be exactly duplicated elsewhere.

SHERRY-LEHMANN, INC.
679 Madison Avenue

In a sense, this is the granddaddy of all wine shops. It claims to stock 2,000 different wines. I will not dispute it. Even if it is a few less than 2,000 it is a lot of wine. Sherry-Lehmann is reputed to have the finest selection in the world of great Bordeaux, better than can be found in the Bordeaux region itself. This is hardly a recommendation to those seeking wines under $4 or $5 per bottle. However, there is a very complete selection of all kinds of wine, including a great many good, inexpensive wines, many of which are here recommended. The store advertises frequently in the local press and its owner, Sam Aaron, writes occasionally for the magazines on wine. The salespeople are trained and knowledgeable.

SIXTY-SEVEN LIQUOR SHOP INC.
179 Columbus Avenue

This store has a large and complete stock and advertises frequently. It does not publish a wine list. The advertised sales are genuine, and a bargain can often be picked up in case lots. The serious wine drinker should watch for its ads.

VENDÔME LIQUOR, INC.
12 East 45th Street

A very well stocked store, with a good range of less expensive, as well as great, wines. Many of the wines are labeled as selections of Frank W. Packard. His selections tend to be very good and many are within our price range. Frank W. Packard is the owner of Vendôme and his selections are available only there, within New York. He is also the owner of a substantial chain of similar stores in New Jersey where Frank W. Packard selections are sold. These can be found listed in the telephone directories for many areas of New Jersey under the name of Packard Liquor and Fine Wine shops and, for those living within reach of his stores, shopping there is recommended.

AUSTIN LIQUORS
71-47 Austin Street, Forest Hills
Among the numerous shops in the other boroughs of New York City and in the surrounding suburban areas, the only one with which I am acquainted personally is Austin. For what is ostensibly just a neighborhood store, this shop has a remarkable selection of wines, always at the lowest allowable prices. Many of the wines recommended here are in stock at Austin and those within reach of the store are strongly advised to shop there.

OHIO

J. L. HUDSON COMPANY
Toledo
A branch of the Detroit store, with a fine wine shop carrying the same selection as the parent store. Please see comments for this company listed under Detroit, Michigan.

TEXAS

CENTENNIAL LIQUORS
5619 East Lovers Lane, Dallas
These are probably the finest wine shops in the Southwest. The range of imported as well as domestic wines is very complete. Centennial boasts that every regular salesman personally tastes more than a hundred new wines every year. No wine list is published, but Centennial advertises every week in local papers and mails very informative monthly fliers to better customers. Many of the wines recommended here will be found at Centennial. There are thirty-two branch stores,

serving all of the higher-income communities of Dallas County.

WASHINGTON, D.C.

Washington, D.C. has the largest per capita sales of wine in the United States. This is probably due in part to the large diplomatic community, but also because of purchases by nonresidents seeking to save because the District levies no tax on liquors or wines. The real savings are in liquor, but some states (including Virginia, a near neighbor to the District) do have sufficiently high taxes on wine to make purchases in Washington worthwhile.

BURKA'S
3300 Wisconsin Avenue, N.W.

This is one of the fine wine shops of the District. The selection is very complete and ranges from the very costly to the very reasonable. Prices are generally lower than in the rest of the East, especially in the case of sherries, ports, and champagnes. Many of the wines are what Burka's calls "direct imports," meaning imported directly from the producer or shipper rather than obtained from a distributor here, and these are lower in price. The staff is trained and fairly knowledgeable. The owner and the manager are wine lovers, not merely wine sellers. Burka's advertises in the local press.

CENTRAL LIQUOR STORE
516 Ninth Street, N.W.

Central Liquor is reputed to be the biggest single retail shop in the United States in terms of volume. It is a fantastically crowded store with low prices, well known to Washingtonians. It has a large stock of wines, with emphasis on the better known Bordeaux and Burgundies, but with surprising omissions, even in French and American wines, let alone those of other countries. The wine manager is quite knowledgeable and could be of help if a time could be found when the store isn't mobbed. On a Saturday afternoon, there are two policemen in the road in front of the store directing traffic and the customers are three to five deep around the counter. A weekday morning is probably the best time to visit this store for browsing and shopping.

PART IV

Table Wines of Many Countries

IT IS EXTREMELY DIFFICULT, SOMETIMES IMPOSSIBLE, TO DESCRIBE A taste to one who has never experienced it. We tend to do so by analogy. For example, a fair description of whale meat might be that it has the consistency of beef with a taste not unpleasantly compounded of beef liver and fish. This description would be meaningless, however, to a lifelong vegetarian.

Actually, only four taste sensations are experienced by the tongue: salty, bitter, sweet, and sour. These four, in endless combinations, produce all the infinitely varied flavors with which people are familiar. How then to describe wine, which can be bitter, sweet, or sour but never salty, and which is also capable of almost infinite variations and subtleties of taste and character?

Some psychologists are at work seeking to devise mathematically precise definitions of given taste sensations. Perhaps they will succeed. Until they do, we must still use the many words of "wine language" for necessarily inexact descriptions that may mean different things to different people. There is a red Bordeaux often described as having an aftertaste of raspberries. A friend of mine insists he can detect this taste. I cannot. Perhaps his palate is keener than mine—or is it his imagination that is keener?

With wine, as with food, description is frequently by analogy, and since French wines are the most varied and the best known, wines of most other countries are usually compared with them. This will be done here, too, and the usual wine vocabulary will necessarily be employed, but it will be kept simple and the more esoteric terms and comparisons will be avoided.

For the complete neophyte, no description by comparison will do the slightest good. Wine can only be compared with other wine, not with liquor or liqueur or fruit juice or soft drinks. (Part IX—"Summing Up" will, however, include advice for the absolute beginner.)

One commonly used term may need explanation for the beginner, namely, "dry." Dry in relation to wine means "not sweet." Labels of imported wines sold in the United States are frequently in English but it is worth knowing and remembering that the French equivalent of "dry" is *sec* and the Italian is *secco*.

Taste is a highly personal thing. It is remarkable what different impressions individuals can receive about the same wine. A particular wine that I shall describe later seems to me to give a slight aftertaste of sweetness. A friend with an educated palate, tasting the wine with me, thought he detected a touch of bitterness. We both found it delectable.

Naturally, the comments made here represent my own tastes. Therefore, there will be what some may consider blank spots. For example, I don't care much for rosés, as must already have become evident, and the reader will find that rosés do not get very detailed treatment here. Similarly, I do not like noticeable sweetness in my dinner wines and again the reader will discover that such wines are not dealt with as exhaustively as they might be.

The purpose of this book must, however, be borne in mind. As regards specific wines, it is to inform the reader about a large number available in the United States, good to fine to great in quality and priced within specified limits. It is not to give a complete description of all wines from every-where, regardless of quality, availability, or cost. It is to be hoped that the advice already outlined as to how to buy wine will be adequate to help any reader ferret out wines, or types of wines, not completely covered here.

For every country, or region, or type of wine discussed here, listings will be found of varying quality. Every one recommended is at least a good drinkable wine. Whenever trying a new type of wine for the first time, you should make it a rule always to start with one of the finer ones, which can be counted on to have the authentic characteristics of the type and should serve as the taste-fixer, that is, the wine that estab-lishes the character of the type on the palate and in the mind. Thereafter, you will be better able to judge the quality of the less expensive ones and choose the best buys intelligently.

The more ordinary method is to start with the lowest-priced first and, by fumbling degrees, to work one's way up. That's the way I did it. It's the hard way. It will be far better and infinitely more satisfying to start with the best quality within our price range and work your way down to the best buys and perhaps, eventually, up also to the best wines.

It must be remembered that wine is an ephemeral thing. No vintage, no supply, lasts forever. Hence a wine mentioned here may no longer be available when you sally forth to buy it. Often enough it is only the supply of a given year that has been exhausted, and the new year's supply comes into the market soon. It is always a bit sad to me, to any wine lover, I am sure, when a wine he enjoys ceases to be available. It is also the occasion for doing a little more trying and tasting, until a new, equally good wine is found. So if you cannot find the particu-lar wine you set out to buy, keep an eye out for its return and, in the meantime, using the methods outlined here, set about finding another instead.

The prices listed here are those generally prevailing in the Northeast in the fall of 1973. They are roughly the same in most of the rest of the country, though there are some states where they are regularly higher because of minimum-price or other fair-trade laws. The economics of inflation being what it is, it is perfectly possible that the prices given will all be out of date as you read this, although I think they may remain steady for a time.

Any reputable dealer will tell you honestly whether there have been general increases in the intervening period. If there have, the given wine will remain proportionately as good a buy as before but you must judge for yourself whether it is worth the new price to you. If there have not, there ought not to be much disparity between the price I list and the one you will find.

If the price appears to be too high, try looking a bit more before you buy. Noticeable differences can often occur. In a single issue of *The New York Times*, in early 1973, Sixty-Seven Liquors advertised a Château Gloria at $4.99 while Gimbel's advertised the same wine, same vintage year, at $6.50. The importance of shopping around a little needs no further emphasis.

One final admonition: Do not sell your own palate short. You have been tasting food and drink of all kinds all your life. Your sense of taste is presumably as keen as the next man's, perhaps keener. Your preferences are your own affair but you do not defer to anyone in ability to judge the quality and flavor of a steak or an omelet, a grilled lobster or a dish of baked beans.

Wine buffs do not have a better sense of taste than you. What they do have is an *educated* palate. Yours will need educating, too, but it is innately as capable as anyone else's of judging and appreciating the fine nuances of wine. Even the professionals, in estimating the probable characteristics of a new vintage, are guided largely by exact and detailed chemical analysis. If you knew how to interpret such data, you might make a moderately accurate forecast too.

The gap between you and the wine buff is not so big as it may seem although between you and the professional wine taster it is big indeed. But wine drinking should be your pleasure, not your living, and for that you need no more than some experience plus reasonable confidence in your own sense of taste.

A word about the alcoholic content of wine: Alcoholic content has become fairly standardized throughout the world and its appearance on the label is of no great significance. Table or dinner wines, as sold in the United States, commonly vary between 11 and 12.5 percent alcohol by volume. Occasionally a dinner wine is found with 13 or even a whopping 14 percent alcohol. Aperitif and dessert wines range between 18 and 20 percent. For those curious to make a comparison with liquor, "proof" in the United States (it is different elsewhere) is twice the volume of alcohol, so that 12 percent by volume would be 24 proof. Conversely, the common 86 proof of whiskey means 43 percent by volume.

France

All discussion of wine begins with France, and for good reason. France produces close to 2 billion gallons a year, sharing honors with Italy from year to year (depending on varying weather conditions) as the largest producer in the world. Most of the greatest wines of the world come from France. Its wines are much imitated in other countries, its vines widely transplanted, its wine industry thoroughly and strictly regulated, and the quality of its wines usually reliable.

The variety is enormous, providing an almost limitless choice of white, red, and rosé, of delicate to robust, of dry to sweet, for all palates and all purposes. Quality, too, ranges from the very great to the very mediocre.

The great wines of France represent a tiny percentage of its total production. Sheer scarcity value is one of the main reasons for their fantastic prices. Most Americans do not realize that France is also guilty of producing vast quantities of mediocre and really bad wines, the kind that have at times been known as "red ink," the kind that make you feel they can take the enamel off your teeth. They have rarely found their way to the United States heretofore, but unfortunately they are beginning to do so now.

Between these two extremes, there is a great supply of very fine, good, and satisfactory wines that do find their way to this country in quantity. For the most part, French wines available here cannot be called bad, although there can be a large step indeed between not bad and really good.

France has enacted some of the most comprehensive laws affecting the production and labeling of wine. (Germany's are even stricter.) The *Appellation Contrôlée* (literally, "Controlled Naming") is the set of control laws dealing with the better wines of France. It specifies such details as the area within which any given wine may be produced, the varieties of grape that may be used, grape-growing and winemaking methods, minimum alcoholic content, and much else.

Labeling is rigidly controlled. The label may bear the simple legend, Appellation Contrôlée. It is more likely that the name of the region or that of the wine will be inserted between the two words: for example, Appellation Beaujolais Contrôlée. Appellation Contrôlée on the label indicates a better French wine. The designation is broad enough to include numerous wines within the price limits set here, as well as the famous ones. It is also broad enough to include many wines that many people would consider far from good. It is a guide to be used with others, not a guarantee.

Another designation that is becoming of some importance in America is V.D.Q.S.—*Vin Délimité de Qualité Supérieur* ("Delimited Wine of Superior Quality"). Wines labeled V.D.Q.S. are considered good enough to require government control, but lower in quality than those of the Appellation Contrôlée. In general, they are what is known here as regional or country wines, connoting, more or less, wines of lesser quality.

Recently, as prices have climbed steeply, the French have begun to send us some of these regional wines, many with the V.D.Q.S. label. Any increase in the availability of less expensive wines should be welcome and there is little reason to doubt that such exportation will continue and grow rapidly.

Still, if the Appellation Contrôlée is not a guarantee of goodness, how much less so is the V.D.Q.S.? Some of these more recent arrivals are proving enjoyable, many are not. Until you have explored the superior wines of France and elsewhere, there need be no stampede to the wines of the V.D.Q.S.

In order to know at least a little about the French wines available in the United States, it is essential to have some understanding of various regions as well as of some producers and shippers. This can be a formidable undertaking, particularly regarding Bordeaux and Burgundy, the two areas that produce the greatest of French wines. It is much simplified for us, since we will deal only with wines within our means, not the entire spectrum from these two regions. Most of their wines are far, far up in the stratosphere and will never come down to within reach of the ordinary buyer.

On the other hand, sometime in the future you may want to dabble just a bit in the lesser greats, which do not command quite such frightening prices as do the giants. If you can occasionally afford to, you should, once your palate has become somewhat educated. It will be a worthwhile experience.

Consequently, while the complexities of wine in these two regions have no place in the body of this book, I have included in the Appendix a quite abbreviated description for those who wish to tackle it. It will have to be studied more than once before it really begins to sort itself out in your mind, but it can be fascinating and can serve as introduction to a more detailed study of the subject.

There is almost no such thing left as a bargain in French

wines, although as recently as a year ago there still were. Here and there, a rather exceptional value for the price still exists but, in the main, the best you can expect is good value for your money in terms of the general level of existing prices. Of such good values there are still a fair number.

Despite the fact that French wines are now far from being best buys among wines in general, it is very important to know about them, their character, the grapes of which they are made. They are so widely imitated, so many of the grapes are grown in other countries, so many wines are sold under the grape names, that it would be equally important to know a good deal about French wines even if there were no longer a single one left at an affordable price.

BORDEAUX

More great red wines are produced here than in any other single region of the world. The drier whites are generally good and sometimes fine. Some of the sweet whites are among the great dessert wines of the world. Production has always been plentiful and, since the great reds constitute a tiny proportion of the total, there has always been a substantial supply of lower-priced ones, many of which remain within our reach today.

Much of Bordeaux wine is bottled under the names of châteaux. *Château* means, literally, "castle," but the Bordeaux châteaux are rarely so imposing, most being comfortable, fairly modest country houses. The term *château* has more loosely come to mean the vineyards around the house, and the most important thing to remember about château bottling is that the wine is made at the château from grapes grown only in its own vineyards. This bespeaks the strong likelihood of greater care and better quality.

There are over 2,000 châteaux in Bordeaux! Some say as

many as 3,000. I doubt whether any one individual knows all of them. I certainly don't, nor do I want to or need to. Listings are available, largely as matters of record. It is perfectly clear that while "château" on the label bespeaks a better wine than just "Bordeaux," it is no guarantee of greatness.

The Reds

Red Bordeaux and claret are the same thing. Claret is the name originally bestowed upon red Bordeaux table wine by the English centuries ago. It is used quite frequently nowadays for lesser wines of other countries seeking to identify themselves with Bordeaux.

Bordeaux wines are generally thought of as light and delicate. Actually, they range from delicate to moderately big. The lesser wines, our concern, are likely to be somewhere in between. In any case, any decent Bordeaux is never thin and has a distinctive grace and charm. All are very dry.

The best of the Bordeaux are usually made of the Cabernet Sauvignon grape alone. Even some of these are made of one or more other grapes as well, the one most often used being the Merlot. The lesser wines can be assumed to be made of more than one grape, which is, by itself, no reason to question their quality. Recently, some Bordeaux labeled Cabernet Sauvignon have been shipped here, and occasionally there is one labeled Merlot. When so labeled, it must be made entirely of that grape.

Bordeaux consists of quite a number of districts, at least one of which boasts several subregions. Three such districts, considered "minor," are of distinct interest to us. They are minor only in the sense that they do not produce any of the famous greats. They do account for very enjoyable and even fine wines, and prices are, as yet, still quite low. If there are any "sleepers" still left among French wines, these are they.

The remaining districts will not be described here. Their wines, for the most part, are far beyond our means; but I do urge you to refer freely to the Appendix, especially since some of the wines still within our limits do have such district designations.

Vintages for Red Bordeaux

These are important for the greater wines, of less importance to us, but not completely without significance.

The vintage of 1967 was very good but not great and hence the wines have been lower-priced. The vintage is rapidly disappearing and prices have climbed, but a few wines at the upper extreme of our range may yet be found.

The year 1968 was a near disaster. Some of the prices among the few wines being offered for sale may look very attractive, but the wines are to be avoided.

The vintages of 1969, '70, and '71 were all excellent. The '70 is great and exceptionally plentiful. It is in these years that most of the wines we are interested in will be found. Any of these three is fine enough for our purposes.

The vintage of 1972 was mediocre. The more reliable vintners and *négociants* should provide satisfactory wines.

Preliminary word regarding the 1973 vintage indicates that quantity is very big (this will help to maintain, perhaps even drive down, prices) and quality about as good as the 1967 year: that is, very good but far from great.

Any '67s that may still be found are not only ready for drinking now, they had best be drunk soon. The modest wines may be drunk young in any case and those of the '69, '70, and '71 vintages are all drinkable at present.

The three districts of particular interest to us are:
CÔTES de BLAYE.

A fairly large district, Côtes de Blaye produces more whites than reds. The whites are minor wines. The reds are on the bigger side, a good deal like St. Émilion, the biggest of the Bordeaux. They are not as good, but are good in their own right and well worth our attention. They are the least common among the three referred to here.

CÔTES de BOURG. This is a smaller district, almost wholly enclosed by the Côtes de Blaye, making a wine very much the same in character as the Blaye, but better. Both are early maturing.

CÔTES de FRONSAC. The reds are bigger than other Bordeaux, approaching the body of Burgundies. They are somewhat slower-maturing wines, are not great, but can be delicious.

All of these are characteristic Bordeaux, all are good to fine, and all are excellent buys. Almost without exception they have very limited distribution. The fine wine shops are almost certain to have one or several of their own brands among their stock.

The following can be found at the shops indicated:

Côtes de Blaye
> CHÂTEAU LA VALADÉ '70—$2.29 at Astor's, $2.99 at Morrell's
> CHÂTEAU GRESSINA '70—$2.49 at Morrell's

Côtes de Bourg
> CHÂTEAU LA JONCARDE '67—$3.25 at Berenson's
> CHÂTEAU LA CLOTE BLANCHE '69—$2.19 at Morrell's
> CHÂTEAU GRAND MAISON '70—$2.99 at Sherry-Lehmann's
> CHÂTEAU GUIRAUD-CHEVAL BLANC '70—$2.99 at
>   Sherry-Lehmann's

Côtes de Fronsac
> CHÂTEAU MOULIN HAUT VILLARS '67—$3.29 at Astor's
> CHÂTEAU MAYNE VIEL '67—$3.49 at Astor's
> LA FONTAINES '70—$3.69 at Sherry-Lehmann's
> CANON de BREM '69—$3.49 at Sherry-Lehmann's

None is specifically recommended. Any would be a very safe wine to sample for those within reach of these stores. It is perfectly possible that, by the time you read this, the specific wines will be gone but, in that case, others of equal quality will surely have replaced them. Others are sure to be found in fine shops everywhere. Try them freely.

There are a great number of small producers in Bordeaux who have in the past dealt with a smaller distributor or, frequently, directly with a larger shop here. It is their wines, often château-bottled, that have always been, and still are, the best buys, if only for the reason that dealing directly eliminates the costs of middlemen. Some of these have yielded recently to the blandishments of the big shippers who, fearing a shortage of supply in the face of constantly increasing demand, have been buying up everything they can lay their hands on. Fortunately, many direct imports can still be found. With few exceptions, each is likely to be available only in a particular shop.

You should not hesitate to try those found in a truly fine shop in your area. At the same time, it would be wise to try first one of those recommended here, if available, or if not, a standard wine whose quality can be relied on. One such is MOUTON CADET, a cousin of, but not to be confused with, the great Château Mouton Rothschild. It is a blended wine, not great but consistently good, and an authentic Bordeaux. At $3.99 it is a very good buy. It would serve excellently as a taste-fixer.

Should it not be available, there need be no hesitation in trying a Bordeaux of one of the big shippers, such as B&G or Cruse. You will overpay but can be sure of good quality and authenticity. Thereafter, the labels available locally should be sampled.

Here are some I know and recommend. The first three listed are the best. The others are all good to very good, and are sufficiently alike in quality so that they do not appear in any particular order.

CABERNET SAUVIGNON '71, Johanneton. This is a supple and excellent example of good Bordeaux, with some of the subtlety of the finer ones, a most unusual buy at $2.99. Quite good enough to serve as a taste-fixer. Johanneton has a broad sam-

pling of Bordeaux, including a rather lovely Bordeaux Rouge at
$2.25, a very good Merlot at $2.99, and an equally good Médoc
at $3.25; also some district and commune wines at prices a bit
too steep for us. The Cabernet Sauvignon is the best buy.

CHÂTEAU ROLLAND. A G. C. Sumner selection, it should be
available wherever his selections are found. There are both a
'70 and a '71. The '70 matured greatly in the two years after it
appeared and ended up as a soft, velvety, and lovely example
of Bordeaux. It is largely gone but, should you still find any,
buy it without hesitation. It will remain at its peak probably
until 1975. The '71 was a delicate, charming, and almost gay
wine early in 1973. Eight months later, it had already matured
along the lines of the '70, but even better. At about $2.49 to
$2.59 for each, this wine is by far the best buy I know of in red
Bordeaux. It can also properly serve as a taste-fixer.

MÉDOC '67, A. de Luze et Fils. This is a very, very good
wine, with some of the subtlety of the fine Bordeaux and a very
true aftertaste. At $4.39 it is far from being a bargain but it
might well be tried as a taste-fixer.

CLUB CLARET '67, A. de Luze. This is a good Bordeaux, in no
way exceptional, but a good buy at $2.79.

CHÂTEAU BELLEVUE '70, Distributed by Austin Nichols, it is
available in New York at Sherry-Lehmann. With moderate
bouquet and fairly good body, it is very pleasant and true to
the Bordeaux type. It is good, not fine, and while not of the
quality of Château Rolland, it is a very good buy at $2.49.

CABERNET SAUVIGNON '69, Frederick Wildman. A very pleasant wine, it is true to type, with good bouquet and body.
About equal to Château Bellevue, it is not as good a buy at
$2.99.

CHÂTEAU LA ROCQUE '66, St. Émilion. It is somewhat light for
a St. Émilion but is mature, of good body, of a quite great
vintage year, and rather a fine buy at $3.19. It will probably
still be at full maturity to the end of 1974. It is carried by
Vendôme in New York but should be available elsewhere, as
well.

POMEROL '70, Auteuil et Cie. This is a true Pomerol, rather

big and soft, a simple, unsubtle wine and a very good buy at $2.59. Auteuil is a brand available only at Vendôme.

BORDEAUX SUPÉRIEUR, Lichine. A '67 and a '70 may both be found. The '67 is a good, not superior, Bordeaux of good bouquet. The '70, now fully mature, is noticeably richer. Both are good buys at $2.99, the '70 being the better.

ST. ÉMILION, Marceau (Macy's brand). Full-bodied, with the true St. Émilion character, it is a very enjoyable wine, not distinguished, but a very good buy at $2.50.

(It should not be assumed that the Marceau label is uniformly a mark of good quality. Different suppliers provide the wines labeled Marceau. I found the Grand Vin Rouge de Bordeaux to be rather thin, sharp, and without character. At $2.50, it cannot compare with their St. Émilion at the same price. Their Margaux '70 is light, like a Margaux, but not delicate and fine. It is rather ordinary and not a worthwhile value at $3.50.)

THE WHITES

Somewhat more than half of Bordeaux' total production is white wine. The best of the table wines are made in the Graves district. Some of the greater châteaux, including Haut Brion and Graves, make some white wine. These are reputed to be very fine indeed. They are also expensive and quite outside our scope.

The name Graves has come to be applied to all of the drier white Bordeaux. For my taste, the driest are still sweeter than I care for, but many are dry enough to be considered dinner wines. Some of those from the southern part of the Graves region are sweet enough to be mistaken for Sauternes, the great dessert wine.

The better whites are most often sold under the name of the châteaux where they were made, whether or not the châteaux are well known. Those sold merely under the designations Graves or Graves Supérieur are likely to be on the sweeter side, with less character. White Graves in general tend to lack the clean-cut freshness of good dry whites of other regions.

The Graves are not in the same class with the wonderful

whites of Burgundy or the excellent whites of the Loire, Alsace, and the Rhône Valley. On the other hand, most of them are less costly, especially as compared to those from Burgundy and the Rhône.

This is not to say that the Graves simply aren't good. They are good but rarely exceptional and need be of interest only to those who especially like less dry wines.

CHÂTEAU GRAVILLE LACOSTE '70. This is an excellent example of a good Graves and, at $2.95, a very good buy. There is a distinct touch of sweetness. It would hardly be the choice for shellfish or delicately flavored boiled or poached fish, but would suit a somewhat more robust dish, such as baked fish or roast chicken. It has the full-flavored mellowness characteristic of good white Bordeaux. I would prefer it for just plain drinking, well chilled.

CLUB BLANC, A. de Luze. This is a good example, characteristic of the type, not exceptional. It is good value at $2.20.

GRAVES SUPÉRIEUR '70, Marceau. Available only at Macy's, it is very pleasant indeed, quite dry, with only the barest taste of sweetness and with the merest suggestion of the beauty of a fine Sauternes. It is an excellent buy at $2.25.

DOMAINE DES PLANTES, Graves Supérieur Sec, Frederick Wildman. Despite the designation of "Sec," there is noticeable but unobjectionable sweetness. A good example of Graves and a very good buy at $2.25.

You should definitely try one of these or one of the many others, some estate-bottled. Your taste may not coincide with mine and you may well find Graves quite suitable as a dinner wine.

BURGUNDY

Small in area and in total production by comparison with Bordeaux, Burgundy's reds share honors with the best of Bordeaux, while its whites are generally considered the greatest dry wines in the world.

Unfortunately for us, the lesser Burgundies, being always in comparatively short supply, have been historically costlier than their Bordeaux counterparts of comparable quality. What this means quite simply is that almost all Burgundy has now become too costly for us to consider. A few reds, a few more whites, are still both good in quality and within our limits. One or two of the whites are rather exceptional.

Burgundies, both red and white, happen to be my favorites. I am sad and angry and frustrated at what has happened to their prices, but I know of nothing to do about it but to go on drinking those I can still afford, hoping that someday prices may come down a bit from their peak, whenever that is reached, and meanwhile occasionally allowing myself a lovely but overpriced bottle as a treat.

If you feel financially able, you too should try one of the costlier ones occasionally. Again, some of the details of the rather complex classifications are included in the Appendix, which I urge you to consult. For our purposes here, it is sufficient to remember that the names of the better, more reliable *négociants*, such as Joseph Drouhin, Pierre Olivier, and J. Thorin, are among the best guides to quality. The "selectors," Frank Schoonmaker and George C. Sumner, are also invaluable as guides.

Unlike those of Bordeaux, the vineyards of Burgundy are usually broken up among many owners. A single vineyard of under twenty acres can have a dozen or more owners. Hence, there are no counterparts to the more obscure Bordeaux châteaux, many of which account for rather exceptional values in the American market. In Burgundy, the best values in lesser wines should be sought among those shipped by the better *négociants*.

Vintages in Burgundy are extremely important for the greater reds and whites both and, in general, the qualities of the given year apply equally to both. However, they are of little consequence to us. Only the more recent vintages need concern us. It is quite enough to know that '67 was a very good year, '68 was a near disaster (particularly with the reds; these wines should be avoided if found), and '69, '70, and '71 were all excellent or great, their lesser wines by now being thoroughly mature. The '72 whites are proving very good; the reds, as they appear, will be spotty, varying from average to very good. The '73 vintage will be enormous and is likely to vary from good to very good, but far from great.

THE REDS

The great red Burgundies all originate in the Côte d'Or, the "Golden Slope." They are by now of purely academic interest to us. Do please, however, consult the Appendix for a description of them.

The second producer of reds is the Mâcon, south of the Côte d'Or. The Mâcon reds are never great, often good to excellent, bigger, fuller, and softer than their brothers to the north. Reds of interest to us are likely to come largely from the Mâcon, whether so labeled or not.

The third region producing mainly reds is Beaujolais, which is in a class by itself and requires, and will receive, special attention.

The grape that gives red Burgundy its distinction is the Pinot Noir. The best are made of that grape only. Those that interest us most are blended wines, but the strength of the Pinot Noir is such that it imparts its special character to all Burgundies.

Burgundies are generally thought of as big, full-bodied, and as red table wines go, slightly sweet. Many of the imitation "Burgundies" of other countries emphasize these characteristics.

I have never tasted a sweet Burgundy, red or white. If some of the reds have a touch of sweetness that the Bordeaux, for example, lack, they are still distinctly dry wines. As for bigness, the biggest of the Burgundies is far from heavy-bodied, and an occasional one, expensive to be sure, is light and delicate.

Here are a few—alas very few—that can be recommended

as authentic and good and, in the context of today's prices in general, worth trying. Not all of these have regional or national distribution. It is probable that their counterparts in quality can be found in fine wine shops. They are listed in approximate order of quality.

BOURGOGNE ROUGE '71 and '72, de Sylou. I hhave not tasted the '72 but have reason to believe it is the equal of the '71. (This is quite likely with blended wines.) The '71, which may not be obtainable any longer, is full-bodied and already mature, with many subtleties of flavor, and a fine example of how good a non-estate bottled, so-called minor wine, actually can be. The '72 could certainly use a year or two of aging in bottle. In absolute terms, the wine is no bargain at about $4.10 but there is no hope of bargains in Burgundy any longer and it is an excellent value.

SANTENAY '69, Pierre Olivier. Santenay is at the extreme south of the Côte d'Or. This wine is a characteristic Santenay, rather big, soft, almost mouth-filling, wholly mature and, while not great as among the greats, it is great among the non-greats. I doubt that it will sell much longer at $3.49 but, even at 20 percent or so higher, and in a younger vintage, it would be an exceptional buy.

SOLEIL NOIR, Joseph Drouhin. It has been a classic among "minor" reds for years. I cannot believe that it will sell much longer at its current price of $3.55 but, as long as it does, it is an outstanding value for an excellent wine.

BOURGOGNE ROUGE, Pierre Olivier. I cannot find any around as of this writing. If it has been discontinued, it is a great pity. I always found it several shades better than Drouhin's Soleil Noir and it always sold at about 10 percent less. Keep your eyes open for it and if you find any at a not outrageous price, buy it.

MERCUREY '70, Lapalus. This is obtainable only at Astor's in New York but is of interest, at least for those in reach of the store. The wines of Mercurey, a close neighbor to Santenay, are usually lighter than this one, which is rather big but at the same time, round, soft, wholly mature and, while not at all subtle, utterly pleasant and truly enjoyable. It is an excellent buy at $3.19.

MÂCON ROUGE '71, Caves de Charnay Bellevue. This is a very good example of red Mâcon, which is never great but capable of being very good. The wine is medium-bodied, with moderate bouquet and a good, true Burgundy flavor. When I last drank it, it was still young and almost refreshing. The '71 would be very mature when you read this. At about $2.35, it is one of the best buys in this group. (The wines of Caves de Charnay Bellevue are all available in the Northeast at Berenson's of Boston and have fairly wide distribution elsewhere.)

PINOT NOIR '69 and '70, Alexis Lichine. Only the '70 may now be available. There is no noticeable difference between the two. It is a rather indifferent Burgundy, moderately full-bodied, with no subtlety or real character. Although nationally distributed and, hence, available almost everywhere, it is not much of a buy at $3.29.

SANTENAY LA FLEUROT, Pierre Olivier. Those who may wish to go to our very upper limits would find this an unusually enjoyable Burgundy. The cost, $4.95. The wine, rather exceptional.

Beaujolais

There is an occasional wine that captures the popular interest, sometimes for no reason of superior quality, merely, perhaps, because the name appeals to that vague and fleeting thing known as the public fancy. Beaujolais, the lovely red wine of the southernmost part of Burgundy, is one of these, perhaps the best known of all, and for very good reason indeed. Unfortunately, perhaps because of this very popularity, Beaujolais has become the subject, if not the victim, of modern merchandising and advertising techniques. Recently it became the victim of the price spiral (or is it the public who is the victim?) to the point where it is now rapidly joining the ranks of so many other French wines as merely a pleasant memory, tinged with the bitterness of present prices.

Beaujolais (I refer here only to the reds; the production of whites is minuscule and they are not of primary importance) is made of the Gamay grape, which, for unexplainable reasons, produces a dull, uninteresting wine a little farther north, but in Beaujolais results in a unique wine that can best be described as light, fruity, fresh, charming, and gay.

The simplest of the Beaujolais, coming mostly from the southern part of the region, rate only the designation of Beaujolais or Beaujolais Supérieur. The production of thirty-five villages farther north may be sold as Beaujolais Villages, a wine of more strength and character. The nine most northerly villages may use their own names, and their wines are known as the Named Crus, or the Commune wines. They are sometimes labeled Grands Crus. They are the best of Beaujolais.

All Beaujolais, with the exception of some of the Commune wines, can and should be drunk young, the sooner after their appearance on the market the better, if the wine drinker is to capture the special qualities of the wine to the fullest. Within four to six months after bottling, much of the fresh sprightliness will have gone. But is nothing worthwhile left? Are they thereafter to be avoided? Not at all.

The fact is that these wines do not spoil or become in any sense undrinkable after those first few months. They merely change, losing most of that special freshness, but always retaining the particular lightness and fruitiness of Beaujolais. Except for the Commune wines, they are not likely to last more than two or three years, perhaps a bit more, but until they fade, they are Beaujolais, not some dull, tasteless imitation. And they are excellent reds for the unsophisticated palate just because they are so light, fruity, and uncomplicated.

Certain terms need definition. Beaujolais Primeur is made of grapes picked at the earliest possible moment, before the end of September, subjected to a quick fermentation and legally not saleable to the French public until November 16, when it traditionally appears in the shops and restaurants of

Paris and Lyons. It is an unusually fresh and fruity wine, but these qualities fade rapidly—within weeks—after which it is quite pedestrian.

Beaujolais Nouveau, or de Nouveau (meaning "new") and Beaujolais d'Année ("of the year") are actually the same thing, the first properly made wine of the newest vintage, on the market in about February of the year following the vintage. Beaujolais Nouveau, however, is a term commonly enough used here to mean Beaujolais Primeur.

This is as confusing as can be to most people, yet must be understood, since some among the American wine industry, for the past few years, have been flying in the Beaujolais Primeur, among much fanfare of advertising, so that it may be on sale here, too, on November 16. The Primeur is no more than an overpriced curiosity and the entire promotion should be disregarded. Above all, avoid buying any wine labeled Primeur later in the season. It may remain on sale for many months after November 16.

The Commune wines, or Grands Crus, are by now mostly beyond our means, and not worth it. Here and there, one can be found at the very upper level of our range. Hopefully, the same prices will prevail for a while, for they are still well worth buying at below $5.

There are nine Communes. Their names should be listed here, even if only for occasional reference. They are Brouilly, Chenas, Chiroubles, Côte de Brouilly, Fleurie, Julienas, Morgon, Moulin-à-Vent, and St. Amour. All may be drunk young, but are best when about three to five years old. Some will last for years longer. Which they are hardly matters. They now command prices commensurate with greatness, but are not great.

Vintages in Beaujolais are not of major importance. Some are of course better than others but none produces great wine and none is disastrous. Suffice it to know that '70 and '71 were both very fine, '72 was modest, and '73 has produced so excellent and copious a vintage that, as of this writing, prices of Beaujolais are actually expected to fall somewhat.

Individual recommendations are not practical, primarily because supplies of a particular year are likely to be exhausted quickly, making an individual listing obsolete by the time it is read and, if the individual wine can still be found at a later date, it may have become anything but a good value. On the other hand, guides are needed, especially because of the abundance of labels on the market—no fewer than 150 by actual count in the bigger shops of Manhattan alone in early 1973, probably several hundred throughout the country.

Also it is a fact, not myth, that a huge quantity of wine leaves the Beaujolais region every year labeled Beaujolais, although it is actually cheap wine brought in from the Midi, Algeria, and who knows where else. Some say these account for fully half of all "Beaujolais" wine. They are poor wines, not better because mislabeled, and they should be avoided. Therefore, attention is centered on the winemakers and shippers whose trustworthiness is certain and whose wines can be relied upon to be authentic.

Among those whose Beaujolais might still be obtained at affordable prices are, alphabetically:

CAVES DE CHARNAY BELLEVUE. G. C. Sumner selections.

JOSEPH DROUHIN

J. LAPALUS. Available only at Astor's in New York.

ALEXIS LICHINE

THE RT. HON. ERNEST MARPLES. A former british political figure (much is made of this but what it has to do with the quality of the wines he grows in Beaujolais I fail to see). In New York his wines are sold by Sherry-Lehmann.

PIERRE OLIVIER. G. C. Sumner selections.

PIAT. A large and well known *négociant*.

FRANK SCHOONMAKER

J. THORIN

Others whose reputations in Beaujolais are excellent, and whose prices are likely to be above our limits, include Bouchard Père et Fils, Paul Bocuse, Dufour, Louis Jadot, Jaffelin, Louis Latour, Prosper Maufoux, and Frederick Wildman.

A listing of some wines still within our range at present is well worthwhile. Possibly none of these vintages will be available any longer next year. In that case, a younger vintage of the same label will serve admirably and may even be better. The price next year is something I do not venture to predict.

BEAUJOLAIS '72, Tête de Cuvée (best of the barrel), Caves de Charnay Bellevue. This is quite a lovely wine and an unmatchable value at $2.89.

BEAUJOLAIS VILLAGE '72, Château de La Roche, Caves de Charnay Bellevue. Somewhat superior to their Tête de Cuvée, it is not as exceptional a buy at $3.25.

BEAUJOLAIS '71, Château des Granges, J. Thorin. A truly excellent wine of a very fine year; an exceptional value at $3.25.

BEAUJOLAIS '71, Frank Schoonmaker. The price, $3.68.

BEAUJOLAIS VILLAGE '71, Frank Schoonmaker. $3.96—His Beaujolais have always been very good, the Beaujolais village a few shades better than Charnay Bellevue's Tête de Cuvée, but the prices—oh, the prices. Still, well worth trying.

CHIROUBLES '71, J. Thorin. Approaching our limits at $3.99 but, for a fine Commune wine, it is not too high in price.

BROUILLY '71, Château de la Valette, Pierre Olivier. At a price of $4.50, worth trying, since it is excellent, but certainly no part of a steady diet.

MORGON '71, Grand Cru Beaujolais, Pierre Olivier. In exactly the same class as his Brouilly. The price, $4.59.

It can readily be seen that Beaujolais can no longer remotely be considered an inexpensive wine. It is easy indeed to drink, but no longer easy on the pocket. However, if prices do not trend still higher, a little of it now and then should definitely be included in your wine repertoire.

THE WHITES

The Côte de Beaune is the home of the greatest dry white wines in the world. Not too long ago, as recently as late 1972, some, though not the very greatest, could still be bought within the prices set here. This is no longer so. The Appendix should be consulted for a description. Fortunately, elsewhere in Burgundy some quite lovely wines that fall within our means are still produced.

With one exception, all white Burgundies are made of the same grape, the Pinot Blanc, more often known as the Pinot Chardonnay. Having said this, I must tell you that some experts say that the Chardonnay and the Pinot Blanc are different grapes. I don't really know, nor does it matter much. What does matter is that all the white Burgundy made of the grape, or grapes, is very dry, with a pleasant floweriness and often a remarkable amount of scent. The exception is the Aligoté grape, which produces a minor white Burgundy of the same name. It is not exceptional.

Even the lesser white Burgundies will last four or five years in bottle. The great ones will mature and grow for ten years, even more. Nonetheless, there is a school, to which I incline, that much prefers the freshness of the younger wines. Any that are not too costly for us may be drunk with full pleasure as early as they appear on the market. And you should try the white Burgundies early in your wine learning process. Even the lesser wines are of a quality among dry whites not too often met with elsewhere.

Mâcon

Large quantities of white wine are produced here. All of it is adequate, some good, some most exceptional. In general character it is dry, perfumed, and flowery.

Wines labeled merely Mâcon Blanc or Mâcon Supérieur are the least expensive of white Burgundies. They can be very enjoyable and very good buys. Special selections can be exceptional.

The glory of Mâcon is Pouilly-Fuissé. It has in full measure the fragrant floweriness of the best of the Burgundies. Made by the wrong hands, it can be only good, almost dull. Made by the right vintner, it is gentle, fresh, and altogether lovely.

This is another name that seems to have captured the American imagination. What with its exceptional popularity, the poor '68 vintage, and the splendid—but for Pouilly-Fuissé exceptionally meager—'69 vintage, the price of this wine had already increased sharply well before galloping inflation and dollar devaluations attacked wine prices in general. By now, most of it is well up in the $5 to $7 range, and simply not worth it.

A new *appellation* has recently been declared by the French government—Saint Véran. The area is close by the vineyards of Pouilly-Fuissé. The first Saint Vérans reached us late in 1972. Some retailers describe the wine as identical in taste to Pouilly-Fuissé and, hence, at a much lower price, an exceptional buy.

Naturally, I tried a bottle quickly. (This, by the way, is exactly how to unearth new, good wines for oneself.) Expecting, or rather only hoping, for something nearly the same as Pouilly-Fuissé, I found what at first sip seemed a thin and almost bitter, unpleasant wine. But I tasted again, and judging the wine on its own merits, I realized that it is not thin but rather delicate, with a noticeable hint of floweriness and a very slightly bitter overlay that I, with my preference for very dry wines, find pleasing and very refreshing. It just doesn't resemble Pouilly-Fuissé. It is a fine wine in its own right and I like it quite well enough to have added a case to my cellar.

The remaining designation of white Mâcon, quite important to us, is Pinot Chardonnay. By French law, every vineyard in the areas covered by the Appellation Contrôlée can bottle only a stated maximum of wine under its own label. In plentiful years there is an excess, which may be labeled with the regional name or with the name of the grape. Most of the excess of Mâcon is sold as Pinot Chardonnay. Theoretically, a wine so labeled might come from anywhere in Burgundy, but practically speaking, all or almost all Pinot Chardonnay is Mâcon Blanc.

Pinot Chardonnay is of varying quality, again depending

on who makes it and, in part, on where within the region the grapes are grown. All of it has the basic characteristics of white Burgundy—scent and floweriness—in differing degree. None of those I have tasted is displeasing. Some is so good that it is at once recognizable as being in the same general class as Pouilly-Fuissé, albeit a few rungs down on the ladder.

Regarding vintages in Mâcon, 1969, 1970, and 1971 were all excellent. The '69s are mostly gone. The '72s are quite good. The '73's will be much better, and rather plentiful. The overriding consideration should be the maker or *négociant* and the price, not the vintage year.

Here are a few white Mâcons still within our budget and varying from very good to excellent.

PINOT CHARDONNAY '70 and '71, Frank Schoonmaker. Both years may be found. The '71 is slightly the better. This is by far the best Pinot Chardonnay I have ever drunk (I certainly have not tasted all). It has in rather full measure all of the delightful characteristics of white Burgundy, is a wine one need not be ashamed to serve even to a connoisseur, and is a most exceptional buy at about $3.10 to 3.25.

MÂCON VILLAGE LA FORÊT '72, Joseph Drouhin. The '70, no longer generally available, was an elegant, aristocratic wine, almost as flowery as a Pouilly-Fuissé, but a far better buy. The '72, somewhat surprisingly, is slightly better still. Even at $3.75, it is a top buy.

POUILLY-FUISSÉ '70, Lapalus. This is quite a good sample of Pouilly-Fuissé, despite the price of $3.99, very low for the type, quite high compared to other fine Mâcons. It is well worth trying for those within reach of Astor's in New York.

BOURGOGNE DE CHAPITRE '71, Jaffelin. Both the typical fragrant bouquet and the fruitiness are there and it is a good buy at $3.49, though not the equal of either Drouhin's La Forêt or Schoonmaker's Pinot Chardonnay.

SOLEIL BLANC, Joseph Drouhin. The '70 and '71 are still available as I write, at $3.09; the '72 is also available, priced at $4.35. At the first price this rather lovely white Mâcon is an exceptional value. At the second, it is clearly not so.

MERCUREY BLANC '70, Regnier. This is a pleasant, soft wine with the typical bouquet and flavor of white Mâcon, but unexceptional and only a fair buy at $2.99.

SAINT VÉRAN '71, Caves de Charnay Bellevue. A lovely example of this new classification and an excellent value at $2.85.

SAINT VÉRAN '71, Les Vignerons de Prissé. Very similar to the one just mentioned, it is an equally fine buy at $2.99. In New York it is carried by Sherry-Lehmann.

SAINT VÉRAN '71, Paul Beaudet. Available at Astor's in New York, it is a very fine example of this type of wine and a good buy at $3.39.

Chablis

This is one of the great dry white wines of the world. It is also one of the most imitated, an outstanding tribute to its stature. It should always be borne in mind that a white wine of any country other than France bearing the name Chablis, while it may be enjoyable, is not Chablis and is unlikely to resemble it.

The best are the Grands Crus ("great growths"), all, with the rarest of exceptions, by now out of our price range. Next in order of quality are the Premiers Crus ("first growths"). The next level of quality is entitled only to the appellation Chablis. The lowest may bear only the name of Petit Chablis ("little Chablis"). I have not seen Petit Chablis on the market recently. Perhaps I look in the wrong bins. It should be avoided.

One characteristic of all Chablis is described variously as hard, stony, flinty, or steely. All of these sound to me vaguely unpleasant, yet there is a distinct taste that is properly so described. It is not in any way unpleasant, quite the reverse, but it is not the wine for the completely unsophisticated palate or the wine drinker brought up, for example, on the much sweeter wines of Germany. It is the ideal wine to be drunk with delicate shellfish, seafood, and fish.

The other characteristic is the scented floweriness of all the wine made of the Pinot Chardonnay. It is not to be confused with sweetness. All white Burgundies are dry, Chablis being the driest and, for that matter, one of the driest of all white wines anywhere.

The Grands Crus are exactly what the name says, great. They have more of everything than the lesser Chablis, more strength, more fragrance, more of the special Chablis characteristics. The Premiers Crus are often wonderful wines, overshadowed only by their greater brothers. Some, quite unjustifiably, sell at prices equal to, sometimes higher than, the Grands Crus. As for plain Chablis, it can be plain pedestrian and it can be rather exceptional, depending on who makes it. If pedestrian, it is inevitably overpriced. Some of the good ones, such as that with the Joseph Drouhin name, are as high in price as the Grands Crus.

Chablis is another French wine that has virtually priced itself out of our limits. An occasional bottle of thoroughly good wine can still be found at affordable prices, and I shall list one or two, but in general, a lower price will mean a poor wine.

The Grands Crus, which are glorious, are almost all in the $6-and-over range. Yet, at whatever cost, I would urge you to try just one, when you are ready for a thoroughly dry white. You will come across so much wine of other countries labeled Chablis that it is, I think, downright important to know the taste of a genuine Chablis of finest quality. Splurge! You will enjoy it. Over and above that, an occasional bottle, at least, of a lesser but good Chablis will always give much pleasure.

There are eight Grands Crus. There are some differences among them, primarily because more than one owner exists for each vineyard and each may make his wine somewhat differently from his neighbor. None will be less than glorious and you should buy the least costly you can find. The Grands Crus are Les Blanchots, Bougros, Les Clos, Grenouilles, Moutonne, Les Preuses, Valmur, and Vaudésir.

The finest Chablis can be drunk with relish two years after the vintage. Anything older than a '69 is unlikely to be found.

If you do come across one, it will almost certainly be a Grand Cru at a high price. It will also still be perfectly drinkable in 1980.

Vintages as such are, however, very important in this northerly region, almost as close to Paris as to the rest of Burgundy. In a poor year, cold and weak sunshine can create a quite miserable wine. Practically speaking, the '70s and the '71s, both exceptional years, are what will be found and can freely be bought. The '72s will be modest. Both the quantity and quality of the '73's will be high.

One Grand Cru, the one I like best, can still be bought within our upper limits, as I write this. It is:

CHABLIS GRAND CRU LES CLOS '71, Ozier. Astor's in New York has it at $4.69. It is a steal. Ozier is available elsewhere but I do not know whether this wine is.

I can tell you of only three other Chablis within our limits. Undoubtedly there are others at fine wine shops and they should be sought after there.

CHABLIS '69, CAVES DE CHARNAY BELLEVUE. This is a G. C. Sumner selection. It is probable that the '69 will shortly be gone but a later year should be fully its equal. The wine is a quite lovely, typical Chablis, exceptionally flowery. While a few steps from a Grand Cru, it is an exceptional value at $2.99. At 50 cents more it will still be rather outstanding.

CHABLIS PREMIER CRU '71, Montée de Tonnerre of Paul Droin—Baudoin. A G. C. Sumner selection, it is a lovely example of fine Chablis and an outstanding value at $3.69.

CHABLIS PREMIER CRU '70, Fourchaumes, Lapalus. This is available only at Astor's in New York. I found it as good as the Charnay Bellevue, but not better. It is a very good buy at $3.39.

CÔTES du RHÔNE

This refers to the slopes of the Rhône River valley for the 140-mile stretch between Lyons and Avignon, on the very border of Provence in the south of France. Sunshine is plentiful; the grapes ripen fully, are therefore rich in sugar, and the wines are therefore rich in alcohol. Very bad and very great vintages occur seldom. The wines, both red and white, are big, robust, often powerful.

The red Rhônes are big and mouth-filling, hard and often harsh in youth, mellow and authoritative in maturity. They are for hearty dishes, for cold evenings. They are almost never sold sufficiently mature.

The whites are deep gold in color, rich, and fragrant. Many, especially those of the north, will remain at their peak for as long as ten years, yet are perfectly ready to drink two years after the vintage. They are not the wines for a delicate broiled fish filet but rather for richly baked fish, chickens roasted and in casserole, and creamed dishes.

Having written this rather glowing introductory description, I must now tell you that, in a single year, between the summers of 1972 and 1973, prices of Rhône Valley wines literally doubled in the area of production, which means almost doubled at retail in the United States. What used to be a group of excellent, often near-great, wines at bargain prices has now joined the ranks of most other French wines—largely too expensive to buy.

Still, the best are much better values than their Burgundy or Bordeaux counterparts of comparable quality, and some among the lesser ones are still affordable and are rather fine wines. It is well worth knowing a bit about the Rhône wines.

The two famous reds are Hermitage in the north and Châteauneuf du Pape in the south.

Hermitage

The vineyards are on a hill rising sharply above the river. In just about every catalog and book on the subject we are told, so therefore I had best tell you, that George Saintsbury (an English man of letters who wrote a book entirely about the wines in his own cellar early in the twentieth century) called this the manliest wine on earth. It is a good description of Hermitage.

It is a beautiful wine when mature. I still have one bottle of the '61 vintage which will last a few years more. It would be useless to buy a recent vintage, such as a '70, to taste. It would be almost unpleasant and would not be mature enough to drink before 1975 or 1976. It is likely still to be perfectly sound in 1983.

Châteauneuf du Pape
This is the most famous of the red Rhônes. It is big and mouth-filling, as are all the Rhônes, and powerful, but softer and earlier-maturing than its northern brother.

Crozes-Hermitage
The village of Crozes and several others nearby may sell their wines under the name of Crozes-Hermitage. They are not as fine as Hermitage itself but sometimes nearly so; maturing earlier, they are less costly and therefore necessarily of interest to us.

Among other lesser red wines there are:

St. Joseph, Cornas, and Gigondas
These are all produced along the river banks between Hermitage and Châteauneuf du Pape. All resemble these to a greater or lesser extent, all are good, and all are lower in price than the two greats.

The lesser reds of the south are sold as Côtes du Rhône or Côtes du Rhône Villages, the latter being somewhat superior in quality. As in the case of lesser wines in general, they have the same characteristics as their finer brethren but are less good, mature much earlier, and can be drunk quite young. Some can be rather exceptional.

As for the whites, production is small. The wines are all exceptionally big and mouth-filling for white wine, especially that of Hermitage. Not much Rhône white is exported but a little can always be found here, mostly Hermitage, very little

Châteauneuf du Pape, and an occasional wine under a name of its own.

As for vintages in the Côtes du Rhône, for each year the same quality comments hold for both the reds and whites. The whites are always mature enough to drink two years after the vintage. The 1967 vintage was very fine, '68 was good, '69, '70, and '71 were all quite great, '69 almost superb. The 1972 vintage was almost fine.

The '67 Hermitages are now ready to drink, the Châteauneufs du Pape past their prime. You are unlikely to find any '68s—they would be past their prime. The '69 and '70 Hermitages will not be ready until at least 1975, and the Châteauneuf du Pape of both these years will be ready when you read this. Younger vintages need maturing.

Most Hermitages now cost over $6, even though immature. Some Châteauneuf du Pape can be found for a little less. Again, despite the cost, I would urge trying at least a bottle of either, or both, as taste-fixers. You will also find drinking them an exceptional pleasure. However, for immediate tasting, there is no point in buying either too young. Nothing younger than 1970 will be mature and, in the case of Hermitage, the '70, too, will certainly not yet be mature, but good enough to drink with pleasure.

As an example of what is available now:

HERMITAGE ROUGE '70, Ozier. Ozier is a label of one of the finest of the Rhône houses. Their Hermitages of earlier years are superb. The '70 certainly will be, too. The price, $6.10.

HERMITAGE RED '70, Frank Schoonmaker. Although its official price right now is $5.80, it still sells as low as $3.99. The '67, if you were to find any still on sale, is the better buy, because it is fully mature. Should such prices still exist in 1974, you should buy the wine without hesitation and, preferably, lay the '70 down for at least a year.

CHÂTEAUNEUF DU PAPE '70, Jaboulet Vercherre. Found at Vendôme in New York, it is a Frank W. Packard selection. Big, soft, and thoroughly mature, it is an outstanding buy at the price, $3.59.

CHÂTEAUNEUF DU PAPE '70, Coulon. Better than that listed ·above, it is perhaps not so good a buy at the price, $4.79 at Berenson's in Boston.

CHÂTEAUNEUF DU PAPE '70, Clos des Papes, Paul Avril. Extremely fine, this is a very good buy even at $5. It is available in New York at Astor's.

CHÂTEAUNEUF DU PAPE '67, Caves St. Pierre. The best of those listed here, at the peak of maturity (and despite the price) well worth trying, it is carried in Boston by Berenson's. It should be available elsewhere, as well. The price, $5.20.

A few of the lesser red Rhônes available now are:

CROZES-HERMITAGE '70, Leon Revol. Available at $2.89 at Astor's in New York, it will also be found elsewhere. It is very big, almost like an Hermitage, but softer and less subtle. When I drank it, it would still have profited from another year of bottle age. When you read this it will be fully mature. It is an outstanding buy at the current price.

ST. JOSEPH '70, Leon Revol. Costing $2.79 at Astor's, softer and rounder than Revol's Crozes-Hermitage, it more nearly resembles a Châteauneuf du Pape. It will be fully mature by early 1974, is very enjoyable indeed, and an outstanding buy.

GIGONDAS '70, Caves St. Pierre. Costing $3.79 at Sherry-Lehmann in New York, it should be available elsewhere, too. It is moderately good but not an exceptional buy at the price.

ST. JOSEPH RESERVE, Ozier. While a fine wine, it is just too costly for its quality and neither as good a buy as others already listed or as a few lesser wines not yet mentioned. The price, $4.75.

The least of the Rhône wines, those simply called Côtes du Rhône, have always included some of unusual quality for the price. All in all, they are the best buys in Rhône wines today, when carefully selected.

CÔTES DU RHÔNE '70, Domaine de l'Enclos. A quite well-balanced, big, smooth wine, it is in all respects very pleasing and a very fine buy indeed at $2.69—at Astor's.

CÔTES DU RHÔNE '70, Chanson. At $2.65, this is in all respects the equal of the one just mentioned. It is very much an exception to my general rule about widely distributed, well-advertised houses. Chanson is such a house. Few, if any other, of their wines are so reasonable in price or such exceptional values.

CÔTES DU RHÔNE '71, La Vieille Ferme. Costing $2.69 at Sherry-Lehmann, it is typical of its kind: decent, and a very good buy at the price, but not the equal in quality of those already described.

CÔTES DU RHÔNE RESERVE, Ozier. It is of the superior quality to be expected of Ozier, the best of those listed here but, of course, costlier. The price, $3.15.

CÔTES DU RHÔNE, Sichel. It is labeled "French Country Wine" although it is Appellation Contrôlée. While characteristic of the type and pleasant, it is nothing exceptional, the least in quality of the group listed, and was a good buy six months ago at $2.50—but at today's price of $3.98? This is a perfect example of how far from a bargin the wines of the big distributors can be.

In fact, it is perfectly evident from the brief listings above that the best buys are almost always the unadvertised, little-known brands. Again, any fine shop can be expected to have its own good labels of this kind available.

Not to forget the Rhône whites:

HERMITAGE BLANC '70, Ozier. This wine is still being sold at Astor's for $3.89. I paid only 30 cents a bottle less a year and a half ago. I had a bottle of it for dinner last evening. Words almost fail me. Do buy it, or an equivalent, if you can find it.

THE LOIRE VALLEY

The Loire River is about five hundred miles long. The area produces some red wine, a moderate quantity of which is exported. Primarily, it is known for its whites. It is commonly maintained that these vary much in character. Among the dry table wines there are certainly differences, but all of them, to me, have a special characteristic in common. Some describe this as charm or gaiety. I find them all to have a pleasant tartness, a refreshing lightness that make them ideal for more delicate foods, particularly in warmer weather.

Loire wines are generally still well within our price range. It is doubtful whether those outside it are worth the price, for these wines, while supremely drinkable, are far from great. Because they have been inexpensive, Loire wines have been growing in popularity, which of course has been making them rapidly more expensive. They are still well worth our attention.

Vintages are of little concern. None earlier than 1969 will be found. All years from then onward are very good, both for reds and whites. The '73's, in particular, will be plentiful of fine quality. Price should be the controlling factor in making a choice.

THE REDS

These are all made of the Cabernet grape, which gives them some of the longevity of the Bordeaux. Nevertheless, they are surprisingly similar to Beaujolais, somewhat drier and less fruity, and entirely enjoyable when young. They are still somewhat overlooked, are therefore rather exceptional values, and it is to be hoped that this desirable state of affairs will continue for a time.

Chinon, Bourgeuil, and St. Nicholas Bourgeuil are all virtually identical. Saumur (also called Coteaux de Saumur, also Saumur Champigny) is made close by the first three mentioned and is like them in character.

An example of what is available:

BOURGEUIL '69, Monmousseau. It costs $3.10 at Berenson's in Boston and elsewhere.

BOURGEUIL '72, Debreuil. This wine costs $2.99 at Sherry-Lehmann in New York. It will not be too young in 1974.

SAUMUR CHAMPIGNY '69, Caves Coopérative de Saumur. The price is about $2.99 at Morrell's in New York.

SAUMUR CHAMPIGNY '69, Couly. It costs $2.99 at Sherry-Lehmann.

CHINON '69, Gouin. Chinon is not noticeably better than the others and this is therefore not quite so good a buy at $3.49 at Sherry-Lehmann.

Many others will be found at comparable prices in other fine shops in New York and undoubtedly at the best shops elsewhere.

THE WHITES

They vary from very dry to dessert-sweet, from still to sparkling. Some are what the French call *pétillant*, the Italians *frizzante*. The closest English equivalent is "effervescent." Such wine will look like still wine as it is poured but, within seconds, tiny bubbles will form all around the inside of the glass. The result is a sort of prickling sensation on the tongue and the refreshing tartness of flavor typical of all Loire whites, even the still ones. Should you come across such a wine, of whatever country, do not think there is anything wrong with it. On the contrary, you will find an unusual and delightful new taste.

Muscadet

This is the name of the grape that makes the wine in the region around the mouth of the Loire River. It is very dry, light, and tart and goes particularly well with fish and seafood. It should be well chilled and is so served in the Paris cafés, where it is delicious for plain drinking while watching the street scene, even though well mixed nowadays with the smell of exhaust fumes. It should be drunk young.

It is difficult to find just Muscadet. Some is sold under

châteaux or other names, which do not necessarily add to its basic charm. Some is the Muscadet-sur-Lie, which is bottled in March following the vintage and is best drunk very young. It is claimed to be superior. Price and youth should be the prime factors in buying Muscadet.

Sancerre

Somewhat finer than Muscadet but surprisingly similar, considering that it is made some five hundred miles upriver. It usually retails for about 50 percent more than does Muscadet but I do not find it 50 percent better. It should by all means be tried for taste, but is not worth its price—to me, at any rate.

Pouilly-Fumé

This wine must not be confused with Pouilly-Fuissé, of white Burgundy fame. As a matter of fact, it is made near the headwaters of the Loire, not more than eighty miles from Burgundy, and is suggested by some as resembling the white Burgundies at lesser cost. I do not find it so, that is, neither the resemblance nor the lesser cost. Rather, the wine has the same basic flavor common to the Loire Valley. It might well be tried for taste but, for me, has never been worth the price and is now much too close to the top of our range.

Vouvray

As it appears on the American market, Vouvray is a soft, somewhat sweet wine, freshened by the characteristic Loire Valley lightness, so that it is not at all cloying. I find it a bit too sweet for my palate but it is perhaps an ideal wine for beginners or early drinkers.

Anjou

Both sweet and dry wines are made here. The dry whites are not as good as the sweet ones. They are not as dry as Muscadet but more so than Vouvray, and always light and fresh. They sell at about the price of Muscadet and are good buys for those who, unlike me, like their wine less dry.

Among all of these, and a few others not often encountered here and therefore not mentioned, the least costly and the best buys are the Muscadets among the very dry and the Vouvrays among the less dry. A sample assortment of very good ones would be:

MUSCADET-SUR-LIE '72, Château Briacé. This is $2.99 at Sherry-Lehmann.

MUSCADET '71, Metraireau. Costs $3.15 at Berenson's.

MUSCADET-SUR-LIE '72, Château de la Sebinière. Costing $2.49 at Astor's, this is the best buy of the group.

L'HUITRIÈRE. This means, literally, "The Oyster One." It is actually a very good Muscadet '72 and, of course, is ideal with oysters and other dishes. I'm not sure who can afford oysters anymore, if they can be found at all. At $3.25 the wine begins to be rather costly for a Muscadet.

VOUVRAY '70, Château Gaudrelle, Monmousseau. A fine example of this fresh, gentle, sweetish wine. The price, $3.05 at Berenson's.

Those in the New York area might care to try:

BLANC DE BLANCS '72, La Tonnelles, Debreuil. This costs $2.19 at Sherry-Lehmann. I have not tasted it. It is described as extremely pleasant, sweeter than a Muscadet, drier than a Vouvray. It could be rather interesting. I intend to try it soon. At that price neither you nor I can go far wrong.

For those who might care to sample the so-called finer Loires at certainly finer prices, here are a few suggestions:

SANCERRE '70, Phillipe Dauphin. The wine is $3.29 at Vendôme in New York. It is a very good example of Sancerre and, at that price, should it still hold in '74, it is not merely worth trying but is an exceptional value.

SANCERRE DE CHAVIGNOL '70. Costing $4.30 at Berenson's, it is a better wine than the one above but, at that price, hardly a very good buy.

POUILLY-FUMÉ '71, Coulbois. A very satisfactory example of the type and, in today's market, an excellent buy at the price: $3.59 at Astor's.

POUILLY-FUMÉ '71, Chatelaine Père et Fils. Undoubtedly a fine Pouilly-Fumé but to me no Pouilly-Fumé is worth the price: $4.90 at Berenson's.

ALSACE

Alsace borders on Germany along the Rhine River and, of course, belonged to it from 1870 to 1918. During that time the Germans planted it to inferior grapes to produce cheap table wines. After 1918, the vineyards were replanted but it was not until after the Second World War, during which the area was fought through again, that Alsatian wines began to come into their own. Today they are excellent. Six months ago they were not yet very well known here, but that is no longer so and their prices, like all the others, are up sharply though still largely within our budget.

Alsace's claim to fame is its white wines. They are made of grapes originating in Germany: the Sylvaner, the Gewürztraminer, and the noble Riesling. But, unlike the German wines, most of which are really too sweet for drinking with meals, those of Alsace are dry, indeed often very dry, and are not to be thought of as really akin to, or substitutes for, the German wines. They have every right to be considered on their own as good and fine dinner wines. In fact, the Germans are by far the largest importers of Alsatian wine, which they use in preference to their own as table wine.

A small quantity of light red wine is made. It is never exported. Some small production also exists of a few other white wines. They are reported to be ordinary and are drunk locally. With almost no exception, the three varieties mentioned above are the ones that will be encountered in the United States.

The vineyards are broken up into multiple ownership.

Most of the wine is therefore produced by cooperatives. There are exceptions, these being usually the better vintners who bottle under their own names. These constitute a good part of what is available in the United States. Regardless of by whom made, the wines are always sold under the names of the grape varieties. Sometimes a "Clos" name or the legend "Réserve Exceptionelle" is added. These may be assumed to be the best of the wines. They are also too costly.

Vintages can vary considerably in Alsace but they have significance only for the better, indeed, the best wines. Those of most interest to us should always be drunk young and, where a later vintage affords a lesser price, it should be preferred. In any case, all the vintages from 1969 onward have been good to excellent; nothing earlier than '69 will be found for sale, hence any vintage will serve.

In the spring of 1973, several Alsatian wine merchants visited the United States. One, when interviewed, expressed the hope that in five or six years, the 50,000 cases of Alsatian wine exported to the United States in 1972 will have grown to 250,000 cases. He also estimated that the best Sylvaners would go up to $3, the Rieslings to between $3.40 and $3.99, and the Gewürztraminers to $4.75. This was a projection for perhaps five or six years later. There is every reason to suppose that this highly reputable merchant meant these forecasts seriously and honestly when he made them. Note, as we go along, what has happened in just six months.

Sylvaner

This is the ordinary wine of Alsace, light, dry, fairly fragrant, not especially distinguished, but very pleasant. The price range today is $2.69 to $3.89, making all but the least costly not worth buying.

Riesling

Riesling is the best of Alsace. It would be difficult to find a bottle of Alsatian Riesling that does not have,.in some degree, the basic qualities of floweriness (some think it the most flowery of French white wines), delicacy, and dryness. The better ones are quite exceptional. The wine sells for more than Sylvaner, not too much more, and is so noble, or nearly so, as to be a far better buy, even at today's prices, and worth our attention.

Gewürztraminer

Gewürz means "spice" in German. I drank this wine for the first time rather recently, after wondering for years how a wine could taste spicy, unless it were spiced. Well it does, and it isn't. To the extent that its character can be judged aside from its spiciness, Gewürztraminer much resembles Riesling, but the spiciness, somewhat like nutmeg or allspice, pervades the wine and lingers on the tongue for minutes afterward. It tends to give an impression of sweetness, though the wine is actually thoroughly dry.

Some may not like its pronounced flavor with a delicate fish dish. I do. It is lovely with shellfish, too. It is obviously a perfect accompaniment for the rich goose and pork and sauerkraut dishes of Alsace. Some find the spiciness cloying after a few sips. I do not. I find the wine delightful to drink with dishes a bit robust for the ordinary white wine, such as casseroles and roasts of chicken, roast turkey, duck, and pork. It is, however, not the equal of Riesling in sheer quality and, in a price range today of $4.29 to $5.45, it is worth trying for its peculiar and pleasing special character, but is not a good buy any longer in money terms.

Among the better producers and shippers of Alsace whose wines are shipped here (this is by no means an all-inclusive list) are DOPFF, DOPFF & IRION (these are two separate firms), HUGEL, TRIMBACH, and WILLM. All their wines may be relied on completely, nor will a given kind of a given year vary greatly in quality from one shipper to another. As elsewhere, wines of less well known shippers will also be found. If good, they will be the best buys.

I see no point in buying Sylvaners at more than $3. They are just not that good. I see little point in buying Gewürztraminers at up to $5.45 but do recommend your trying a lower-priced one, if only to savor the unusual flavor. The Rieslings are so lovely that a few might well find their way into your repertoire, if only prices don't go up still further.

The best buys I know of as of now from personal drinking are:

SYLVANER, Domain Hauller. $2.49 at Vendôme in New York.

SYLVANER, Dopff & Irion. $2.69.

RIESLING, Domain Hauller. $2.99 at Vendôme.

RIESLING RESERVE, Crus d'Eguisheim '69. $3 at Berenson's in Boston.

RIESLING, Dopff & Irion. $3.15.

RIESLING '69, Hugel. $3.29 at Sherry-Lehmann's in New York, although officially priced at $4.25.

GEWÜRZTRAMINER, Hauller. $3.39 at Vendôme.

GEWÜRZTRAMINER, Trimbach. $4.29.

COUNTRY WINES

This is an exact translation of the French *Vin de Pays*. It has a rather vague meaning in the United States. Some authorities include among country wines the reds of the Loire Valley, the wines of Lirac in the Côtes du Rhône, even those of Alsace. Irancy, a light and rather lovely red wine, with the Appellation Contrôlée label, is advertised by one shop here as a country wine, at well over $4. You have seen that Sichel's Côtes du Rhône is labeled a country wine, at almost $4.

I think of the country wines as the French wines of regions other than those already described. These regions produce more than half of all French wine, but none of its great ones and few fine ones.

Country wines started to come into the United States as a trickle only about a year ago. They are rapidly becoming a flood. Most of those now available here are V.D.Q.S. and, if you have any doubt of the comparatively lesser quality of V.D.Q.S., just taste a wine so labeled.

Some are quite enjoyable, just the same, and a good deal less costly than most other French wines. Some are perfectly mediocre. A few that I can describe are:

COTEAUX DE LANGUEDOC-BESSIÈRE. A simple, somewhat thin red wine, unpretentious, it is a pleasant drink and a fair buy at $1.69. It is a V.D.Q.S. The label bears the word *friand*, which, according to the dictionary means "fond of delicacies." The wine certainly is no delicacy. Or does it mean that it goes well with delicacies? That would be no way to treat delicacies.

CHÂTEAU MONTFORT '69. A V.D.Q.S. red costing $1.99, it bears the grandiose labeling for which the maker, Henri Maire, is well known, reading like a French version of some of the worst in American advertising. Furthermore, there are no châteaux in the Jura, where the wine is made. It is a fairly light, somewhat thin, slightly sharp wine, moderately enjoyable but a far cry from the lesser Bordeaux and the good red wines of other countries not yet discussed.

CHÂTEAU DE SERAME '70. This is a Corbières, a red that tends to be better than many other country wines. This one is a fairly light wine with quite good body, moderately fruity, dry and fresh on the palate. Its quality is not surprising in view of the fact that it is a G.C. Sumner selection and is bottled and distributed by Pierre Olivier. It is a very good buy at $1.95.

CARTIER BLANC DE BLANCS. This is a rather enjoyable white costing $1.98. Distributed by Monsieur Henri, it is a Loire Valley wine, labeled "Estate Bottled," which I would consider doubtful. It has a faint but noticeable touch of sweetness, with fairly good bouquet and fruitiness. It is somewhat like a Vouvray in character.

A recent but well advertised and widely distributed brand of country wine on the American market is ÉCU ROYAL. It is sold in half-gallons at $3.99. There is no classification on the label. It is all advertised as being of the 1971 vintage. What can a vintage year mean with so minor a wine?

There are inevitably two reds, two whites, and a rosé sold under this brand name. Some fairly extravagant claims are made for them. The Blanc de Blancs is described as similar to a Pouilly-Fuissé! Also, they are all described as "good, honest" French wines. I have long since learned to duck when "honest" is used to describe a wine. Altogether too often, the only honest thing about it is the money we pay for it.

Actually, they are reasonably drinkable. The Bordeaux-type red is rather sharp, the red Mâcon has a trace of fullness and less sharpness. The Blanc de Blancs is characterless and pleasant and in no way resembles a Pouilly-Fuissé, I need hardly say, while the Graves-type white is a bit sweeter, equally without character, and perfectly decent. They are better, at any rate, than some American "jug wines" at higher prices. The rosé I have not tasted.

It should be evident why I suggested earlier that there is no need to rush to the French country wines. There are simply too many good and excellent wines, of many other countries, at comparable and not too much higher prices. Some are even lower in cost.

I must also sound a note of warning. A year ago I came across a French red (I can no longer remember the name) with an Appellation d'Origine Simple (A.O.S.) on the label, at 94 cents a bottle. Curiosity impelled me to buy it and, after due observance of all rules of proper handling, to taste it. Maybe some would consider it as at least drinkable. I would not.

This classification, "Wine of Simple Origin," denotes the *vin ordinaire* of France, the wine that French workingmen drink, not because they don't know better but because they can't afford better. I do not feel that the American wine drinker can afford no better.

To my horror, just a few weeks ago I found a red wine of the Appellation d'Origine Simple on sale at one of New York's fine stores, at $1.99. The name of the wine is unimportant. This is already scraping the bottom of the barrel and, as you will find as we go on to examine wines of other countries, there is not the faintest need for any of us to sink so low.

Avoid wines of the A.O.S. at all costs, and hope with me that none of us will ever have to come to them.

Despite the sharp increases in price, against which I have inveighed throughout this description of French wines, it is perfectly evident that there are still quite a few genuinely good French wines at affordable prices. How long they will remain so is another matter. It is still my belief, not merely my hope, that most French wine prices are stabilizing now and will not go up—for a while, at least.

It may have appeared to those many of you who do not live in the New York–Boston area that too many of the wines recommended are obtainable only there. This is an unavoidable consequence of two facts: the first, that the best buys in French wines are very commonly the more obscure labels; the second, that I am necessarily most familiar with the wines of that area.

Aside from the fact that other obscure brands of equal, perhaps superior, quality will be found in fine shops everywhere, be assured that, as we proceed with wines of other countries, there will be recommended a great many more wines of broader distribution.

Italy

Italy's total annual production, close to 2 billion gallons, is frequently larger than that of her neighbor, France. (The year 1972 was disastrous, most unusual for Italy, where production tends to be stable. Only about 1.5 billion gallons were produced.) But Italy was until recently, and still largely is, the land of the individual peasant producer, to whom wine is wine and who ever heard of modern methods or controlling quality?

The vine grows literally almost everywhere. Much of the wine has no name. It is simply known as *vino locale* and is so ordered in the restaurants. A good deal of it is drunk by the makers and never finds its way even into the local market.

The *vini locale* are almost always enjoyable when drunk where they are made. Many, probably most of them, will not travel. They can be better made so that they will survive shipment, and many are. They may lose their fresh charm in the process but usually gain in quality. A great many of the Italian wines available in the United States are made by the local cooperatives, called *cantine sociale*, which use the modern methods beyond the means of the peasant, and produce good, clean wines that are very satisfactory but by no means great.

However, all is far from mediocre in Italy. Some very fine wines indeed are made, and a few that have every right to be called great and are equal to all except the very best of the Bordeaux and Burgundies. Such wines are always made by individual vintners, not by *cantine sociale*.

The government has a quite comprehensive set of control laws and, in the past several years, has been getting tough. All of the wines recommended here have been included in the *Denominazione di Origine Controllata* ("Controlled Denomination of Origin") and those words on a label are an assurance of minimum quality. There is no longer any justification for the wine snob to turn his nose up at all Italian wines or, for that matter, at all non-French wines. Besides, only a rich wine snob can afford to any longer.

Italian wines are among the best buys available in the United States. A good many of the finest are still within our budget. In the mad scramble to acquire the "name" wines of France, Americans have largely overlooked some of the wonderful wines made in other countries, including their own, for that matter.

In order to purchase intelligently, some understanding of the various wines and their qualities is needed. It is important to be aware of the maker or shipper and of his reputation, as well. Some make or ship the wine of a given region only, but frequently a selection of different wines is offered by the same shipper, as indeed it is in France often enough, and very commonly in some other countries.

What lovely names the wines have, so graceful and sonorous. And why not? Italian is the most musical of European languages. But beware of buying wine because of its euphonious name rather than its quality. There are some bottles with beautiful names on the labels, but I would not buy the wine inside.

Vintage years have some significance for the great wines, and only for them. Such wines are generally not in ample supply, in the United States or anywhere else, and there is not likely to be any choice. It is usually a case of taking what you can get. Hence vintage years among the fine wines are largely just a way for the buyer to know their age. As regards all other Italian wines, vintage years mean exactly nothing. The Italians seem long since to have discovered that Americans set great store by vintages, so it is almost impossible to find an Italian wine, no matter how minor, not so labeled. Such labels should just be disregarded.

TUSCANY

Tuscany is the home of Chianti, a wine of importance to us. Red Chianti is one of the best known wines in the world, the straw-wrapped *fiasco* (flask) being almost its trademark. It is also one of the least understood and most maligned of wines, often referred to derogatorily as "spaghetti wine."

In the past, much of the ordinary Chianti that sold here was pretty bad. With stricter government supervision quality has improved and little is likely to be really poor, while some is definitely good. But the glory of Tuscany is the wine made in a specific manner in the region lying between Florence (Firenze) and Siena and entitled to the government-controlled designation of Chianti Classico.

Chianti Classico
One of the finest wines Italy produces. The oldest and best are known as Riservas and are remarkable. If not great, they

certainly approach greatness. Some fall within the very upper limits of our budget. The Classici as such are less expensive, all within our means, and they vary from very good to very fine indeed. Some are shipped in the familiar fiasco but most come in Bordeaux-shaped 24-ounce bottles.

Chianti Classico is a fairly light wine of good body, powerful and lovely fragrance, and clear ruby color; it is well balanced, moderately fruity, always dry. It is most nearly comparable to the better Bordeaux in character, although no comparison is needed. Italy's better wines are quite capable of being judged purely on their own merits. Chianti Classico is an aristocrat among wines everywhere, not merely Italian ones.

All Classici bear the emblem of a black cockerel on a gold background around the neck of the bottle. Without this emblem, it is not a Classico. Look for it. Also, the individual bottles are always numbered. I suppose this tends to indicate quality. I find it impressive.

Vintages rarely go back farther than '67. Some are younger. They are mature enough for immediate drinking, although any of them would improve with age up to as much as ten years.

The most pleasing thing about Chianti Classico to us, who are interested in good and fine wines at reasonable prices, is not merely that it is one of the best buys in red wine but that there is a wide choice of both wines and prices. Among those most commonly available, in order of how well known rather than comparative quality, are:

BROLIO '69. The maker is Barone Ricasoli, whose ancestor established the method of making Chianti Classico more than a hundred years ago. It is unusual, unorthodox almost, but of no concern to us. Our concern is with what is in the bottle, and Brolio is a fine example of the type. At $3.25 per quart it is an excellent buy.

RUFFINO '69. This Chianti is not labeled Classico but certainly is one in quality. It tends to be somewhat bigger than the others, but is equally excellent. It is, however, far from a best buy at $3.75 per quart.

VILLA ANTINORI '67. It is one of the best, austerely dry and rather delicate. At $3.99 for a 24-ounce bottle it is hardly a bargain, but well worth sampling.

SERRISTORI-MACHIAVELLI '66. This is a Frank Schoonmaker selection. Count Serristori is the vintner but the wine is usually identified as Machiavelli, since a line drawing of that famous (or notorious) statesman, who once owned the vineyard, appears on the label. It is a very good buy at $3.32 for a 24-ounce bottle. (It should not be confused with Chianti Serristori '70, selling in a 59-ounce bottle for $3.79. This is a much more ordinary wine from the Serristori cellars. It and its white counterpart, Bianco di Toscano '70—white Tuscan wine—at the same price, are fine buys in their own class. They are also Frank Schoonmaker selections.)

MELINI. Among the best of the Classici and a good buy at $3.45 for a quart, Melini is one of the shippers of fine reputation and will be mentioned again.

There are numerous other excellent Classici not so well known, but many of them quite widely distributed. Among them, in order of quality, are:

COUNTS CAPPONI '69. This wine comes in a 24-ounce bottle. The label states in English: "Estate Produced & Bottled." It is the best Classico I have come across, truly subtle and velvety and better than many a French wine called great. At $2.95 it is an outstanding buy.

MONTEPALDI RISERVA '67, MARCHESI CORSINI. This is a fine example of Classico and an excellent buy at $2.39 for 24 ounces.

PALAZZO AL BOSCO '69, FREDERICK WILDMAN. It is the equal of the Marchesi Corsini but not as good a buy at $3.25.

LA QUERCIA '70, GIOVANNI CAPELLI. At most, it is only a shade less good than the two previously listed, though clearly somewhat young. At $2.49 for a 23-ounce bottle, it is a very good buy.

CASTELLI DEL GREVEPESA '68. This comes in a straw-covered quart fiasco. The label says: "Bottled at Vineyard." It is surprisingly good for what looks like an ordinary fiasco of Chianti. It is a fairly fine Classico and, at a price of $2.50, it is the best buy of the entire group.

CANTINA DEL PAPA. '66. It is rather light, with good fruitiness and balance. The price was recently raised a full 20 percent, to $3 for a 24-ounce bottle. It is obvious there are far better values.

SUALI '69. This is a very satisfactory example of Classico but far from a bargain at $2.99 per quart.

Any of these can be bought with the confidence that it is an exceptional wine. But, if you feel in a mood for greatness (I hope you will), try one of the Riservas, too. You will enjoy the experience. Some within our upper limits are:

Brolio Riserva—$3.75
Melini Riserva—$4.55
Ruffino Riserva Ducale—$4.49

The Chianti Classici are hardly for ordinary drinking. They are special-occasion wines. Ordinary Chianti is also well worth exploring. There are altogether too many Americans who somehow equate Ruffino with Chianti and buy only Ruffino for their ordinary drinking. They are buying an excellent wine but it is too good and much too costly for day-to-day purposes. It is time they learned of the large variety of ordinary Chianti available in the familiar 1-quart fiasco.

Until the government put teeth into the control laws, almost any Tuscan red wine went to market under the name of Chianti. It could be almost anything, good or bad, heavy or light, rough and coarse or moderately fine. This is no longer the case. Six areas in Tuscany have been granted the right to label their red wine Chianti and fairly strict control is maintained.

It would merely be confusing to list those areas here. The names do not lend themselves to easy memorization to one who does not speak Italian. It is enough to remember that if the wine is called Chianti and Denominazione di Origine Controllata appears on the label, it may be assumed that it is Chianti. The areas that make the best of the ordinary Chianti are those centering around Florence and Siena. Rufina (not to be confused with the shipper, Ruffino) is reputed to be as good. The label will always bear the name of the nearest main city.

There is still much variation in quality among Chianti wines. They should not be bought at random. The good ones are thoroughly enjoyable, considerably better than just everyday drinking wines, yet ideal for that as well, since they sell generally in the range of $1.80 to $2 per quart.

Specific labels have a tendency to come and go, to disappear after a few years, sometimes to reappear later. If those listed here cannot be found in a particular part of the country, you must try others on your own, but with caution and only after your taste in wine has been somewhat established. A really good Chianti can form the staple of your wine diet—for everyday meals, for guests, for everything, in fact, but the special occasions.

GIUNTI, RICARDO. Giunti is located in Poggibonsi, near Siena. The wine is moderately light, with fair perfume, good body, dry, uncomplicated, and utterly pleasing. It has been my "staple" wine for some ten years. It is always good and never fails to please. I consider it only a small step or two removed from the lesser Classici in quality. Yet it has been selling for only $1.79 per quart up to the time of this writing and, in gallons, the way I always buy it, at about $5.25. Recently, alas, it has been unavailable. It is to be hoped that this is no more than a temporary interruption in shipment or, perhaps, a prelude to a price hike (we've become very used to that recently) rather than an abandonment of the American market. Perhaps it is due to the sparseness of the '72 vintage. Have an eye out for this wine and buy with alacrity any you can find. Centennial in Dallas still has Giunti. I intend to keep in touch. So should you.

CAVALIERE. Somewhat lighter than Giunti, it is smooth and mellow and just about as good. The price is about $1.90 for a quart. It is distributed in New York by Wines of All Nations.

BORGHINI. Quite smooth, perhaps a shade less good than the two preceding, it is still an excellent value at $2 a quart. It is distributed nationally by Leonard Kreusch.

BARDI. It is rather light in color and body for a Chianti, with a pleasant tartness associated with slight effervescence, though it is not fizzy. It is a very pleasant wine and a good value, though I prefer Chianti to be somewhat bigger and more robust. The price is a modest $1.89 for a quart.

CHIANTI RUFINA, SOCIETÀ VINICOLA RUFINESE. A creditable Chianti, but lacking, to a slight degree, the smoothness of those listed above; nonetheless, a good buy at about $1.80 for a quart.

One Chianti I drank recently and found pretentious and far from good is:

LEONARDO '70, CANTINA SOCIALE DI VINCI. It comes in a 24-ounce bottle, pretending to be a Classico, but it is not, nor is it so labeled. It is decorated with a drawing of Leonardo da Vinci on the label, but is very ordinary, hardly undrinkable but not nearly as good as any of those previously listed. At $2, it works out to be about $2.50 a quart and should not be mentioned in the same breath as, for example, a Castelli del Grevepesa, a quite fine Classico at $2.50 a quart.

Some white Chianti is also made. It is common enough in Tuscany but has never been in great supply in the United States. It is generally perfectly pleasant, very dry, and somewhat hard. Where it is found at prices approximating the reds, it may safely be bought, but it will not be of much distinction.

I did once drink an extraordinary white Chianti, at the Trattoria alla Romagna in Fiesole, in the hills overlooking Florence. I was in the company of a Florentine-transplanted-to-America, his childhood native Florentine friend, and our respective wives. A 2-liter fiasco was brought in, well covered with cobwebs. Whether the bottle was old or just plain dirty, the wine went so well with the superb food and the operatic arias played by an itinerant and capable accordionist, that both my Florentine friends, expatriate and native, dissolved in tears of nostalgia. The only reason I did not was that I was far too busy singing the arias in competition with another thwarted opera singer from the next table who ended up joining us, along with his wife, children, and grandchildren, for coffee. But unless you can recreate such a background, don't expect anything exceptional from most white Chianti.

Brolio, Ruffino, and Antinori, as well as one or two others of the best vintners, make white wine, always shipped in 24-ounce bottles. They are fine, especially that of Brolio, which certainly is one of the best white wines of Italy. They are not expensive for wines of quality. Current prices are:

Brolio Bianco—$2.75
Ruffino Bianco—$2.59
Villa Antinori Bianco Secco—$3.19
Chianti Machiavelli Bianco, Serristori—$3.32

You could do worse than to try one.

NORTHWESTERN ITALY

It is in the northwestern part of the country that the finest Italian wines are made. The reds, along with the Chianti Classici Riservas, can hold their own against most of France's finest. Here, too, is made the famous Italian sparkling wine, Asti Spumante, of which more later in the appropriate place. From Piedmont come:

Barolo
This is unquestionably one of the world's great wines. Big and full-bodied, it is highly scented and mouth-filling. It is always quite dry. This is a wine that needs aging and should not be drunk when it is younger than five or six years old. It does not come fully into its own until about ten years old and

will last much longer than that. A truly mature Barolo is a dark brick-red in color and so powerful and intense that it seems to catch at the back of one's throat.

Gattinara

It is made of the same Nebbiolo grape as the Barolo and is its equal in character and quality. Very little is found here, but there is some. All I have seen is above our limits. If it can be found at an affordable price, it should be bought unhesitatingly.

Barbera

This is the name of the grape, and the wine made of it is fairly big-bodied and satisfactory, without any claim to greatness. Italian Barbera is not overly plentiful in the United States and is not an exceptional buy when found. California Barbera is another story and is described in the appropriate section.

Grignolino

A light, fruity wine, it is somewhat comparable to Beaujolais, but not as good. It is perfectly enjoyable but not more than a decent buy.

Other wines come from Piedmont, but none is of primary interest.

Some Barolos are priced in the stratosphere, but a good many are well within our limits. Here are a few:

BAROLO '64, BOSCA. This is a lovely example, thoroughly mature, smooth and mellow, with beautiful bouquet—a great wine and a steal at $2.99. There was a '61 having more of everything, with an intensity that was almost throat-catching. None is left in the New York area, except for two or three bottles in my cellar that I'm loath to open. Burka's in Washington, D.C. still had the '61 in the fall of 1973, at $4.99. If you can find any at an affordable price, buy it.

BAROLO '65, BARBERO. Excellent in all respects, this is a great wine and an excellent buy at $3.75.

BAROLO '66, ANTICHE CANTINE TENUTE GALAREY. A Frank Schoonmaker selection, this is a fine example of Barolo: big, fairly mellow, with much perfume. It would undoubtedly profit from being laid down for two, three, or five years. At $3.99 it is an excellent buy.

BAROLO '68, SCANAVINO. This is darker in color and somewhat more full-bodied than most, exceptionally big and mouth-filling. It lacks the mellow smoothness of fully mature Barolos, yet is enjoyable now. It might well be laid down for several years. It is a very good buy at $2.89.

From Valtellina, a narrow valley at the foot of the Alps in Lombardy, some remarkable red wines are beginning to come in. Sometimes they are labeled Valtellina, sometimes with the picturesque names of Grumello, Inferno, and Sassella. They are all the same wine, are all made of the same Nebbiolo grape of Barolo fame, and, when fully mature, are the equal of Barolo, somewhat more delicate and with not quite so much bouquet. To be fully mature, these wines can use six or seven years in cask, followed by three or four in bottle. As is too usual nowadays, they do not always get it. I have not tasted any called Grumello. Some that I have drunk are:

VALTELLINA, RISERVA DELLA CASA PELIZZATTI '61. A very smooth, almost velvety wine, thoroughly mature and aptly called great, it is not a bargain at $4.19 but an excellent buy. The bottles are individually numbered.

SASSELLA '61, CASA PELIZZATTI. Here was an opportunity to make a fair comparison, two differently named wines of the same vintage year and the same vintner. I could note no difference. This is the better buy of the two purely because its price is somewhat lower, $3.99.

INFERNO '67, CASA PELIZZATTI. I found this very similar to the first two except that it noticeably needed maturing. An excellent buy at $2.89, especially to lay down for some years.

INFERNO '67, NEGRI. Though this was of the same vintage year as the one above, the vintner is different. The wine was somewhat sharp, otherwise typical. It clearly needs more maturing. It is far from a bad buy at $2.82.

I suspect that more of the Valtellina wines will arrive here as time goes on, in response to our now chronic shortage of fine wines at reasonable prices. Try any of those listed above if they are available and keep your eyes open for others.

OTHER ITALIAN WINES

Bardolino
A red wine from Lake Garda in the north with no pretensions to greatness, it is light-bodied, soft, often delicious, and very drinkable. It might be compared with Beaujolais, but with much less bouquet and fruitiness. For all its goodness, the wine does not merit the prices often charged here. It is light enough to be drunk slightly chilled.

Valpolicella
Also a red wine, somewhat subtler and a trifle more full-bodied than Bardolino, it is the pride of Verona where it is delightful as the carafe wine of the city. What is sent to the United States is, within my experience, never as good and, in most cases, overpriced for its quality. Valpolicella has a tendency to be *frizzante*, or slightly effervescent. Should you find the characteristic bubbles forming on the inside of the glass, do not fear that the wine is spoiled. On the contrary, it will be better than otherwise. Valpolicella also may be served slightly cool.

Soave
This is the best white wine of Italy, with the exception only of the very special Tuscan whites already mentioned. Depending on who makes it, Soave can vary from very delicate to moderately robust. It is always fresh, never thin, thoroughly dry, and never great. Some can be found at prices that make it a very satisfactory wine for ordinary drinking. Some is quite delicate and fine enough to serve as a party wine.

Italian shippers frequently put up what I call the triplets, that is, Bardolino, Valpolicella, and Soave, under their own labels, at the same price for each of the three. Among those who do so are:

BOLLA. This is the heaviest advertiser of them all. Their wines are among the most expensive, $3.25 for each of the triplets. They are good of their kind, but I do not think them worth such a price.

RUFFINO. The Ruffino name is much more famous for Chianti. Their price is $2.95 for the triplets. Quality approximates that of Bolla.

BERTANI. Bertani's price per bottle is $3.25; the wines fall into the same general quality class as the first two.

RICASOLI. Ricasoli is best known for Brolio. They have entered the triplets field rather recently. Their quality is not quite comparable with those above but they are good and enjoyable and best buys at $1.99.

I find it hard to make a case for Bardolino or Valpolicella at $3.25 for 24 ounces, when compared with a very good Chianti Classico at $2.50 a quart or a most excellent one at $2.95 for 24 ounces. They are not the same type of wine, granted, but the Chianti Classici are so much better value. Still, your taste may not coincide with mine and you should try them, by all means.

You might well start with the best, as taste-setters, if you wish to try at all. Ruffino is the best buy among those of top quality, purely because it is lower in price. If unavailable, Bolla or Bertani certainly will be.

Ricasoli at $1.99 is the best buy for each of the triplets. The Soave is particularly appealing, a light-bodied wine, not thin but delicate and almost aristocratic. It is very much a "party" wine but must be used with care. It should not be served even with more robust fish or chicken dishes, but it shines with broiled fish and shellfish.

Frank Schoonmaker has two selections called Rosso di Verona ("red wine of Verona") and Bianco di Verona ("white wine of Verona"). The red is an authentic Valpolicella of no extraordinary quality. The white is an authentic Soave of equally modest quality. They are perfectly enjoyable and both are excellent buys at a cost of $2.06 for a liter bottle (about 33.5 ounces).

Orvieto

This is the white wine that so often comes in a squat 22-ounce version of the Chianti fiasco. There are two types, *abboccato* ("sweet") and *secco* ("dry"). Be very careful to read the label, where one of the two terms will appear. The abboccato is much too sweet to drink as a table wine. The secco is never completely dry and is soft and pleasing, a good dinner wine. It is well worth serving occasionally.

There is not a great deal available but some can always be found. There is also not too much choice. Most common are Melini in the 22-ounce fiasco at $2.99 and Ruffino in a 23-ounce bottle at $3.15. Both are excellent examples, neither is inexpensive, and either will prove enjoyable occasionally. Again, remember that there is both *secco*, which is a rather lovely dinner wine, and *abboccato*, too sweet for drinking with meals but highly enjoyable chilled for plain drinking.

Here ends the list of Italian wines that I recommend. There are a good many others, any of which you may try if you wish, but none of which excites me. You will inevitably come across them. Hence, a few brief comments about some:

Lambrusco

This is a red wine, more nearly sparkling than effervescent, made a few miles from Mantua. I have drunk it there, where it is at its best. What I had was a rather dry wine of only 7 percent alcohol, light, refreshing, very enjoyable as a curiosity. What is sold in the United States is a wine of still only 9 percent alcohol, sweet and frothy and more like an American soft drink than a wine. Try it by all means if you wish—the most common label is Riunite—but don't expect wine in the normal sense.

Frascati

The white carafe wine of Rome, where it is as enjoyable as most of the *vini locale*, rather fragrant and strong, as the southern wines generally are. In the United States the price range for Frascati is fairly wide, though all within our limits, but I have never tasted a Frascati here worth the price or other than ordinary in quality.

Verdicchio

This is a white wine whose greatest claim to distinction is its fancifully shaped bottle. It is pleasantly dry but otherwise has little character. If I had a choice only between Verdicchio and no wine, I would not be unhappy with Verdicchio but I just see no purpose in choosing it among so many other wines.

Ravello

Its wines do not begin to equal the serene beauty of this paradisiac village, which was once the summer retreat of the wealthy of the Republic of Amalfi. Most of what is shipped here is rosé but some red and white may be found. The only brand I know of is Gran Caruso. The wines have deteriorated sadly. In the summer of 1972 I found the Gran Caruso wines poor, right at the Hotel Gran Caruso. The other Ravello wines I tried there were equally unenjoyable. Ravello wines are specifically not recommended.

Segeste

This is a red wine from Sicily. In so hot a climate as that of Sicily, wines are never great, seldom delicate. The reality of Segeste, unlike its ads, is rather heavy and coarse. It is perfectly drinkable, but much more nearly approaches the derogatory appellation of "spaghetti wine" than any of the other reds discussed here. For myself, such an appellation also derogates spaghetti and all pasta. Properly made, and in the enormous variety of styles possible, it is perhaps Italy's greatest contribution to wonderful cuisine.

These are hardly all of the Italian wines you may come across. Almost every time I walk into a wine shop, I seem to find another I've not heard of before. Do not be enticed by low prices and perhaps the handsome, odd-sized bottles. By all means, try such a wine here and there. I have not tried them all, I could hardly find the time, and I cannot comment on any I have not tasted. Just be sure that you start with some of those recommended and leave new and unknown ones for later, when a disappointing wine will not "turn you off."

Germany

It is unnecessary to distinguish between East and West German wines. To the best of my knowledge, East Germany produces no wine. All German wine is West German in origin.

Germany produces some of the greatest white wines in the world. This is no mean feat, considering that her famous vineyards are among the most northerly in the world and that growing conditions are so uncertain that in many years there is not enough sunshine and warmth to ripen grapes properly. In addition, some of the vineyards are situated on hillsides so steep that no beast can make its way to and among them, only man.

Under such conditions, winemaking is an art as much as a commercial enterprise. The cost of making wine in Germany is many times that in France or Italy. Total production is perhaps 10 to 12 percent of the wine made in the latter countries. Consumption is far greater than total native production. Small wonder that German wines are not low in cost. On the other hand, largely because of the challenge of making wine at all, the quality of German wines is exceptionally high.

Although red wine is made, the whites account for about 85 percent of the total production. The reds are reputed to be good but never more than that and they are almost completely consumed at home. A few have found their way to the United States, but they are unimportant in the American market and should be disregarded.

As with French wines, Americans have been misled, and have misled themselves, into believing that the fine estate-bottled German wines are the only ones worth drinking. It is time that we recognize that there are highly enjoyable German wines within the reach of people of moderate means, that the very fine wines are by now far beyond our limits, and that the great ones have always been among the most expensive in the world. Today's higher costs are, of course, in good part attributable to upward revaluations of the German mark, as well as to inflation and dollar devaluation. And the full impact of the mark revaluation may not yet have been felt.

I came late in my wine life to German wines. From some tastings of a long time ago I had formed the belief that German wines were all sweet and simply outside, if not beneath, my consideration. Vigorously, almost belligerently, I resisted the conception that they are dinner wines. I have had good reason to change my beliefs more recently, and have experienced much enjoyment in doing so.

It is true that there are many people, especially Americans of German extraction or origin, who seem to believe that anything short of the honey-sweet wine is the proper wine to drink with a meal. It is certainly true that many of the wines, especially the Rhines, are really much too sweet to serve at dinner. But it is equally a fact that many, many Rhines and Moselles are fairly dry—never as dry as, for example, a Chablis, but quite sufficiently so to drink with meals.

Some of these are dry purely because there was so little sugar in the grapes that the alcoholic content of the wine is as low as 8.5 percent. These are perfectly enjoyable but totally unexceptional. There are, however, many others, including some of quality, that have more body, more alcohol, and are good to excellent with food.

However, thought and care are needed in matching such wines to meals. They are so light and delicate that they can very easily be overpowered by foods that are at all robust. A sweeter wine can more readily cope with heartier foods, but it is almost walking a tightrope to determine beyond what degree of sweetness the wine is no longer a dinner wine. That degree is reached earlier for me than for some others. From that point onward, the German wines are better suited for just drinking, or as highly enjoyable aperitifs.

The German generally treats his wines in much that way. The finer wines are drunk just for the pleasure of drinking. They are really just too good to "waste" with food. They are light and not strong and will not go to one's head. At mealtimes he is likely to have one of the simpler wines of the district, or a red German wine from farther south, or an imported wine.

German wines have a character unique unto themselves. Whatever the type, they all lack the rather big, mouth-filling quality of most French whites. Instead, they are so light and delicate that, tasted side by side with, let us say, white Burgundy, they would seem thin and watery. They are nothing of the sort but are, in fact, among the most delicate, and delicately well balanced, of all white wines.

German control laws are the most complete and rigid in the world. Quality of wine is graded in three classifications. There are minute descriptions of the characteristics for each grade (and subgrade) and specific legal requirements for each. For anyone who wishes to cultivate an interest in German wines, it is important to have at least a working knowledge of these classifications, even though many relate to wines far beyond our means. Simply, rather than legally described, they are:

TAFELWEIN ("Table Wine"). Essentially, this is wine with a minimum 8.5 percent alcohol content. Very little reaches the United States; most is consumed in Germany. Such a wine is light, pleasant, and simple.

QUALITÄTSWEIN ("Quality Wine"). This is just what its

name implies and includes the better among the regional wines and some estate bottlings. This grade is well worth our attention.

QUALITÄTSWEIN MIT PRÄDIKAT ("Quality Wine with Special Attributes"). This is superior wine; the classification includes everything from fine wines up to the very greatest, from dry to honey-sweet. The individual special attributes are also spelled out and, again, it is worth getting an understanding of them.

KABINETT (sometimes appearing on the label in English as "Cabinet"). This used to denote wine from the best cask of the vintage, with no sugar added in fermentation. Its meaning is less definite nowadays, but still indicates a better quality.

SPÄTLESE ("Late-picked"). The wine will be richer and fuller because the grapes have more sugar. It may also be sweeter.

AUSLESE ("Selected Picking"). The wine is made from the ripest bunches of grapes, specially selected as they are brought in from the vineyard. These are sweet wines, unsuitable for drinking with meals, quite sweet enough to serve as dessert wines.

BEERENAUSLESE ("Specially Selected Berries"). Overripe, partially shriveled grapes are individually picked off the bunches. The sugar is highly concentrated and the resulting wine is almost syrupy.

TROCKENBEERENAUSLESE. This is the latest picking of all, of grapes shriveled almost into raisins. The wine is obviously the sweetest and richest of all.

All of the last three types of wine are far too sweet to be considered table wines. Most of them are also far too expensive to be considered here at all. They will be discussed later in the section devoted to dessert wines.

We come now to bottle labels. You may as well learn the elements of German wine labeling now, too. They can be mastered with very little effort. German wine labels are the most revealing of all. They are also the most difficult, because they are often printed in hard-to-read Gothic characters, the descriptions are usually in German (although more and more

English words are appearing), and because, in fact, they reveal as much as they do. German law requires detailed and accurate information on wine labels so that, if you know how to read them, you will know everything about the wine inside. If you don't, the sheer amount of verbiage will be confusing.

There are a few simple things to remember. The suffix *er* at the end of a word means "of." *Bernkasteler* means "of Bernkastel." A vintage year, *1971er*, means "of the 1971 vintage." It is the same use of the suffix as in "New Yorker." The label will always indicate the classification, such as Qualitätswein, and any special attribute, such as Kabinett or Auslese. It will also show the region, such as Mosel-Saar-Ruwer, and, if the wine is estate-bottled, it may say so in English but is more likely to carry a legend such as *Original-Kellerabzug* or *Original-Abfüllung*.

That is not all of it, but it is the uncomplicated minimum that you should know, and it will fall into place mentally after you have examined a few actual labels. A bit more that you will need to know will be explained when individual wines are described. As though to make identifications a bit easier for us, Moselle wines all come in long-necked green bottles and Rhines in similarly long-necked brown ones.

There are some ten wine districts of any note. They cluster along the two rivers, the Rhine and the Moselle (the French and English spelling is usually used outside of Germany, where they are called the Rhein and Mosel) and their various tributaries, among them the Neckar, Nahe, Saar, and Ruwer. The Moselle itself joins the Rhine at Koblenz, not far south of Bonn. We need be concerned with only three of these districts.

VINTAGES IN GERMANY

Vintages are of the greatest importance in a land where sunshine is so scarce a commodity. The less than great wines with which we are concerned should, however, be drunk young. Hence, only the past few years will matter. They have been kind, on the whole. The vintage of 1969 was very good to great; '70 was an exceptionally large vintage of very good quality; '71 was superb—also, for that very reason, expensive; and '72 was better than in most other countries—production was average or almost so and the wines are very pleasant but, unfortunately, high in price. The weather was poor in '73, with so little sunshine that there will be none of the sweeter wines at all. The drier ones will not amount to much. So poor a year can mean higher prices for earlier vintages.

THE RHINE

Most Rhine wines are made of Sylvaner or Riesling grapes. The Sylvaner produces a pleasant, soft, and wholly enjoyable wine, with moderate fragrance. It is by no means great. Wines made of the noble Riesling grape are round, rather full, with much richness and floweriness, both of flavor and bouquet. They range from fine to very great.

The two regions that produce most of the Rhine wines exported to the United States are RHEINGAU and RHEINHESSEN. The label will always show the region.

The Rheingau accounts for most of the best Rhine wines. Most of its vineyards, and all of the best ones, are planted to the Riesling grape. Rheinhessen is more a producer of quantity than of great quality. Most of its vineyards are planted in Sylvaner grapes. The small proportion that grow the Riesling produce most of the best wines of the region.

One of the best known of the Rhine wines, indeed of all German wines, is Liebfraumilch. It is not the wine of a particular vineyard. It is simply Rhine wine. Most of it is made in Rheinhessen of Sylvaner grapes.

Liebfraumilch should not be bought indiscriminately. Those of the great shippers, such as Sichel, Kreusch, and Deinhard, are sure to be well blended wines of good quality, slightly sweet, soft, of good body and fragrance, and thoroughly drinkable. There are, of course, many other shippers whose quality can be trusted equally, but Liebfraumilch of an unknown shipper can be rather awful stuff.

The finest of the Rhines are, as usual, far beyond our means. There are still a fair number of excellent to good quality that are reasonable in price. Here are a few, in order of price:

NIERSTEINER DOMTAL '70, Ludwig Seifert—Rheinhessen. It has slight bouquet, is very light but not thin, and is mild, pleasant, and quite dry. It is a very good buy at $1.69, although the wine is far from great.

LIEBFRAUMILCH '70, Ludwig Seifert—Rheinhessen. It is quite similar to the Niersteiner above, having a bit more body and power. Again, just a pleasant dinner wine, but a very good buy at $1.69.

NIERSTEINER GUTES DOMTAL, Leonard Kreusch—Rheinhessen. Just a little more of everything—power, body, bouquet —than the Niersteiner Domtal. The price is $2.49 and it is worth the extra cost.

RUDESHEIMER ROSENGARTEN '70, Leonard Kreusch. It has a noticeable touch of sweetness, but is still satisfactory as a dinner wine. With moderate bouquet, good body, and balance, it is a very good buy at $2.49. This is a product of a Nahe vineyard and is not to be confused with Rudesheim of Rheingau, which produces much better and more expensive wine.

LIEBFRAUMILCH '71, Von Plattenberg (a family associated with some of the finest of Rhine wines)—Rheinhessen. It is labeled Qualitätswein and is a G. C. Sumner selection. It has lovely bouquet, body, and balance, and is a best buy at $2.69. It also has enough sweetness to rule it out as a dinner wine for me, but certainly not for many others. I enjoy it as an aperitif.

JOHANNISBERGER ERNTEBRINGER '72, Leonard Kreusch. The label says it is a Rheingau of Riesling grapes, and a Qualitätswein. Erntebringer is one of the well known, good vineyards of the region, a close neighbor to the famous Schloss Johannisberg. The wine has very good balance, is delicate and quite dry, with excellent bouquet. It is rather lovely, a most enjoyable dinner wine and a fine example of good Rhine. At $2.89 it is a very good buy.

HATTENHEIMER STABEL '70, Schloss Reinhartshausener—Rheingau—Qualitätswein. Hattenheim produces excellent wines. This one is very fragrant, light, and of good balance, and for me, on the sweet side. For many it would be a satisfactory table wine, but I would rather just drink it on a warm afternoon. An excellent buy at $2.60.

LIEBFRAUMILCH SPAETLESE '70, Leonard Kreusch—Rheinhessen. This wine is labeled *Natur*, which means that no sugar was added in fermentation. Beginning with 1971, the new laws have eliminated Natur as a description. As might be expected from a Spätlese, the wine is richer, yet still delicate and well balanced, with fine fragrance, and noticeably on the sweet side. A very good buy at $3.25 for those who care for that much sweetness in a table wine.

SCHLOSS VOLLRADS '70, Green Cap. This is one of the famous vineyards of the Rheingau and its wine doesn't really need the label of Qualitätswein which it bears. The vineyard produces six or seven qualities of wine, each with a differently colored cap. The Green Cap is the least of them, despite which this wine, of only a very good vintage year, not a great one, is a joy to drink. It is also the only wine of this vineyard still well within our price range. It is beautifully balanced, with lovely bouquet, but again, on the sweet side for me. Whether as a dinner wine or just for elegant drinking, it should be tried. The cost, $3.29.

JOHANNISBERGER KLAUS RIESLING '70, Landgraf von Hessen. This is a nearby neighbor to Schloss Johannisberg in the Rheingau, both producing among the loveliest, softest, and lightest of the Rhines. Those of the Schloss are no doubt better, but probably not enough better to justify the sharply higher prices. Johannisberger Klaus is the better buy of the two—a wine of sheer, delicate loveliness, not inexpensive at about $4.89, but well worth trying once, at least.

THE MOSELLE

The Moselle and its two main tributaries, the Saar and the

Ruwer, are often treated as a single area of wine production. Labels of wines from this region usually carry the legend *MOSEL-SAAR-RUWER*. There are differences in character among the three, but no greater than those among the wines of any one of them alone. This is especially true of the less costly ones. Virtually all Moselle wines that are exported come from Mosel-Saar-Ruwer.

All Moselles are made of the Riesling grape. The better ones have a powerful fragrance, so intense that it almost pours out of the bottle as the cork is drawn. They are drier than the Rhine wines, all in all, although they range from quite dry to intensely sweet. Even a Moselle as sweet as an Auslese still leaves a hint of underlying dryness on the palate.

The Moselles are characterized by a lightness and delicacy that is matched by their pale golden color. Withal they are fruity and almost as flowery as the Rhines. The drier ones are true dinner wines and some of the Spätlese are by no means too sweet to drink with meals.

In the same way that there is a liebfraumilch for Rhine wine, there is a MOSELBLUMCHEN, "little Moselle flower", for Moselle. It is a regional blend and has never achieved great fame.

Much better known among the blended Moselles are several named after and produced within a radius of nine miles of a well known town or vineyard of the region. These are ZELLER SCHWARZE KATZ ("Black Cat Vineyard of Zell"), BERNKASTELER RIESLING, and CRÖVER NACKTARSCH ("Bare-Bottom Vineyard of Cröv"). With the German penchant for colorful pictorial labels, it is not surprising that the first is illustrated by a sinister black cat and the last by a scene depicting a child being spanked on its naked bottom.

Here are a few of the Moselles well worth your attention, again in order of price.

MOSELBLUMCHEN '70, Hans Bach. It is labeled 8.5 to 10 percent alcohol. As might be expected, it is very mild and light. It has small bouquet and fruitiness, is quite dry and very easy to drink, and is a good buy at $1.99 but no more than that.

CRÖVER NACKTARSCH '72, Kreusch—Qualitätswein. This is labeled 10.5 percent alcohol and is noticeably bigger than the Moselblumchen, with good fragrance and balance and quite in a different class. It is a very good dinner wine and an equally good buy at $2.79.

ZELLER SCWHARZE KATZ '72, Kreusch—Qualitätswein. It is very like the Cröver Nacktarsch, with a noticeable touch of sweetness. It is still suitable to my palate as a dinner wine. A very good buy at $2.69.

PIESPORTER GOLDTRÖPFCHEN '70, Kreusch. The actual Goldtröpfchen vineyard has become so well known that all vintners in Piesport have taken to using the name. Apparently the wine laws permit it. I doubt that this wine is a product of that vineyard. It would have to cost more. Nonetheless, it is a delicate, well balanced wine of fine bouquet, a very good dinner wine and an excellent value at $2.98.

BERNKASTELER RIESLING '70, Stephen Studert. A wine of fine bouquet, good balance, considerable floweriness, with a touch of, to me, unobjectionable sweetness, a rather lovely dinner wine and a very good buy at $2.95.

ZELTINGER HIMMELREICH KABINETT '71, H. Ehses— Qualitätswein mit Prädikat—Erzeuger Abfüllung ("Estate-bottled"). It is also so labeled in English. It has a rich, powerful bouquet and a noticeable touch of sweetness, yet not too much for a table wine. This begins to approach greatness, with subtle overtones, and lovely balance. It is an excellent buy at $3.50.

ZELTINGER HIMMELREICH KABINETT '71, Winzer. It is possibly somewhat more readily available than the one above, but otherwise I find no noticeable difference between them. The price, too, is the same, about $3.50.

GRAACHER HIMMELREICH KABINETT '71, S. A. Prüm. The Prüm family make some of the finest and greatest of the Moselles. This is also estate-bottled. It is somewhat better than the two above, rounder, with more balance. At $3.80 it is not the better buy, however.

WEHLENER SONNENUHR '69, S. A. Prüm—Sonnenuhr ("Sundial") is perhaps the most famous of the Moselle vineyards and dispenses with some descriptive labeling. It is, however, labeled *Original-Kellerabzug* ("Estate-Bottled") and *Naturwein* ("no sugar added"), the latter since it is a pre-1971 vintage. Everything said about the previous three estate-bottled wines may be said of this one, plus 10 to 15 percent. You will not find many Moselles finer than this outside the Spätlese class, and even though the price, $3.98, is somewhat steep for us, the wine is well worth it and should be tried.

FRANCONIA

Franconia (Franken) is the one remaining region producing wines of some quality. They are often referred to as *Steinwein*. They are always bottled in a *Bocksbeutel*, a roundish, flagon-shaped bottle. The wines are reputed to be much drier than those of the Rhine and Moselle, with some of the strength and stoniness associated with Chablis.

Very little Franconian wine is shipped here, so little that I do not recall ever having seen a bottle of it. Most of what is available is quite expensive, well above our limits, for example WÜRZBURGER STEIN RIESLING, Julius Spital, at more than $7.50 per bottle. I have heard that BANFI distributes a Frankenwein at about $3. Try it, by all means, or any other you may find within our price range, but I am unable to recommend any.

The United States

Twenty-six states of the United States produce wine commercially. Surprised? American wine is frequently thought of as coming only from California and New York. Yet good wine is made, for example, in Oregon, Washington State, and Ohio, which was the largest producer of premium wines a century or so ago.

There is no doubt that much more will be heard from the lesser wine-producing states as time goes on and interest in wine increases. Ohio is now revitalizing what had become a rather moribund industry. Oregon and Washington are clearly only in the early stages of viticulture of good to high quality. Michigan has the elements of a thoroughly respectable industry. Missouri, too, for example, has a small but quite decent wine industry. This is to mention only a few. The other states will not be backward about increasing production and promoting their wines. At present, however, they are a factor primarily only in their own areas and are largely unknown elsewhere.

In 1972, 71 percent of all wine consumed in the United States was California wine, 15 percent was from all other states, and 14 percent was foreign wine. New York State accounted for much of the 15 percent for all other states. The remainder was consumed largely in and near the producing states.

With California wine representing almost six out of every eight bottles drunk in the United States, it is evident that any discussion of American wines must center primarily on that state, despite the fact that California's *share* of the total market appears to be decreasing, while total *sales* of their wines continue to increase. New York State's wines are also nationally distributed and will be described here, but those of the other states must be left to a later time, when they will undoubtedly represent a more significant part of the national market.

Parenthetically, figures for foreign wines are rather interesting. They appear to be quite a minor factor in the U.S. market, but the increase in 1972 over 1971 was 30.1 percent. The American industry is concerned. They see a trend. So do I. Wine producers from all over the world have been intensifying their efforts to penetrate the American market during 1973. If the industry's concern results in increased competition, the consumer will profit. If it seeks to express itself in restrictive legislation, and succeeds, it will be at the consumer's expense in more ways than one.

CALIFORNIA

Although the vine was brought to Southern California by the Spanish centuries ago, wine making in the modern sense has flourished for little more than a hundred years.

In 1851, Colonel Agaston Haraszthy, a Hungarian political refugee, introduced about a hundred cuttings of European vines to California. Sent to Europe by the governor of the state some ten years later, he selected and had shipped to California cuttings of about three hundred more varieties. From among these a true native Californian viticulture has developed.

Prohibition ruined what had become a flourishing industry. After its repeal in 1933, production began again, but for about two decades it was concentrated on cheap dry wines and perhaps even cheaper sweet ones. This is not to say that some lone spirits did not preach against such a trend while themselves producing, and promoting the production of, quality wines. It was really only about twenty years ago that wide emphasis on the production of premium wines began. In that very brief time, near miracles have been achieved.

California is blessed with some of the finest grape-growing country in the world. A great quantity of wine of satisfactory quality is produced. The region around San Francisco in the north is ideally suited to the grapes that make fine and great wine. Napa and Sonoma counties are the best known. There are other areas, including Santa Clara County and the Livermore Valley, where the best of the European grapes flourish. The lesser wines and most of the sweet ones are produced in the hot central valley and in the southern parts of the state.

The industry, which originally consisted of many small, occasionally moderate-sized vintners, has long since succumbed to big-business trends. This is not unusual on the

American business scene. Today a few giants dominate California wine making and distribution. There remain a number of medium-sized wineries, many of which emphasize premium wines.

At the other end of the scale, there are, and probably always will be, numerous small wineries, with minor production. Many of these may not make more than 1,000 or 2,000 cases per year. Some are reported to be passionately devoted to making exceptional wine. Their distribution is limited, at best, to the locality of the vineyard or not far beyond, perhaps as far as the nearest big city. If I were to take up residence in California I would be out hunting up a few such vineyards right after laying down the carpets, but they are of no significance outside their immediate localities.

California's (in fact, America's) table wines are of two main qualities. Those which are merchandised as European types, that is, Burgundy, Claret, Chablis, Sauterne, Chianti, are the lesser and lower-priced wines, rarely having more than a remote resemblance to their European counterparts and varying from satisfactory to rather poor. These are known as generics and the lesser among them are often referred to as "jug wines."

The better wines are, for the most part, named for the grape varieties that predominate in the wine and are therefore called "varietals." They include such names as Cabernet Sauvignon, Pinot Noir, Pinot Chardonnay, Chenin Blanc, Sauvignon Bllanc, and many others.

These are the pride of California and of America. They range in quality from good to superb. In recent years, the best among them have taken honors from the great European wines. Needless to say, the best varietals are far beyond our price limits. Many, however, remain thoroughly affordable.

Almost a hundred years ago, an experimental grape-growing station was established by the College of Agriculture of the University of California at Davis. Research and teaching, there and elsewhere in the state, has continued ever since and has made immense contributions to viticulture.

In 1934, after the repeal of Prohibition, both the state of California and the federal government established standards of quality and legal requirements for the industry. For that matter, all of the wine making states maintain measures of control. Consequently, the American wine industry is quite thoroughly, and often rigidly, policed. The consuming public tends to be unaware of this, principally because there are no labeling requirements for such qualifying terms as the French Appellation Contrôlée. The requirements exist just the same and are adhered to perhaps more faithfully than in some European countries.

The biggest of the wine makers produce a complete range from generics through varietals to aperitif and after-dinner wines and champagne. Some of the medium-sized producers do somewhat the same, usually limiting themselves to less variety, and some specialize only in varietals, often in a limited range only. Still, there is just no such thing as an American vintner of any size that produces a single wine, or a red and white only, as so many European vineyards commonly do.

To the uninitiated, this is a jungle. It is made even worse to find some "Burgundies" moderately dry and then to come on one so sweet that it is unpleasant. It does not help to find that some Sauvignons Blancs are as sweet as dessert wines and others wonderfully dry. It certainly complicates life when one vintner makes both a light, almost delicate, Zinfandel and a robust, full one.

Fortunately, there are ways of finding a path through this maze. First, it is important to know something about the producers. Second, it is essential to know a good deal more about wine types and individual wines.

There is no enormous number of producers of national significance, but quite enough to make it profitless to try to list and describe them all. I will refer only to those that are best known or most important for our purposes. Nor are my descriptions intended to be exact ratings as to their size or the overall level of quality of their wines. Each seems capable of making good and bad wines, or at least, good and less good.

ALMADÉN, one of the half-dozen largest producers, makes some of everything, including varietals. Their ordinary wines are good, for ordinary wines. Some of their varietals are rather superior.

CHRISTIAN BROTHERS, another large winemaker, is owned by a monastic order. Their wines tend to be better than average in quality.

FRANZIA is among the ten largest producers. Their wines are all low-priced, and of satisfactory quality in their price range.

GALLO is the biggest of all, accounting for more than one third of all California wine production. They make some of everything except varietals. Much of their production is of jug wines. As ordinary wines go, their quality is good, but nothing exceptional should be expected.

PAUL MASSON at one time produced excellent wines, then went along the too common path of quantity rather than quality, and in recent years have been doing much to recoup. Many of their wines are now of better than average quality.

We come now to a group of smaller vintners, whom I class loosely as medium-sized, only in the sense that they are not among the giants. These are known for good to exceptional quality. Among them, they produce most of the better California wines which are our special interest.

BEAULIEU VINEYARDS produce both generics and varietals, with emphasis on quality in both. Their reputation for excellence is well deserved. Their wines are easily identified by the prominent BV symbol on the label.

INGLENOOK VINEYARDS are known for quality, at least in their better wines. They have established three classifications. Estate Bottled Wines are vintage varietals, Vintage Table Wines are vintage generics, and the Navalle Series are jug wines. The first two groups tend to be very good to excellent. The Navalles are unimpressive.

KORBEL produces a small selection of good generics and varietals both, and some jug wines as well. They are best known for their excellent champagne.

CHARLES KRUG offers a number of good generics and fine

varietals, the best of which are at the upper limit of our price range or beyond it. Their line of jug wines is marketed under the name of C. K. Mondavi.

LOUIS M. MARTINI offers a rather extensive selection of varietals, generics, and jug wines and is noted for quality among all of them.

ROBERT MONDAVI makes fine varietals only, most of them, though not all, beyond our price limits.

SONOMA VINEYARDS is a very recent arrival on the scene. They began national distribution only in 1972. Their wines can now be found in a limited number of shops in most larger cities. They grow only the fine varieties of grapes. They offer an unusual promotional device of personalized labels that has much appeal for gift-giving. Their wines are good but more time is needed to determine just how good.

WENTE BROTHERS are far and away the best makers of fine white wines in California. They produce a few reds as well but their outstanding achievement is their whites, some of which are authentic reproductions of European varieties and often much better than their European counterparts of like price.

A few other producers are worthy of mention.

FREEMARK ABBEY, HANZELL, HEITZ, MIRASSOU, MARTIN RAY, MAYACAMAS, RIDGE, and SOUVERAIN. These, plus one or two others, produce probably the best of all American wines, quite capable of holding their own in competition with the fine wines of Europe. Their prices, with very few exceptions, are beyond our limits, but it is at least worth knowing of the exceptional excellence they have achieved in the making of American wines. Should you sometime feel like splurging, your money would be well spent on one of their wines.

SAN MARTIN is a smaller vineyard that makes the more ordinary wines and some varietals and makes most of them well. It is by no means as widely distributed as the better known brands but can be found, at very least, at Hoffman's in Denver, Berbiglia's in Kansas City, Central Liquors in Washington, D.C., and Astor's in New York City.

CONCANNON is a small vineyard that makes wines of excellence. Production is not great but their wines can be found in most parts of the country. They are more common in the West than on the East Coast. There are some varietals, a few of them being quite exceptional and much too costly for us. Most of their wines are well within our limits.

THE VARIETALS

The finest grape varieties of Europe flourish in California. They make the best wines of America, an entirely different breed from the generics. A great deal of work has been, and is being, done on hybrids as well, often with much success. Indeed, in this respect we are no different from, though perhaps more advanced than, European vintners. Hybrids will become increasingly important in winemaking. For now, our main attention will center on the more traditional varieties.

These wines are often in short supply. A very small part of total California wine-grape production is devoted to the fine varieties. More vineyards are being planted all the time, but constantly increasing demand prevents accumulation of any surplus. Some experts in the field predict that, by 1980, but not before, supply will have finally caught up with demand.

This, plus restrictive tax laws on wine inventories, commonly causes the reds to be brought to market not yet mature. Some varietals bear vintage years, some do not. Since many of the vintage wines, whose age is known, are not yet mature, it may fairly be assumed that all non-vintage wines would profit from a year, preferably two or three, in bottle. Those who can should lay down one or two varietals, even if only a bottle or two at a time, thus establishing their own cellars.

Though there tends to be less difference in year-to-year growing conditions than in the fine wine areas of Europe, there are certainly differences. We have not yet learned to control the weather and assure a regular supply of grapes of unchanging quality. Very simply, however, there is seldom available any range of vintage years of a given wine. You must take what you can get. Hence, vintage years become of little importance.

However, it is worth mentioning the last two years. 1972 was a vintage of fair to good quality but of meager quantity. Undoubtedly this contributed in part to the price increases of 1973 which, by comparison with the soaring costs of French wines, were very moderate indeed. 1973 will probably be magnificent—and it was huge, with a record grape crush. This should help keep prices of California wines down.

Varietal wines are legally required to be made of at least 51 percent of the grape variety after which they are named. Vintage varietals are also required to be made at least 95 percent of grapes grown in that vintage year. Many vintners use much more than the 51 percent minimum as a matter of principle, and at least one, Beaulieu Vineyards, uses 100 percent. I am sure they do not stand alone. I just don't know personally who the others may be.

Three varieties account for most of the red wine production and much of the best of all the reds.

Cabernet Sauvignon

The principal grape of Bordeaux, the Cabernet Sauvignon, makes far and away the finest of all California red wines and some of the best in the world. Naturally, the best among them require painstaking effort, the area in which they are grown is limited, they are in short supply, and are expensive. Like Bordeaux, the wine starts in life hard and almost harsh, though less so than the French wines. More than any other varietal, it needs aging and often enough has not had it when you buy it. It is likely to retain a sharpness that is not a characteristic of the wine, merely a sign of its youth. It should be judged with that in mind and, when at all possible, it should be laid down for a year or more.

Some that I like among those not too costly for us, in order of ascending quality, are:

CHRISTIAN BROTHERS Cabernet Sauvignon. It has good bouquet and fruitiness, is very dry, and begins to display a bit of the subtlety of which this wine is capable. It is also a trifle thin, probably a sign of immaturity. A good buy at $3.39.

ALMADÉN Cabernet Sauvignon. It has the true claret flavor, very dry, very good bouquet, delicate but not thin, with considerable finesse. I consider it the best buy at $2.80, though not the best wine in the group.

LOUIS M. MARTINI Cabernet Sauvignon '68. It has a bit more of everything than the Almadén, appears to be quite mature, and is by all means an excellent value at $3.20.

BEAULIEU VINEYARDS Cabernet Sauvignon '69. The label states: "Produced entirely from Cabernet Sauvignon grapes" and "Estate Bottled." It is the best of all in this group and even though the costliest, $3.82, should be bought for its quality, regardless of the greater cost. I am not sure whether it can still be found. The '71 is now available and is clearly not mature but already enjoyable, and would profit greatly from up to two years of bottle aging. If you are ever in the mood to find out what the really great California Cabernets are like, you might try Beaulieu Vineyards Georges de la Tour Special Reserve, in whatever vintage year it may be available. The '66 was superb, the '67 nearly so. The '68 is reputed to have been the greatest ever produced by BV. The price at present is officially $5.81, although I was horrified to see a bottle of the '67 in a New York wine shop in December, 1972, priced at $9.95.

One Cabernet Sauvignon I definitely do not recommend is:

ELEVEN CELLARS (California Wine Association). The bottle is capped, not corked. Imagine that in a $3 wine! The wine is thin and sharp, tastes only a little like a Cabernet Sauvignon, has meager bouquet, and is distinctly poor in quality.

Pinot Noir

This is the great grape of Burgundy but, in California, it is by no means the success that Cabernet Sauvignon has become. The wine made of it does not approach the quality of the better French Burgundies, which are, however, beyond our price range. In fact, some of the better California generics labeled as Burgundy are superior to the Pinot Noir I have tasted. They, too, tend to be marketed young and, as a general rule, any that you do buy can profit from a year or two of bottle aging.

Among the few I have drunk, I have enjoyed:

KORBEL Pinot Noir. A big, full wine with moderate bouquet and fruitiness, it is a fair facsimile of genuine Burgundy. It could clearly use more bottle aging. It is a good buy at $3.40.

LOUIS M. MARTINI Napa Valley Pinot Noir. A full-bodied wine, clearly resembling a true Burgundy, rather robust and fairly smooth, with good bouquet, it is a better buy than most Californias of this variety at $3.59.

Some that I have found unsatisfactory are:

PAUL MASSON Pinot Noir. It has moderate body, little bouquet, and, while resembling French Burgundy in taste, it is without character. The price, $2.98.

ALMADÉN Pinot Noir. It is a somewhat thin, fairly decent wine, with meager bouquet and no character at all. I have tasted better jug wines. The price, $2.80.

Zinfandel

There is more of this grown in California than of any other red grape variety. Its origin was for a long time unknown. Colonel Haraszthy is credited with having brought it from somewhere in Europe in the early 1850s. It produces an excellent wine, not comparable to any European wine and peculiarly Californian. Recently the origin of the grape appears to have been traced to Sicily, where it is still grown.

Zinfandel is a very agreeable, light, and light-bodied wine, of good bouquet, very dry, extremely pleasant but never great. The grape is grown throughout California but the best wines come from the north. Like Beaujolais, which it does not resemble except in being light and uncomplicated, it should be drunk with less robust dishes. It has the further virtue of being fairly inexpensive. Most of the fine wines cost well under $3.

The wine can generally be drunk young. The occasional

big, full-bodied Zinfandel will profit from bottle aging but there are not many made, they are often unavailable, and they cost more, sometimes almost as much as vintage Cabernet Sauvignons. They are not likely to be worth the price.

Some that I have enjoyed greatly are:

INGLENOOK Vintage Zinfandel '71. Although the label says it is medium-bodied, I find it quite light but in no way thin, with moderate bouquet. It is very dry, very fresh, and thoroughly drinkable. It is the best buy of the group at $2.15. I understand that Inglenook also produces an estate-bottled Zinfandel, big and full-bodied. It is probably quite a fine buy at $2.85 but it is not readily available. I have been unable to find any.

LOUIS M. MARTINI Mountain Zinfandel '69. Light in body, with moderate bouquet, the wine has the slightly tart taste associated with effervescence, though it is perfectly still. It is a sprightly, very drinkable wine, and an excellent buy at $2.45.

CHRISTIAN BROTHERS Zinfandel. It is much like the Martini, without the special tartness, and a very good buy at $2.80.

SONOMA VINEYARDS Zinfandel. Bigger and fuller than the others, it yet has the basic lightness of character of this wine. In absolute quality, it is the best of those listed here and an excellent buy at $2.69.

Among the other red varietals that California produces, I am acquainted with:

GAMAY BEAUJOLAIS. (It also appears as GAMAY. It is not clear whether these are two different grapes or two names for the same grape.) The wines do not particularly resemble Beaujolais but some are light, very pleasant and enjoyable. Some can be quite big and Burgundylike, much better in that respect than the Pinot Noir.

INGLENOOK GAMAY '69. This is a fine example of the lighter wines, dry and almost sprightly, and a very good buy at $2.85.

PAUL MASSON Gamay Beaujolais. It is an exceptionally good example of the fuller wines. I cannot forbear from commenting on the label, which says, "brisk but serious vivacity, youthful delicacy, and it is deep red in color." It certainly is deep red in color, but what does the rest mean? Just typical publicity, using meaningless terms that conjure up pleasing images. The wine is actually rather big, with very pleasant bouquet, and thoroughly delicious. It would have been far more accurate to describe it as an excellent Burgundy-type wine. It is a very good value at $2.88.

Barbera

The Barbera grape comes from Piedmont in Italy, where it produces a big, vigorous wine, reminiscent of Barolo, but in no sense great. There does not appear to be a great deal of it grown in California, but its reputation is as good as that of the Italian original. A fine example is:

PAUL MASSON Barbera '69. This is very big, rather smooth, with just enough of the sharpness or "bite" (just as in the original) that is actually welcome in such a wine. It is somewhat reminiscent of Barolo and is a perfect accompaniment for robust, spicy dishes. Though it displays no lack of maturity, I suspect that about two more years of bottle aging would produce something very fine indeed. It is an outstanding buy at $2.45.

There are still other red varietals. Explore them by all means, after you have learned something of the fine ones listed here.

The white varietals are made generally of the grapes responsible for the fine French and German wines. There is so much variation from dry to sweet in wines made of the same grape, sometimes by the same vintner, that it is more convenient to group these by vintner rather than by variety.

Almadén

BLANC FUMÉ. This wine is made of the Sauvignon Blanc grape. It is a dry, slightly tart wine, with the freshness typical of the Loire Valley, quite distinguished and an excellent buy at $2.80.

GEWÜRZTRAMINER. It is a rather impressive, true Gewürztraminer, with a spiciness somewhat subdued compared to the Alsatian examples, but definitely there. It has good, spicy bouquet and is just a bit sweeter than the Alsatians, which probably makes it preferable to most drinkers. An excellent value at $2.80.

JOHANNISBERG RIESLING. This is the name given in California to the true Riesling. The wine is light, quite dry, with a faint, pleasing overlay of sweetness, much resembling the Alsatian rather than the German Rieslings, but just a bit less vigorous. A good buy at $2.80.

Beaulieu Vineyards

BEAUFORT PINOT CHARDONNAY '71. Very dry, with rather full bouquet and fruit, this is a distinguished, quite true white Burgundy. It is hardly inexpensive at $4.15, but well worth trying as one of the finest of California wines.

Inglenook

CHENIN BLANC '71, Estate Bottled. There is much of the Loire Valley taste here. It is quite similar to Pouilly-Fumé but a trifle less dry, with good bouquet and fruit, and an excellent buy at $2.65.

DRY SEMILLON. This is the grape that, with Sauvignon Blanc, makes white Graves and Sauternes. The wine is rather dry, much more so than most Graves, with much of the same distinctive flavor. It is a much better value at $2.65 than most Graves.

Paul Masson

PINOT CHARDONNAY. A dry, moderately flowery wine, a close first cousin to a French white Burgundy and a very enjoyable dinner wine in all respects. It is a good buy at $3.29, but, when compared to Frank Schoonmaker's Pinot Chardonnay (French) at $3.19, it comes off second best.

EMERALD RIESLING. Made of a fairly new hybrid grape, this

may be considered a uniquely Californian wine. It is perfectly delicious. It has the slight fresh tartness typical of Loire Valley wines, a noticeable but wholly pleasant touch of sweetness, fair bouquet, and moderate lightness. It is an excellent accompaniment to chicken and other light meats. At $2.35, this is one of the best buys I know of among California whites.

Mirassou
CHENIN BLANC '71. Fairly full-bodied, with a faint touch of sweetness, it is a lovely and distinguished facsimile of a fine Loire Valley wine and, for its quality, a very good buy at $3.49.

Wente Brothers
PINOT BLANC '70. This is a true white Burgundy in all respects, fragrant, flowery, altogether fine. An excellent buy at $2.80.

PINOT CHARDONNAY '71. This also is essentially a true white Burgundy, very dry and with good bouquet, but with just a bit less floweriness than I think it ought to have. A really lovely wine but, at a cost of $3.80, not as good a buy as their Pinot Blanc.

LE BLANC DE BLANCS. Made of Chenin Blanc (the grape of the Loire wines) and Ugni Blanc (a white wine grape of France and Italy), this wine has a lovely bouquet and fruitiness, is somewhat sweet, and is quite similar to a Loire Valley Vouvray. A lovely wine for those who prefer less dryness, and a bargain at a cost of $2.50.

SAUVIGNON BLANC '71. This is a simply lovely wine, extremely dry, with very good body and fine bouquet, much like a Pouilly-Fumé, but a far better buy. It is truly fine and the best buy I know of in California whites for those who prefer their wines dry. The price, $2.80.

DRY SEMILLON. There are both a '69 and a '71. There is no noticeable difference between them. The wine is quite full-bodied, drier than a French Graves, yet with a faint touch of sweetness, and with the characteristic Graves flavor. This is a wine of distinction, lovely, and a much better value than any Graves I know of. The price, $2.55.

GREY RIESLING. This is not made of the Riesling grape at all but of a descendant of the French Chauché Gris. The wine is very dry and quite good but, unlike most of Wente's wines, it is rather undistinguished and no more than a fair buy at $2.55.

There are many other white varietals but you must be careful in trying them. They can range from very dry, as you have seen, to sweet enough to be dessert wines, and there is seldom any way of telling without buying and tasting. Whenever you are ready to go beyond those listed here, get the advice of a reliable dealer, if you can, or of someone else whose knowledge can be relied on.

THE BETTER GENERICS

In general, these are produced only by the better vintners. There is no restriction as to which grapes may be used in making generics, and the jug wines are almost uniformly bland and undistinguished. This is no longer true of the better ones. They begin to show signs of character, begin to bear at least some resemblance, and sometimes a fairly close one, to the European wines they seek to imitate.

Their general price range is about $2 to $2.50. A few are put up in half-gallons also, at some saving in cost. They are not nearly so readily found as are the jug wines and, in the upper end of their price range, comparison must be made with values in varietals at little more cost.

A few worth trying are:

BEAULIEU VINEYARDS Burgundy. Made mostly of the Pinot Noir grape, with only a bit of the grapiness so common in the jug wines, this is a fair facsimile of a French Burgundy and a very good buy at $2.43.

CONCANNON Red Dinner Wine. It is described on the label as Burgundy like and it is so, with little grapiness and not enough sweetness to detract from its basically dry character. It is an excellent buy at $1.89.

CONCANNON Burgundy. It is everything that the Red Dinner Wine is, just more so, but at $2.40, while a better wine, not as good a value.

PAUL MASSON Rubion. This does not bear a generic name but is a claret type and belongs in this group. It is light in color and body, rather fragrant and fruity, and very pleasing. It does somewhat resemble a claret and is a good buy at $2.39.

BEAULIEU VINEYARDS Chablis. It is made largely of Chenin Blanc grapes and has the distinct taste of a moderately dry Loire Valley wine. It is a good wine and a good buy at $2.43.

INGLENOOK Vintage Chablis. Thoroughly dry, with moderate bouquet and body, and more than a hint of the true Chablis flavor, it is a very pleasant wine and an excellent value at $2.15.

CHARLES KRUG Chablis. The wine is really like Chablis, with some of the characteristic flavor and dryness, and a good buy at $2.44.

MIRASSOU Chablis. There is a good deal of the genuine, steely character of Chablis in this wine and, while it is the best of the group listed here, its price, $2.99, must be considered.

THE JUG WINES

There is no precise definition for the term. In a general way, it means the equivalent of the Frenchman's *vin ordinaire*, the everyday drinking wine, the carafe wine. These are the wines almost always served in restaurants here that sell wine by the glass and in carafe. No wonders are to be expected of them. They are mass produced, may legally be made of any or all kinds of grapes (although other standards of alcoholic content and minimum quality are rigidly applied), and, as a group, have no distinctive character of their own.

Generally these wines are pasteurized so that, while they are thus protected against spoilage, they cannot improve even in the slightest while in bottle. Hence, the fact that many are capped instead of corked is meaningless.

Most, regardless of maker, resemble one another considerably, while hardly ever bearing any resemblance to the European type. The Burgundies are big, often heavy and somewhat sweet. The clarets are lighter, often rather sharp and still somewhat sweet. They all tend to have a strong flavor of grapiness. At best they lack any positive character but are pleasant and drinkable.

The whites are likely to be somewhat better. They are generally labeled Chablis and Sauterne (the "s" at the end of the French *Sauternes* is deleted) but are not different from one another purely because of the name. Again there is a tendency to sweetness but some are dry enough to be quite enjoyable. At best they are without special character but clean, refreshing, and agreeable.

There is certainly a place in wine drinking for the jug wines, a place directly related to their price. They are usually fairly easy on the pocketbook, although there are still some European wines available here that are no more expensive and, to my taste, better. They are not, however, inexpensive, as are the European ordinary wines in their own countries. They are lower in cost than the better wines, that is all.

Jug wines should be of interest only to the comparatively rare wine lover who really drinks wine with meals daily, or almost so, and naturally, to those to whom economy must be the first consideration. For others, I would emphasize better wines, at least at first. Jug wines need not be disregarded, but should be of secondary importance.

There must be hundreds of them. Any larger city is likely to have fifty to a hundred available. With few exceptions, the fifths range in price from about $1.40 to $1.80. Most come also in half-gallons in a range of about $2.75 to $4 and in gallons in a range of $4 to $7.75. Some, in fact, come only in the larger bottles.

I have not tasted them all. I wonder whether anyone has. Those that I have drunk and list here are numerous enough to give more than adequate choice to any reader. They are not listed in any special order of quality. In fact, they are sufficiently alike in character and price so that selection might well be made on the basis of cost and availability.

Among the reds, I like best:

LOUIS M. MARTINI Mountain Red Wine
C. K. MONDAVI Burgundy
KORBEL Mountain Red Wine
CHRISTIAN BROTHERS Burgundy

I give passing marks to:

SAVANT Burgundy
SEBASTIANI Mountain Burgundy
GALLO Hearty Burgundy. I am really of two minds about this one. I find it both too grapey and too sweet. Every so often it is reported as having been selected as best or near best in blind tastings of lower-priced American and European wines. It is evident that the standards of the experts differ from mine. I do think that a beginner, not yet accustomed to extreme dryness, will find it fairly palatable.

I do not like:

ALMADÉN Mountain Claret
ALMADÉN Mountain Burgundy
CHRISTIAN BROTHERS Claret
PETRI Burgundy
G&D (Gambarelli and Davitto) Fior di California Burgundy Scelto. *Scelto* means "choice" or "exquisite" in Italian. The wine is neither, nor good at all.
SAN MARTIN Mountain Red Burgundy. I think this would be quite good if it were not so sweet. Genuine sweetness in a red wine, especially a bigger one, is almost literally unpleasant.

Among the whites, I like best:

GALLO Chablis Blanc. In France the Chablis is all white. In the United States, Gallo and one or two others make rosés named Pink Chablis, and so must distinguish white from rosé.

KORBEL Mountain White Wine
CHRISTIAN BROTHERS Chablis
ALMADÉN Mountain White Chablis
SAN MARTIN Mountain Chablis

Louis M. Martini Mountain White Wine
I give passing marks to:

Romano Cucamonga Chablis
Petri Chablis Blanc

I do not like:

Villa d'Este Chablis
Sebastiani Mountain Chablis
Almadén Mountain Rhine Wine
Roma Rhine Wine

If the total of what I have recommended tends to overwhelm you, remember, first, that California wines alone represent a cross section of practically all the wine types produced in France and Germany and some of those made in Italy; and second, that a summation at the end of this volume will suggest some guides that should make selecting particular wines not at all difficult.

NEW YORK STATE

Wine has been made commercially in New York State for the past 140 years. The wine grape is grown in the Hudson Valley and in the Niagara area in the western tip of the state. There has even recently been established a small vineyard, growing only fine varietals, on the northern fork of Long Island. But the main wine-making area is around the Finger Lakes, where the large bodies of water have a moderating effect on the harsh winters of upstate New York

New York's wines were once made entirely of native grapes, originally found growing wild and colloquially known as "fox grapes." Native grapes impart a very decided flavor known as "foxiness." There is no way of describing the foxy taste, other than to say that it is strong and somewhat coarse. It must be experienced. More recently, much success has been achieved with hybrids.

There are no neutrals among wine drinkers on the subject of foxiness. Many dislike it. Some obviously find it enjoyable, else how could 35 million gallons of New York State wine have been consumed in 1972?

For a long time, the efforts of the industry have been directed at eliminating foxiness. Sweet and sparkling wines are most successful in doing so. It is no accident that a very large part of the total production is sweeter table wines, aperitif and dessert wines, and champagne, for which the state is noted.

There has been some success with hybrid varieties of vines that are better able to withstand the severe winter cold than the true European vines. The wines may contain up to 25 percent of California wine, and many do. A few New York vintners, in fact, own producing acreage in California.

Sugar may be added to the wines, as indeed it quite often is in France and Germany. But water—up to 53 percent of water and sugar combined—may also be added. It begins to sound as though the state's wines are a rather polyglot mixture, and some of them are. Still, none of these additions is harmful or dangerous, and if the end product is a palatable wine, something worthwhile has been achieved.

The experimental station at Geneva, part of the New York State Agricultural College, has functioned for a long time in much the same manner as does the University of California's College of Agriculture at Davis, and also with much success.

Most of the New York State wine industry is represented by a small number of comparatively big producers who offer a moderate range of wines, largely sweet, and who use mostly the native grapes, such as Catawba, Delaware, Concord, and Elvira. What else the wines contain besides California wine, sugar, water, or even sometimes Algerian wine, only the makers know.

There is also a group of small vineyards pioneering in producing fine wines, some of them varietals. In quantity their total production is not significant. In quality, and in the ultimate effect on winemaking, their influence may prove incalculable.

TAYLOR WINE COMPANY is the largest of the vintners. They produce a cross section of generic wines, all priced at $1.90 per fifth and $3.79 per half-gallon. They also make aperitif and dessert wines and champagnes. Over a period of years I have drunk most of their wines, of all types, and have found them always mediocre. Recently I have renewed acquaintance with their claret and Burgundy. The first is somewhat thinner and a trifle drier than the second. Otherwise they are the same, a strong aroma of Concord grapes, very noticeable foxiness (I am one of those who do not like it), quite dry, and, in fact, very much like dry versions of kosher Concord grape wine. That is not meant to be praise. No serious or would-be serious wine drinker should include Taylor's wines in his repertoire.

GREAT WESTERN is the trade name used by Pleasant Valley Wine Company. It is situated right beside the Taylor Wine property and has been owned by Taylor for the past twelve years or so. Great Western continues to operate separately. While best known for its champagnes, the winery has a broader selection of dinner wines than its parent company.

Their Burgundy, costing $1.95, is made of several grapes, including the Baco Noir, a French Burgundy-like hybrid. The foxiness is there, but comes through only slightly and not unpleasantly. The wine has fair bouquet, is somewhat on the thin side, rather dry, and quite satisfactory, a good buy compared with other New York State wines, nothing great in absolute terms. The Chelois, which costs $1.95, described as a hybrid of French and American grapes, is reminiscent of the Concord grape, and is very dry, foxy, thin, and sharp, almost vinegary. It is not at all enjoyable. The Chablis, at $1.95, is austerely dry and would be quite good if it were not for the strong foxy flavor. The combination of foxiness and almost sharp dryness is, to my taste, actually unpleasant.

WIDMER WINE CELLARS produce probably the best of the

wines made of native grapes. That, alas, does not make them good. They also have aperitif and dessert sherry, which are their best wines, and port. Their Burgundy, costing $1.95, is very similar to that of Great Western, with a hint of a sweet overlay, but equally unacceptable. Their Dry Sauterne, at $1.95, if one goes by the label, is really an all-purpose wine. They suggest it be served with "seafood, fish, fowl and other light meats," also as a light dessert wine. Why not as a hair tonic as well? I don't like to be caustic, but the publicity boys can be downright silly. The wine is actually much too sweet for anything but a dessert wine, the sweetness rendering the quite noticeable foxiness palatable, but it is wholly undistinguished and uninteresting.

GOLD SEAL is the brand name of Urbana Wine Company. They also produce a broad range of wines and are best known for their excellent champagne. I have not had their wines recently, with one exception, but have the impression of a shade or two better flavor than those described above. The exception is their one varietal, Pinot Chardonnay at $3.49. It is quite good, somewhat suggestive of a true white Burgundy and, in New York State terms, a good buy but, beside some of the Californias at like or lesser prices, no bargain.

It must be very clear by now that I am not a loyal son of New York State. In the realm of wine, my loyalty is to good wine and, with the exception of the few fine winemakers, little, if any, acceptable table wine is made in New York State.

VINIFERA WINE CELLARS is the property of Dr. Konstantin Frank who, having grown grapes and made wine in the Soviet Union's harsh climate, derided the idea that European grapes could not survive New York's winters. He set out to prove it only ten years ago, and has succeeded resoundingly. His wines are reputed to be most exceptional. Therefore, naturally enough, they are costly, starting at the very top limit of our price range and going up from there. Total production is small and the wines are virtually unavailable. If you ever come across any, particularly the Pinot Chardonnay or the Johannisberg Riesling (his best wines are the whites), splurge and buy one.

BULLY HILL is the vineyard of Walter Taylor, Jr., grandson of the founder of Taylor Wine Company, who left his family's company some years ago in an ongoing disagreement with their winemaking practices. In particular, Mr. Taylor vigorously deplores adulterating the New York product with water and California wine.

Bully Hill's first wines were marketed only in 1967. It has grown since, but total production is no more than 20,000 gallons annually. Mr. Taylor looks upon Bully Hill primarily as an experimental winery. Despite limited production, the basic red and white Bully Hill wines, at least, appear to be quite readily available and are distributed in most parts of the country.

BULLY HILL RED '71 is made of seven grapes, some of them native. There is no trace of foxiness. It is very dry and light, with a hint of sharpness that does not enhance its quality. A year or two more of bottle age might eliminate that. The wine has moderate bouquet and is thoroughly pleasant but not distinguished. It is infinitely superior to the more ordinary New York reds but is not the equal of some California and European wines at the same or lower cost. The price, $3.25.

BULLY HILL WHITE '71 is made of three grapes and has no trace of foxiness. It is very much like a good Moselle wine, a bit too sweet for my taste but in all respects very good, with some distinction. Again, at $3.25, it is not the equal of others at similar and lower cost. Along with the red, it is well worth trying, if only to see how far from the run-of-the-mill stuff a New York State wine can be.

In 1972, Bully Hill brought out a group of varietals, some hybrids, some native varieties. They disappeared so quickly that I, for one, never got a chance to try one. I believe that their cost is the same, $3.25 per bottle. You might like to try one for yourself if you can find any.

BOORDY VINEYARDS was originally a Maryland vineyard,

owned by Philip Wagner, formerly a writer on the Baltimore *Sun*. The Maryland operation was experimental at first, but soon became a successful, if limited, producer of hybrid and varietal wines. In 1968, a Boordy Vineyard was established in New York (it is now owned by Seneca Foods) and another in the state of Washington.

There can have been little actual production as yet from the New York vineyard but the wines are comparable in quality to those from Maryland. There are both a Red Wine '70 and a White Wine '70, each at $1.89. I have found them pleasant and well balanced. The Pinot Chardonnay and the Chenin Blanc, each at $2.79, are somewhat reminiscent of the respective Burgundy and Loire Valley originals and have noticeable character but are not the equal of many California varietals of like price.

HIGH TOR VINEYARD was established in Rockland County, only thirty miles north of New York City, in 1951. The owner is Everett Crosby, a playwright. High Tor produces premium wines, namely Rockland Red, White, and Rosé, all at a cost of $3 per bottle. I have drunk both the red and white, but not for some years; the price was a good deal lower. I then found them pleasant but not impressive.

BENMARL is a new, tiny vineyard of only fifty acres (twenty more were to be added during 1973) in the Hudson Valley, a few miles north of Newburgh. The owner is Mark Miller, an artist and illustrator. Production is minuscule. Mr. Miller lived in Burgundy for some years and if he absorbed there the native winemaking ability, Benmarl's products may turn out to be exceptional. I am not familiar with the wine.

I have described these quality vineyards in some detail, despite the comparative non-availability of their wines, because a curious fact emerges. They were established by an interesting group of non–wine establishment individuals, a maverick ex-European vintner, a wealthy "renegade" from a big wine family, a newspaperman, a playwright, an artist and illustrator. These are people who obviously love wine and perfection in wine. The young couple who have just begun a twenty-acre vineyard on Long Island are kindred souls. If New York State is ever to become a substantial producer of quality wines, and I believe it will happen over the next twenty years or so, it will probably be because the big wineries will have seen the light. But the torch has been lit, and is being carried, by this small group of pioneers.

Spain

Spain is one of the world's great producers of wine, some of which ranks among the great wines of the world. The best known and most famous is sherry, which, as an aperitif or dessert wine, not a table wine, is reserved for later discussion. Wine is made in almost every part of the country. Most of it is not exported to us, not known to me, and reputed to be of no great excellence. Those wines that can easily be found here come from two of the winemaking regions, Rioja and Catalonia.

The term "Spanish wine" tends to be associated in the mind of the average wine buyer with half-gallon and gallon bottles, frequently found in the back of a wine shop, covered with beautifully woven wicker, and bearing prices at which no wine could possibly be any good. Many Spanish wines are not, though the bottle may well be worth the cost to some as the base for a lamp. Some of these wines, surprisingly, are quite good, at the price. Here and there one can prove exceptional. What most buyers do not know is that Spain also produces truly great wines, readily available here at remarkably reasonable prices.

For some years now, the Spanish government has been carrying forward a program of establishing place names, the *Denominación de Origen*. It is only partially complete and not nearly so vigorously enforced as the controls existing in other countries, such as the French Appellation Contrôlée. The tiny rectangular stamp on bottles of the wines of Rioja, where the program is most widespread, is a reasonable guarantee of authenticity.

Spain's finest wines are produced in the region of Rioja in the north, not far south of the Pyrenees, along the Ebro River and the Río Oja (Oja River), from which the region takes its name. Although winemaking in the area goes back many hundreds of years, the quality of its wines is undoubtedly partially traceable to the settlement there of many French vintners after the phylloxera (plant lice) destroyed the Bordeaux vines about eighty years ago. For the most part, the French are long since gone. The quality remains.

Rioja has been so much emphasized as making the best of the Spanish wines that too little attention has been given those of other regions. Perhaps some of those not shipped here are exceptional. I do not know. It is certain that Catalonia, on the northeastern coast, producing more than twice as much wine as Rioja, sends us some that rank among the best.

Spanish wines really should not be compared with French or any others. They have a character of their own that is delightful, but different from Bordeaux, or Burgundy, or Chianti, or any other wines. Yet, for lack of any better way to describe them, some comparisons have to be made. Those other than the finest are frequently labeled Spanish Chablis, or Riesling, or Burgundy, or Claret. Any resemblance to the original would be purely accidental.

Vintage years as such mean little in Spain. Vintages are "established" when the growers feel the year has been very good. The vintage year has importance, though, in determining the age of the wine. Spanish wines start out in life big and harsh and require much aging, in cask and bottle, to produce the utterly velvety smoothness of which they are capable. A ten- or twelve-year-old Reserva can be a thing of beauty. Dollar for dollar, I believe that the old, mature Reservas are the best buy in great red wines today. They can still be bought for under $4 a bottle and are the equal of French wines selling at twice and three times the price.

Most important in identifying Spanish wines is the name

of the *bodega*, which is usually the grower, maker, and ship-per. Wines do not have vineyard or "château" names. Many bodegas have distinctive designations (that have no special significance) for their various wines. The designations serve, in effect, as brand names and are in no way descriptive of the wine. Those listed here can generally be found in better-stocked stores everywhere.

BODEGAS RIOJANAS

This is one of the large bodegas of Rioja. Their Rioja Monte Real '52, a Gran Reserva, is superb. It is moderately full-bodied, mellow, and velvety and, though fully mature, will last for many years to come. It is the equal of French châteaux wines in the $9 to $10 range, yet can still be purchased at $3.79. It is an outstanding buy for present drinking.

The Viña Albina '66 is not labeled a Reserva but has all of its characteristics. It is light, delicate, and very smooth, extremely dry, with lovely bouquet and a true aftertaste. With my eyes closed, I would think I were drinking a rather fine claret of the delicacy of a St. Julien or a Pauillac, the kind that today would cost as much as three times the price of this wonderful wine, $2.25.

The Rioja Superior '70 is light and rather fine, in all respects agreeable and in no sense great. It is somewhat similar to a very delicate Bordeaux. It is ideal with dishes that are just a shade too robust for a white wine, such as a casserole of chicken. At $1.69 per bottle, it is an exceptional value.

MIGUEL TORRES. Torres is the best known grower and ship-per in Catalonia. The Gran Coronas '55, now, alas, all gone, was in every respect as great as the Monte Real '52 described earlier. The Gran Coronas '61 is also gone but fortunately there is no trouble in finding the '62, the equal of the '61 and second only to the Monte Real '52 for present drinking. A big wine, like a very fine Burgundy, it is supple and marvelously smooth. The price is $3.79; it is an outstanding buy, and generally available.

Sangre de Toro ("Bull's Blood"), also like one of the bigger

Burgundies, is sturdy and well made but a bit rough, although not unpleasantly so. At $2.79 it is a good buy.

Viña Sol is a white with the character and bouquet of a fine Burgundy. It is dry, moderately full-bodied for a white, and while there is a suggestion of a refreshingly bitter aftertaste on the palate, with some foods, remarkably enough, there is also a hint of sweetness. A delightful wine, bottled sunshine, and at $2.59 an excellent buy.

MARQUÉS DE RISCAL. The most famous of the winemakers of Rioja, and the only vintner employing strictly French methods, three years in cask and then bottled. The oldest Reserva available is the '68 though, with luck, you might still find a '67. Properly aged, it would undoubtedly be the greatest of the Spanish reds. Fortunately, unlike the greater Bordeaux, which it most closely resembles, it is not astringent and downright unpleasant in its youth, but very agreeable and clearly hinting of greatness. For present drinking, I consider it to rank just below the Torres Gran Coronas and it is an outstanding buy at $3.59. Those who can would be well advised to lay down a few bottles or a case or two for even a year. Five years would be even better.

MARQUÉS DE MURRIETA. This is another of the great bodegas of Rioja. There is available here a '66 red with the Ygay name used by this vintner. It is not labeled a Reserva but has all the fine qualities of one. It is rather lovely, perhaps like a St. Émilion, with softness and finesse, and is a very good buy at $3.59.

BODEGAS BILBAINAS. This is one of the ten or so leading firms of Rioja. Their Vendimia Especial '55 is a wonderful, silky wine with great breed and finesse, somewhat like a Volnay in Burgundy. It is almost as good as the Torres Gran Coronas '62 but is not nearly as good a buy at $4.52. Their Viñā Pomal '66, somewhat bigger than the Vendimia Especial, is very smooth, very good and fragrant, and an excellent buy at $2.56.

They produce a delightful white wine, Viña Paceta Blanco Seco. Both the '68 and the '69 are to be found. There is no noticeable difference other than that the '68 has a slight sediment. This can happen with whites. The wine is very dry, with good bouquet, somewhat big, slightly flowery, and utterly lovely. It is the best I have come across among Spanish whites and an outstanding value at $2.56.

Another white wine of theirs is Brillante at $2.69. I have never bought it, since it is a sweeter wine, just how sweet I do not know. Knowing the quality of their other products, I do not hesitate to suggest that those who prefer sweeter wines try it.

COMPAÑÍA VINÍCOLA DEL NORTE DE ESPAÑA. Considered by some the best of the Rioja bodegas, it is commonly referred to as Cuné. The bottles may bear either name. I am not as familiar with their wines as with those of some of the other bodegas. I have found their Imperial Reserva '59 a lovely, velvety wine, but it has quite recently risen in price to $5.45, well beyond our budget. The best buy in Cuné wines, and still a rather exceptional value, is Viña Real '66 (a '67 is also available), a fairly full-bodied Burgundy type of wine, with fine bouquet and good fruitiness. It is not quite so balanced and velvety as a fine Reserva but is pretty wonderful, and costs $2.75. Others, such as their claret-type and Rioja Blanco at $2.35 and their Corona Semidulce (semisweet white) at $2.59, might well be tried. I would expect them to be excellent for their respective prices.

RENÉ BARBIER. A French family that settled in Catalonia and has remained there. Available are a Vino Tinto (meaning red) '67 and a Vino Blanco '69. Both are rather light, somewhat thin-bodied, in no way distinguished, but just plain pleasant and much better buys at $2.15 than many a French wine at higher prices.

FEDERICO PATERNINA. This is one of the well known bodegas of Rioja. The wines are selections of Frank Schoonmaker; they are quite widely distributed and are therefore mentioned here. I specifically do not recommend their purchase. The Reservas are in any case all far above our limits, the lowest-priced being $5.99. None is remotely worth the cost. The prices of Paternina's wines have not leaped or soared. They have taken off like a moon rocket. For example, the Reserva '59 sold at $2.99 as recently as the end of February, 1973. By June 1, only three months later, it sold (if anyone was foolish enough to buy) at $6.49, an increase of a mere 117 percent. The dollar devaluation plus inflation here and in Spain hardly account for this. What is left? I guess it must be greed, and I try to avoid feeding other people's greed with my hard-earned money. So should you.

I found the Banda Azul, a moderately big, sturdy red, more enjoyable than the Reservas, but it is no bargain at $2.98, up $1.25 in a few months. The only one I consider still a fairly good buy is the Banda Dorada, a light white wine with a touch of sweetness, resembling a good white Graves. It is priced at $2.59.

There are many lesser, low-priced wines, both red and white. These are the ones usually labeled, quite meaninglessly, as French regional types. Some of the reds I have tried are coarse and harsh and not to be recommended. Yet I have also come across French and Italian wines that were even worse, at much higher prices. There is at least one notable exception that I will describe shortly and there may well be others. I urge you to try freely, even among those I do not care for. At prices of under $1.50 you can afford to do so, and remember, tastes differ.

As for the whites, none that I've drunk has been unpleasant. Unhappily, some that are labeled "Chablis," which should be very dry, turned out to be as sweet as Sauternes. Many are remarkable values at their low cost.

YAGO is a common brand. Their wines should not be confused with their Sant'Gria, a mixture of wine and fruit juices for making the famous wine punch. Their red is not recommended. Their Spanish Chablis, surprisingly, does somewhat resemble Chablis. The price, $1.69, is too high by comparison with others equally good. It is hardly a best buy at that price but is still much more so than many a French or American white at higher prices and it is recommended where other, less expensive Spanish whites cannot be found.

Having mentioned Sant'Gria, it is worth discussing further. This is the famous wine-fruit punch of Spain, delightful to drink with meals, or by itself, primarily in warm weather. Almost any kind of citrus fruit juice and fruit and dry red wine will do. A simple recipe, well worth trying is: 1 bottle of red wine; the juice of 1 orange and 1 lemon; several slices of orange, or lemon, or both; sugar to taste; ice. Brandy may be added, as may other fruits. Your own taste, and what's available in the refrigerator, should prevail. It seems unnecessary, as well as more costly, to buy Yago's Sant'Gria or any of the many other brands, imported and domestic, which have appeared recently. They are only wine plus citrus fruit juice.

While on the subject of wine punches, the simplest and still one of the best is claret lemonade. Make a quantity of lemonade, well sweetened to counteract the dryness of the wine. Fill a tall glass about two-thirds full. Add ice and top off with any dry red wine, preferably a light one. Delicious!

But to return to wines:

GOMEZ CRUZADO. This is one of the big bodegas of Rioja, but only a very few low-priced wines can be found here. The red is not recommended. The white, labeled "Chablis," is a different matter. It is just the kind of simple, good country wine that those who have traveled in Europe remember as having drunk at that particular inn or *osteria*, a remembrance compounded of wine, exotic surroundings, good food, and nostalgia. It is a decent, everyday drinking wine and should not be expected to be more. At about $1.49 it is an excellent buy. It can also be found in half-gallons and gallons.

JUAN HERNANDEZ. Here, also, red and white are available. Again, the red is not recommended. The white, also labeled "Chablis," is very similar in all respects to that of Gomez Cruzado except that it is a shade the lesser in quality. It sells at about $1.19 a bottle and is an extraordinary buy at that price. It is also available in half-gallons and gallons.

MARTINEZ LACUESTA. This bodega had, and presumably still has, a white that they had the courage and good taste to label "Spanish white wine," instead of giving it a French name. It has been unavailable in the New York area for the past three years or so. It was much like the white of Gomez Cruzado but a shade better in quality. If it is to be found in this country at all, I do not know its price. When I last bought it, it sold at the same price as the Gomez Cruzado. Should you happen upon it, buy it.

LA TARRA. These wines come from Tarragona, in Catalonia. There are a "Burgundy," a "claret," and a "chablis." The Chablis is a light, almost delicate wine, not at all resembling real Chablis, but highly enjoyable and superior to the Gomez Cruzado. For everyday drinking it is highly recommended. The claret is actually fairly similar to a Bordeaux, light in color and texture but with good body, fair bouquet, and excellent for the price. It might well be served without hesitation to anyone but a wine snob. The Burgundy is indeed like a Burgundy, big and quite smooth and, despite the faintest touch of sweetness, the overall impression remains of a completely dry wine. It is my favorite everyday red wine.

All three sell at the unbelievable price of $1.49 per bottle. The Chablis and Burgundy can also be bought in half-gallons at $3.29 and in gallons at $5.15, the latter equal to all of 97 cents per 24-ounce bottle. The claret does not come in larger bottles.

These are perfect examples of wines carrying a price at which no wine could be any good, but turning out to be not only good, but excellent. For this very reason, I urge you to try freely others than those mentioned here. You too may make a discovery.

La Tarra is sold mostly in restaurants in the New York region. It can be found in some wine shops, including Austin's in Forest Hills. The importer and distributor, Knickerbocker Liquor Corporation of Syosset, New York, will gladly ship to any retail dealer on request. I do not know whether the wine is available outside the New York area. I hope so, for I consider La Tarra, particularly the two reds, to be among the best buys in wine to be found today in this country. You should make every effort to find them.

Portugal

Portugal is by no means one of the minor wine countries. Its annual production almost equals that of the United States. As a wine consumer, it is right at the top of the list, sharing honors, if honors they be, with France and Italy, with an annual consumption of about 30 gallons per person.

While Portuguese wines do not reach the heights of the great wines of other countries, the average standard is fairly high. A good deal of far better than ordinary wine is produced, as well as great quantities of country wine, often unnamed, and reputed to be delightful when drunk locally, young and fresh.

Yet, for reasons beyond my understanding, or perhaps for no reason other than happenstance, a very limited selection of Portuguese wines is imported here. With the intensified, and now probably never-ending, search for new sources of good wine at affordable prices, it seems to me that what Portugal has to offer will not take too long in beginning to appear on the American market.

The most famous wine of the country is, of course, port, which is an after-dinner wine and will be dealt with later. Port aside, the other substantial import into the United States is Portuguese rosé wine, of which there is considerable variety and which is referred to in the section on rosés.

Of all the other many good wines of Portugal, only a few are found in the United States.

Dão. This is pronounced like "don," more or less, with a

nasal ending and the "n" not quite sounded. It is mainly because of the availability of this wine that I list Portugal as a primary source of wine supply, rather than lumping it with a good many other countries whose wines are of minor interest here.

There are both a red and a white. Very little white is made and not much is available here.

Red Dão is a big, robust, mouth-filling, sturdy wine, a wine for hearty dishes like pasta and stews. It is not a great wine, although I suspect that if a Dão fifteen or twenty years old could be found, it would be most remarkable. Those that are to be found in the United States frequently do not show a vintage year. As with Spanish wines, vintage years mean little beyond an indication of the wine's age.

Red Dão is in the same general class as the Rhône wines and the Egri Bikavér of Hungary. Any decent wine shop will have Dão available, but even the best shops rarely have more than one brand. However, that is enough. I have been unable to find a red Dão that is other than very enjoyable.

White Dão is not nearly so easy to find, but it occasionally can be. It is a dry wine of pleasant bouquet, and big, almost like a white Hermitage, withal soft and clean. It is by no means a long-lived wine and older ones should be avoided. Where a very dry white is called for, white Dão is an excellent choice and an unusual buy.

Among the reds most commonly found are:

GRÃO VASCO. It has the reputation of being the best of the Dão. It is the best among those I have drunk. It is also the most expensive, yet hardly truly expensive at $2.99 for a 25-ounce bottle. It is everything that a Dão should be, with power and authority. This wine comes in a roundish flask, similar to the Franconian *Bocksbeutel*. Many Portuguese rosés are shipped in the same kind of flask. I find it hard to handle and recommend that the wine be decanted.

DÃO CABIDO. This is not quite the equal of Grão Vasco. It is in all respects a very good example of Dão, merely lacking a trifle of the powerful bigness of the first. At $2.59, it is at least as good a buy in money terms.

SANTA REY DÃO '64. This is almost indistinguishable from the Dão Cabido, except in price, $1.85. It is the best buy of the three mentioned.

As for the whites, there are:

SANTA REY DÃO WHITE '66. It is to be hoped that a more recent vintage is now available, for I found the '66 to be a bit past its prime, with just a suggestion of flatness. A younger vintage would be a sound, very good wine, and an excellent buy at $1.85.

GRÃO VASCO WHITE. This is a fine example of white Dão and a good buy at $2.99.

Another red, not well known here and possibly not widely distributed, is:

Evel.

This is a brand name, the property of the Companhia Vinicola do Norte de Portugal. The distributor is Austin, Nichols, who describe it in their official listing as a claret type. Nothing could be further from the fact. Evel is, like all the red wines of Portugal, a big wine, and could only be conceived of as less than that by comparison with Dão. The Evel I have been drinking is a 1959 vintage. I suspect that in its youth it may incline to sharpness but age has turned this into a smooth, rather mellow, mouth-filling wine, very dry, with good bouquet. It is a steal, not a buy, at $2.59, if you can find it. If not, the '64 is available and is virtually indistinguishable from its older brother.

Vinho Verde.

The remaining wine that is well known and available in the United States is Vinho Verde. This does not mean green wine but young, fresh wine. In Portugal it frequently contains no more than 9 percent alcohol and is always light and refreshing. I am told that it is no trouble at all to drink a whole bottle at a time.

Such wine is never likely to travel well. Still, with some scientific help and a touch of added sweetness, large quantities are successfully exported. I have never drunk it in Portugal, only because I have never been in Portugal, so I cannot say whether the version available here has suffered in transportation.

I find Vinho Verde to be very pale, very light and fresh, almost gay, with a slight but noticeable touch of sweetness. It is a very easy wine to drink and a very enjoyable one. However, I am not sure that it is worth the price it fetches, generally in the $2.65 to $2.99 range. In absolute quality it is not to be compared with others of similar price, such as white Dão, Spanish whites, and the American varietal whites. Still, the wine is so pleasant that, if you don't care for my pennypinching, by all means try it. You will certainly enjoy it. Some good, less costly examples are:

VINHO VERDE, SOLAR DO MINHO. Monsieur Henri, at $2.45.

LAGOSTA VINHO VERDE. Distributed by Austin, Nichols. Price, $2.69.

Hungary

Hungary alone among East European countries is famous for fine cuisine and fine wine. The two frequently go together. I have not had much opportunity, alas, to sample genuine Hungarian food. What little I have eaten was wonderful. I have been more fortunate with the wines. A number of them are available everywhere in the United States and, if not literally wonderful, they are all good to excellent and merit our enthusiastic attention.

Strict controls and quality production have been a fact of the Hungarian wine industry for a very long time. I do not know what exists in Communist Hungary, but there is every reason to assume that the present government has in no way relaxed winemaking standards. Certainly the excellent quality of the wines tends to confirm this. Never having drunk pre-World War II Hungarian wines, I cannot make a comparison.

Most Hungarian grapes are native varieties, producing wines with their own special character, different from those of any other country—but deliciously different. This holds true even for the occasional variety that is also grown elsewhere, such as the Riesling. In Hungary, it has a quality all its own.

The most famous wine of the country is Tokay (in Hungarian, *Tokaj*), known throughout the world and much imitated, although very unsuccessfully. Since Tokay is a dessert wine and occasionally an apéritif wine, it will be discussed in the appropriate section later.

Vintage years mean exactly nothing, at least in the United States, and should be disregarded. At present, all the wines I've seen bear the 1969 vintage label. It is most unlikely that any will be found in more than one vintage year. You simply buy whatever is available. None will be too young.

For a person with no knowledge of the language (that includes me) Hungarian wine names are almost a penance. But there they are, and I am not being sadistic in discussing them. There are a few clues, very few, that I can offer you as a buyer.

There are usually two words to the name. Almost always, the first is the place of origin or wine type, the second the name of the grape. For example, Badaczonyi Kéknyelü is a wine made of the Kéknyelü grape, from Badaczony. The "i" at the end of the word means "of." *Badaczonyi* means "of Badaczony." The "cz" is pronounced like our "ch." An "sz" is pronounced like a "z."

Here ends my knowledge of Hungarian names. You will be able to struggle through them just as well as I can and that is, at least, no worse than the ability of most wine dealers. All that matters is being able to identify the bottles and to know what is in them.

More white wine is produced in Hungary than red. The

whites are somewhat better, on the whole. Many of the whites, of whatever grape they are made, have a suggestion of a special flavor, peculiarly Hungarian, entirely unusual, and completely enjoyable. It is the flavor particularly characteristic of Tokay, which is made of the Furmint grape. I have no way of describing it, although some have tried to do so. You must taste for yourself. You will enjoy it.

Hungarians like their white dinner wines on the side of bigness, with a noticeable touch of sweetness. It is common to drink white wines with rich, spicy dishes. I have been so served in a wonderful Hungarian restaurant in London, where I allowed the maître to choose our food and our wine, to our delight. Because they are usually both big and slightly sweet, the whites can cope successfully with fairly robust dishes.

A single state agency, Monimpex, exports all Hungarian wine. There is therefore no choice, nor any of the problems of choosing, any particular wine. A dozen or more dinner wines are shipped to the United States. All come in 23-ounce bottles. I have not tasted all of them, which reserves for you the joy, and it will be a joy, of exploring for yourself.

THE REDS

It should not be supposed from what I have said in praise of the whites that Hungarian reds are inferior. Quite the contrary. In fact, the best known and one of the best of all Hungarian table wines is—

Egri Bikavér

. This means "Bull's Blood of Eger". The label bears a dramatic line drawing of a bull's head against a black background and the English legend "Bull's Blood," as well as the Hungarian name. The wine is very big, soft, and almost velvety, mouth-filling, a wine for sipping, not gulping. It is quite dry, yet with a suggestion of sweetness, a wine for hearty dishes and cold evenings. It is a deep, dark red in color and I suspect that a year or two more of aging would develop hidden fire. It falls short of being great but, even with a very recent price increase, it is nevertheless a great buy at $3.69.

Szekszárdi Vörös

This is a lighter red wine, thoroughly dry, fairly smooth, very pleasant and enjoyable without being at all a fine wine. It is well worth trying but, at $3.19, as the result of a recent price hike, is no more than a good buy.

Nemes Kadar

The remaining Hungarian red likely to be found here is Nemes Kadar, made of the Kadarka grape, the most common red wine grape of Hungary. I have not tasted it but understand it to be quite light in color, rather big, and somewhat on the sweet side. You might try this one for yourself.

THE WHITES

The best whites come from the Lake Balaton area and the best of these from the slopes of Mt. Badaczony, an extinct volcano.

Badaczonyi Szürkebarát

(Gray Friar of Badaczony) This is probably the most popular, both here and in Hungary. To my mind, it is certainly the most typically Hungarian. It is described on the label as "light" but is actually big and rather robust for a white. It is quite noticeably sweet, though only slightly so and, even to my dry-oriented palate, marvelously pleasing. It has the reputation of being the perfect wine with goose. It certainly complements goose and duck extremely well and is equally enjoyable with many other dishes normally calling for lighter reds, such as a well browned chicken casserole. At $3.45 it is a most excellent value.

Badaczonyi Kéknyelü

This has almost nothing in common, except for that unmistakable thread of Hungarian flavor, with the Szürkebarát except the place of origin. I have found it described in many ways, one of them as a dry dessert wine. Actually, it is a fairly big wine, thoroughly dry, quite delicious, and in every respect a dinner wine that goes exceptionally well with fish, seafood, and other lighter, delicate dishes. I simply do not understand how it can be described as a dessert wine, dry or otherwise. It is an excellent buy at $3.45.

Debröi Hárslevelü

This, too, has the inimitable Hungarian flavor. I have read that this wine is sometimes as sweet as Sauternes. If so, the sweet ones are not exported to us. It has a distinct but rather slight touch of sweetness, less of it, for example, than Badaczonyi Szürkebarát, and is round and rather full. It is a delightful dinner wine and is still a very good value at $3.29.

Hungarian Rizling (Riesling)

The name appears thus on the label. Its resemblance to other Hungarian whites is mostly in the lovely bouquet. For a Hungarian wine, it is light in body with a most interesting series of tastes. It seems very slightly sweet, with a mere hint of the typical flavor, as it is sipped. It turns entirely dry in the mouth and, after swallowing, leaves a distinct suggestion of bitterness. It is nothing like a Riesling of the Rhine or Moselle, nor of Alsace either, except for the dryness. I think I might identify the other whites as Hungarian in blind tasting, but not this one. It might sooner be mistaken for a Saint Véran, the white wine of Mâcon. It is extremely pleasant to my palate, and a good buy at $3.10.

These wines should be included in your wine diet. They are excellent, not too costly, readily available, and not difficult to select. If you find those recommended as enjoyable as I do, by all means go on to try the few others to be found in this country. I intend to, as time goes on.

Other Countries

The wines already described, and others of the countries so far dealt with, are far, far more than enough to last the most devoted and enthusiastic wine lover several lifetimes. However, the American wine market being probably the most diffuse, as well as profuse, in the world, some representation of the wines of almost all countries that make wine is likely to be found.

Just about every country in the world seems to make at least some wine. A hardy experimenter or two make some in England. Perhaps surprisingly, Canada has a small and flourishing wine industry. Now that the United States has again acknowledged the existence of China, we learn that the Chinese produce grape wine, too, and we may get to know something about it in the future.

Over and above the production of the countries already described, I look upon other wines as "curiosities" in the sense that they are not needed to make up any part of a basic wine diet. But since you will come across them, they require some comment. Many are good, some better than that, most are quite inexpensive, and they should be considered as wines to be tried here and there in the never-ending search for good buys. It goes without saying that they should be experimented with only after your tastes in wine have begun to be established. Never assume that, for example, a Yugoslav Cabernet has the true Bordeaux character. Sample it only after you know the true Bordeaux character, from drinking true Bordeaux.

SWITZERLAND

Both red and white wines are made. The whites are better; they are well made, clean, rather dry wines, somewhat like those of Alsace. They are decidedly dinner wines. The best is the Fendant, named after the grape. There are Fendant du Valais (a district) and Fendant du Sion (a town). They, and Swiss wines in general, are priced toward the upper limit of our price range and beyond. None is worth the cost compared with the white wines of most countries already described, and none is recommended. For the adventurous spirit, a Fendant or a Neuchâtel (usually a bit less expensive than the Fendant) would be best to try. An excellent producer is Bouvier.

AUSTRIA

If there are any reds made in Austria, I have never heard of them. The whites should be compared with the German wines; they are not nearly so delicate and full of bouquet but are nonetheless flowery and, to my taste, all on the sweet side. Austrian wine too is essentially for just plain drinking, not for meals. The wine goes with Vienna's public gardens and Strauss waltzes.

The best known in the United States is Gumpoldskirchen, light, pleasant, and noticeably sweet. Good examples can be found in the $3.50 range. Grinzing, a suburb of Vienna, produces a similar wine. A good example is Lippizaner Grinzinger Garten of Lenz Moser, named after the gardens in Vienna, and undoubtedly commonly drunk there. It can be found at Astor's in New York at about $2.35 per bottle.

YUGOSLAVIA

A great deal of wine, both red and white, is produced in Yugoslavia. The white is reputed to be the better of the two. I have personally found neither white nor red of distinction although I may not have tried hard enough. One great virtue of the Yugoslav wines is their price; they are almost all just under or a bit over $2. One has no right to expect unusual excellence at such prices.

The Yugoslav Riesling, somewhat similar in character to Alsatian Rieslings, is considered the best of the whites. Among reds, the Cabernet is undoubtedly the best. Unlike other East European countries, Yugoslavia appears to have more than a single cooperative as maker and shipper combined. Adriatica is the principal shipper. I have found their

Cabernet '67 to be somewhat thin and, while having some of the characteristics of a Bordeaux, rather indifferent. You might well try for yourself, especially in view of the low cost, about $1.98.

RUMANIA, BULGARIA, THE SOVIET UNION

The vineyards of these countries are all grouped around the Black Sea. All are substantial wine producers. I have tasted none of their wines, but they may represent fruitful areas of exploration for you and for me.

Rumania is reputed to make quite good red and white wines, the white, which tends toward sweetness, being better than the red. Bulgarian wines are reputed to be generally somewhat on the dull and heavy side. A small quantity of both can be found in some shops, usually one red and one white. Again, as in the case of Yugoslavia, there is the virtue of low cost. Bulgarian wines are in the under-$3 range, the Rumanian ones slightly higher. I know of no Soviet wines presently available in the United States, but they will be quite soon, perhaps before you read this, as a result of a general broadening of trade relations but primarily because of a recent agreement between Pepsico and the Soviet Union. In return for selling Pepsi there, a good deal of Soviet wine will begin to be available in this country.

GREECE

The best known Greek wine is retsina, which is not a specific wine or type. It is the result of maturing white wine (sometimes rosé, never red) in resinated casks. The reason is obscure. There are tales about it, but they are unimportant. The wine smells of turpentine! That is exactly as far as I ever got with retsina. The smell was enough. I've never tasted it. It is certainly an acquired taste for those who can stomach it. Several friends of mine who have spent time in Greece like it, or profess to. About 50 percent of all Greek wine is retsina.

I have tasted other Greek wines, white and red, and have found them to be entirely without distinction. They do have the virtue of being low in price, mostly not much over $2 a bottle. I would recommend disregarding them, except where one may have some special reason, such as being a sentimental scholar of ancient Greece, or being of Greek origin. In such a case, someone who both knows wine to some degree and who also knows Greece would be a better guide than I.

ISRAEL

The fact that wine was made here as early, probably, as anywhere in the world means little in terms of today's quality. The fact that wine production was religiously prohibited, and, at best, not encouraged in the Muslim world, means more.

Israel's wine industry, for practical purposes, is a twentieth-century phenomenon. The hot climate is not conducive to very fine wines. On the other hand, the Israelis have a habit of doing things well and some good beginnings have been made with drier whites and even with Cabernet Sauvignon.

Many of the wines are still on the sweet side, some rather sickly sweet. This may be conscious catering to the tastes of traditional Jews (Israel's exported wines are all kosher) who are accustomed to sacramental wines, at Passover particularly, which rather justify Schapiro's advertising motto, "The Wine You Can Cut with a Knife."

For their quality, Israeli wines are not particularly low in price, ranging from the upper-$2 to the mid-$3 range. For the present, I would recommend them only to those for whom kashruth (dietary laws) is more important than price or quality. Carmel is a common brand here, and a good one. For the future it is likely that we will all have to re-examine Israeli wines because of greatly improved quality.

NORTH AFRICA

The former French possessions of Morocco, Algeria, and Tunisia all make wine. An occasional bottle of Moroccan wine finds its way to the American Market. Moroccan wines can be fairly good and may become a factor in our wine drinking in the future. Some Algerian wine used to be sent to this country, but no longer. It appears to be marketed primarily in France and Germany. Perhaps Algeria also will ship to us again. Algerian wine has the reputation of being coarse and most of it is, but I had the good fortune to get some Royal Khebir '49 in 1964 at the even then ridiculous price of $1.79 a bottle. It was a big, Côtes-du-Rhône type of wine, with a delightful smoothness. I do not know Tunisian wines at all and have never seen them on the American market.

CHILE

Chilean production is substantial and the wines are widely exported. Although their quality is often extolled, I have found none of great virtue. Those exported usually bear the name of the grape. The most common are Pinot Noir and Cabernet Sauvignon among the reds, Pinot Blanc and Riesling among the whites. Government supervision of the industry is quite strict. There seems every reason to suppose that Chile can and will emerge as a plentiful producer of good and fine wines but her greatness still lies in the future.

Nonetheless, Chilean wines should be tried. Their cost is generally in the low-$2 range. One of the good shippers is Undurraga, whose Red Pinot '67 is clearly Burgundy-like, very dry, not distinguished, though perfectly drinkable and better than some California Pinot Noirs. Another fine shipper is Concha Y Toro, whose Cabernet '70, made of Cabernet Sauvignon grapes, is surprisingly big for a Bordeaux type, enjoyable, but somewhat muddy, that is, leaving a taste almost as of sediment on the tongue. I suspect that laying it down for about three years would produce a rather fine, big wine of the St. Émilion character and, at $2.29 a bottle, it is well worth doing so.

Chilean wines usually come in squat, roundish bottles that I find difficult to handle and easy to drop. My solution in the case of all wines in this shape of bottle is to decant into a carafe upon opening.

ARGENTINA

Argentina is the largest producer in the Western Hemisphere, as well as the largest consumer. This could be due to the considerable population of Italian derivation. In any case, Argentines appear to consume most of what they produce. They still export a good deal, but very little is to be found here. That is a pity, since Argentine wines are inexpensive and have the reputation of being good and pleasant, without being remotely great. Rodas Cabernet at about $1.99 is smooth, pleasant, thoroughly enjoyable, a good buy at the price.

AUSTRALIA

The Australian winemaking industry is about 150 years old and rather parallels that of California in the sense that there were no native grapes; all wines are made of imported varieties, mostly European, and the climate in the grape-growing areas, while somewhat diverse (it is a big country), largely approximates that of California. Australia produces, to use American terms, generics, varietals, and some hybrids.

Australia's production of wine increased from 34 million gallons in 1966 to 62 million in 1972. Of the latter figure, about half was distilled into brandy, so that actual production of wine as wine was about 31 million gallons, most of it consumed at home. In the 1970-1971 fiscal year (I believe the Australians use a fiscal year from April 1 to March 31, but am not sure), fewer than 11,000 gallons were exported to the United States. In 1971-1972, this rose to 38,000 gallons, more than their total production. Their reserves cannot last forever and all of this is still a drop in the bucket of U.S. wine consumption.

With Britain's entry into the Common Market, Australia finds it both less profitable and more difficult to sell to Britain, its main export market. Canada and the other Dominions are its best market, but it will intensify efforts to export to the United States. When you consider that Australia's total plantings about equal California's *annual new* plantings, it is evident that Australian wines will be no great factor here for some time to come.

This should not deter us from drinking these wines, if they are good. I really do not know whether they are or not. They are reputed to be so, some as good as all but the great French château and estate-bottled wines. I have tasted only a few, all from Thomas Hardy & Son. Their St. Thomas Burgundy '70 is medium in everything—bouquet, body, flavor, and character. It bears little resemblance to Burgundy. It is a decent wine, no more. Their Nottage Hill Claret '70 has no particular resemblance to a Bordeaux but, aside from somewhat lighter body, it is very similar to their Burgundy. Their Moana White Burgundy is moderately full-bodied, with fair bouquet, pleasantly dry, with an interesting combination of tastes resembling both a Muscadet and a white Mâcon; it is a very enjoyable wine. All three are priced at $2.49 and, at that price, must compete with American, Spanish, and even some French wines, which are, to my taste, superior.

You might well try Australian wines, especially the varietals, which are not low in price. The generics run in the range of $2.49 to $2.80 or so, the varietals close to $4. Some of the shippers whose wines are available in the United States are Lindeman, Ltd., B. Seppelt & Son, Ltd., and Barossa Cooperative Winery, Ltd., the latter distributed by the Safeway supermarket chain.

PART V

Rosé Wines

A YOUNG MAN SEEKING AN EXTRA-MARITAL LIAISON ONCE WROTE TO
Benjamin Franklin, asking his advice on the choice of a mis-
tress. Franklin replied, "Marriage is the proper remedy" for
the "inclinations you mention," and went on to expound why.
He continued: "But if you will not take this counsel and persist
in thinking a commerce with the sex inevitable then, . . . in all
your amours you should. . . ." His advice and his reasons are
vastly amusing, but have no place here.

I feel much the same way about rosé wines. If your inclina-
tion is to drink wine, reds and whites are the proper "remedy." But if you will not take this counsel and persist in a
desire to drink rosé, I must do what I can to advise you.

I have already indicated that I do not care much for rosés. I
have plenty of company. Many wine drinkers feel, as I do, that
rosés can serve no purpose not equally well or better served by
reds and whites—which has not prevented rosés from becoming extremely popular in this country and elsewhere.

In fact, rosé wine can be perfectly pleasant, although never
anything more. The trouble lies with the American tendency
to go overboard in the reaction to many things. I have not
drunk rosé in Europe, but I am told that in such countries as

France and Italy it is often of better quality than those we have here and that it is drunk only in summer, instead of red wine, with the lighter dishes often made there in hot weather. In this country, however, it is drunk all year round, is the exclusive wine of many drinkers, and is often unhesitatingly drunk with such robust foods as roasts and stews.

I have already described how rosé is usually made (see page 16). The very manner of making it insures against the wine's having any real character. This is not the only method. Another, having the same effect, is simply blending red and white wines in given proportions.

Rosés should be drunk young. There is no virtue in age. If they bear a vintage year, always try the youngest and avoid any that is more than about three years old. If they do not show a vintage year, avoid the less well known brands entirely. They may have been on the dealer's shelf a long time.

As a general rule, contrary to what I have suggested for other table wines, buy the less expensive rosés. There is often little relationship between price and quality. And, as a general rule, stick to the domestic rosés. There is enormous variety to suit every taste, they are frequently just as good as the imported ones and sometimes better, and they cost less. Perfectly good ones can be found at under, and just over, $2 a bottle.

Rosés should always be served well chilled. There are no exceptional nuances of taste to be killed by overchilling, and most rosés are so light that they need thorough cooling. Moreover, if drunk as they really ought to be, they will be consumed primarily in hot weather when chilled liquids are most pleasant.

Basically there are two kinds of rosé, the dry and the sweet, the latter varying from slightly sweet to semisweet. The dry can vary from thin to rather full-bodied and from quite good to sharp and even astringent.

Among the dry rosés, I do *not* like:

TAVEL. Made in the Rhône Valley of several grapes, Grenache predominating, Tavel is the best known of the dry rosés and the most full-bodied of all the rosés. If there is anything that justifies rosés, it is lightness. Tavel is a contradiction in terms, and its price, ranging up to well above $4, does not help me to like it.

LANCERS. A famous Portuguese rosé, it is also dry and in all respects unenjoyable. Its reputation is genuinely puzzling. It is thin and sharp and astringent. Perhaps its pseudo-earthenware jug (it is really glass) makes it so popular. Or perhaps most buyers assume that it has to be good because it costs so much, $3.80.

I do like:

LIRAC, '71, Ozier. This is a G. C. Sumner selection, costing $2.90. Lirac is a close neighbor of Tavel but the wine is less full-bodied and without Tavel's almost offensive bigness. Ozier's '71 is an excellent example, very dry, not sharp, light enough to be quite enjoyable, and a rather satisfactory accompaniment to chicken, pork, or veal.

PAUL MASSON'S VIN SEC ROSÉ. Made of the Grenache grape, it is not dissimilar to Ozier's Lirac and a considerably better buy at $1.99.

BEAULIEU VINEYARDS GRENACHE ROSÉ. This is a shade better than the Paul Masson, with the same general character. Cost, $2.09.

I give barely passing marks to:

ALMADÉN MOUNTAIN NECTAR ROSÉ. This wine is very mild and quite characterless, with just a touch of sweetness. It is no match for Paul Masson's Vin Sec Rosé, despite the same selling price, $1.99.

CHRISTIAN BROTHERS VIN ROSÉ. Rather similar to the Almadén just mentioned, it sells at about the same price, $2.

RODITYS. This is a Greek rosé and a fair buy at $2.15. It has a touch of sweetness, enough to cover up most of the sharpness. Some claim that it has a slight taste of resin. I have not noticed it.

All of the sweeter rosés that I have tasted are, to me, too sweet to serve as dinner wines, aside from whatever other virtues they may have or lack. I would recommend them, if at all, purely for drinking on a hot afternoon.

MATEUS. This is a Portuguese rosé that claims to be the largest-selling wine in the world. If so, it is the result of magnificent merchandising, not the quality of the wine. In common with all the sweeter rosés, Mateus is perfectly pleasant, but it is equally innocuous and tastes more like grenadine-flavored water than wine. At $2.99 it is almost a dollar cheaper than its famous competitor, Lancers, but still much too expensive.

MYRANDA. Myranda is another Portuguese rosé (there are many) that is much like Mateus in all respects except that it sells for $1.79 and is worth buying for those who desire such mildness.

ROSÉS D'ANJOU. These are all among the sweeter rosés. The best known is perhaps Nectarosé, no bargain at $3.25. I would prefer that of Alexis Lichine at $2.49.

CHRISTIAN BROTHERS NAPA VIN ROSÉ. This is quite different from their Vin Rosé. It is a sweeter wine, quite pleasant, and a satisfactory buy at $2.10.

SAN MARTIN VIN ROSÉ. This wine has considerable bouquet, more body than the Portuguese rosés and, among all the sweeter rosés I have tasted, is the only one that I could contemplate drinking with a meal. It is an excellent buy at $1.39.

NEW YORK STATE produces the sweetest rosés of all. By no stretch of the imagination would I consider them table wines. They all have the characteristic foxy flavor to one degree or another. WIDMER'S LAKE ROSELLE, the rosé partner of their white Lake Niagara, selling at $2.09, is a perfectly pleasant wine for just drinking. GREAT WESTERN'S PINK CATAWBA and their ISABELLA ROSÉ, both at $2.19, are quite similar to one another and to other New York State rosés.

There is a simply enormous number of other rosés. I think more than enough have been mentioned here to start you off, but—

If you are a complete beginner who has never yet tasted

rosé, don't—at least until you have gotten to know what enjoyable reds and whites are like. You won't know what you've been missing until you do. Then by all means try a rosé or two. If your taste does not agree with mine, you will find a new dimension of flavor but you will not have run the risk of judging all wine by the taste of rosé.

If you happen to be one of those who have fallen into the rosé trap and drink nothing else because you have found it easier to believe that rosé goes with everything than to try other wines, then please, please, start using this book. That's exactly why it was written.

PART VI

Sparkling Wines

THE GREATEST AND MOST FAMOUS SPARKLING WINE IS, OF COURSE, champagne. Technically, only sparkling wine made in the Champagne region of France is champagne. Much to the chagrin of the French vintners, who surely would do something about it if they could, American sparkling white wine is always called champagne. In the other countries, other names are used.

Sparkling wine is always expensive in the United States because of the high tax and duty imposed on it. Federal duty on a gallon of still wine is 37.5 cents and tax 17 cents, a total of 54.5 cents. On sparkling wine, duty is $1.17 per gallon and tax $3.40, a total of $4.57. This comes to 91 cents per fifth of sparkling wine as compared with 11 cents for still wine.

American champagne is proportionately even worse off. It is not subject to duty but is subject to the tax of $3.40 per gallon, compared with only 17 cents for still wine, or, per fifth, 68 cents, compared to just over 3 cents for still wine. The extrra cost over still wine per fifth, 80 cents for the imported, 65 cents for the domestic, when subjected to percentage markups along the way, comes out to probably at least double these figures as part of the eventual retail cost.

To a large extent, therefore, French and American champagnes, both, are beyond our price limits. However, champagne is an "occasion" wine, the greatest of them all, and I will in this case go beyond our normal limits.

Champagne (I use the term generically for all sparkling white wines) is not a dinner wine, although it is too often so used. With the exception of the very sweet ones it is a wine to be drunk as an aperitif or just to be drunk at a celebration. It is the sheerest mistake or pure ostentation to drink it with filet mignon. About twenty years ago, American airline companies used to serve it so. Fortunately, they have long since discovered red wine.

Champagne achieves its sparkling character because of a secondary fermentation that occurs in the bottle. Carbon dioxide is formed and, having nowhere to go, it dissolves in the wine, forms the lovely bubbles in the glass, and then promptly goes to your head.

A mass production method has also been devised and is in considerable use in the United States. This, in brief, consists of pouring the wine into a pressurized vat for its secondary fermentation, then bottling it. It can make a very acceptable wine but not quite the equal of that produced traditionally. Some U.S. makers label their wine "fermented in this bottle," to distinguish it from vat-fermented champagne.

A bottle of champagne must be opened with care. It is potentially a dangerous weapon. A popping cork is supposed to be lots of fun, but it's been known to cause severe eye injuries and can do other less unpleasant but unenjoyable things.

The best place to open a bottle is over the kitchen sink. The wine will often spurt out as the cork comes out. Have a glass handy and, with luck, you can get the wine to spurt into it instead of being wasted.

Fold a kitchen towel over the top of the bottle and then work the cork up with your thumb. When it pops, it won't fly, being restrained by the towel. It takes speed and a very deft hand, though, to get the towel out of the way in time, should the wine spurt out.

Sometimes there will be neither pop nor spurt. This does not mean the wine is flat. It just happens that way occasionally. But, if the wine has lost its sparkle, and you have bought it only recently, take it back to the shop.

Despite the powerful cork used in champagne bottles, it is possible for a cork to dry out and the wine to go flat. Hence, if champagne is to be kept for any length of time, it, too, should be laid on its side. Most people buy champagne as needed, so that storage is no problem. As a matter of fact, more and more sparkling wine, foreign as well as American, is being bottled these days with plastic "corks" that are perfectly effective.

Champagne should be served cold. Some experts believe that too much cold freezes the taste and aroma and that French champagne (and I include the best American ones) are too good to be so treated. This makes perfect sense to me, yet I confess that I like my champagne frosty cold. At the very least, I like it chilled two hours in the refrigerator. Four or five are better. A half hour in a wine cooler is best.

French Champagne

Champagne is ordinarily made from two or even three grapes, only one of which is white. More recently, some emphasis has been placed on "Blanc de Blancs." There is no special virtue in champagne made of white grapes only. It is a bit lighter and more delicate, but ordinary champagne is quite light and delicate enough.

The driest champagne is called *BRUT*. It is very dry indeed and it should come as no surprise that this is my preference. Strangely enough, *sec* in champagne is less dry than brut, slightly but noticeably sweet, in fact. *Demi-sec* (half dry) begins to be quite on the sweet side.

As with so many other French wines, champagne prices

have climbed into the stratosphere in just the past two years. In 1971 it was still possible to buy Moët et Chandon (the biggest and best known of the fine producers) for $6 or $7 a bottle, not too much for an occasional celebration. As I write, their run-of-the-mill champagnes are in the $10.75 to $12 range. It is entirely pointless even to talk of the more expensive vintage champagnes, or of the exceptional ones.

There are still some French champagnes that sell in the $6 to $7.50 range. Some are very good, all are authentic. The best of the sparkling wines of other countries are not quite the same as champagne and therefore, at least as taste-setters, one or two ought to be tried first. Many shops have a brand or two that are their own specialties. Those I am familiar with may not be generally available. You are almost certain to find the special brands of truly fine wine shops very acceptable.

HENRI MARTIN. Carried by Berenson's in Boston, it sells at about $5.75.

RUINART BRUT RESERVE. This wine is featured at Astor's in New York at $6.99. Ruinart is one of the twenty or so finest houses of Champagne, and the oldest. It is now under the same ownership as Moët et Chandon.

MERCIER BRUT. This can be found at Morrell's in New York at $7.79. Mercier also is now under the ownership of Moët et Chandon.

LANVIN BRUT '64. This is the specialty of the Vendôme in New York, at about $6.99 per bottle.

Other French Sparkling Wines

Sparkling wines are made all over France but, unlike champagne, the intention is too often to make poor wine palatable and hennce salable, not to create an exceptional and beautiful wine. None has, or should be expected to have, the quality of genuine champagne but prices are commensurately lower.

The best is sparkling Vouvray from the Loire Valley. It needs no apologies for not being champagne. It does not try to imitate champagne. It can claim excellence in its own right. If it lacks a bit of delicacy, it has a fullness and softness many may prefer. The driest sparkling Vouvray, like its still brother, has a noticeable, but very pleasant hint of sweetness. At a cost in the $5 range, it is much easier on the pocketbook than champagne and is a better buy.

Excellent examples of sparkling Vouvray are:

VAVASSEUR, SPARKLING VOUVRAY GRAND RESERVE. It is sold at Sherry-Lehmann's in New York at $4.99.

MONMOUSSEAU SPARKLING VOUVRAY. Berenson's in Boston carries this wine at about $4.30.

Sparkling wine is also made in Anjou in the Loire Valley. It is rather on the sweet side, like the still wines of the same area and, at about the same price as the Vouvray, is not its equal or as good a buy.

There are numerous others available, frequently below $4 in price. When the ultimate cost represented by tax and duty alone at retail is considered, it is obvious that they cannot be great, but they can be rather good. Certainly if you want to taste and learn about sparkling wine you should not start with these. Equally certainly, it makes good sense to try one or two, once you know what real champagne is like. Every good wine shop will have several available. You might well go by their recommendations.

One of the regions of France that produces fine sparkling wine is Seyssel, in the north. There is a noticeable difference in flavor and bouquet between their wines and real champagne but, truly, not very much. They are quite a good substitute for champagnes costing twice as much and more. Examples are:

CUVÉE DU CENTENAIRE '69 BRUT. The label bears the legend "Fermented in this Bottle." The price is $4.69 at Astor's in New York.

SAINT GERMAIN '69 BRUT. It sells for $4.25 at Berenson's.

Both are extremely dry, the Saint Germain somewhat fizzier, and both are excellent alternatives to champagne.

American Champagne

The two states that produce champagnes of note are California and New York State. The best, in each case, are not equal to the best of French champagne (I am sure the American vintners will dispute me), but the best of France are well up in the $20-a-bottle range and most of the best of the United States are still in the $6 and $7 range. Furthermore, the American champagnes are not just a comparatively good buy. They are excellent in their own right, superior to the French ones in the same price range, and owe no apology to anyone, including the French.

By all means, try French champagne first, to be sure you have the taste of true champagne in your mind. But try American champagne soon afterward. It is somewhat different, but so nearly the same that an uneducated palate may not notice it at all.

The finest come from California. Among the best of these are:

KORBEL. Korbel is better known for its champagne than for its other wines. The price range is $5.59 to $6.39.

INGLENOOK. Its champagne is among the best and, like most of its wines, among the more expensive. The price, about $7.30.

BEAULIEU VINEYARDS. Also very fine, its champagne is in the $5.65 to $6.65 price range.

ALMADÉN. Almadén's Blanc de Blancs is reputed to be the lightest of all. As I have indicated, I do not think such lightness to be a special virtue and it always costs more—in this case, a price of $6.49, compared with $5.20 for their Champagne Brut.

PAUL MASSON. Masson offers a Brut at $4.99 and a Blanc de

Pinot at $6.95. I assume the latter to be a Blanc de Blancs, made of the Pinot Chardonnay grape.

Your choice among these and other California champagnes might well be dictated by cost, or by what is in stock in the shop you visit. All are generally available. I like Korbel best.

New York State champagnes, like their other wines, are made of native grapes, largely Delaware, Catawba, and Elvira. They taste less like French champagne than do the Californias. They have a tendency to "foxiness" which, in the champagne, resembles the flavor of muscatel to some. I cannot describe it. The makers of fine champagne have done a good job in overcoming this.

Vat fermentation is used fairly commonly in New York. Most of the wines so produced are not good. Beware of New York champagnes selling as low as $2 up to about $2.89. Still, some that are labeled "fermented in this bottle" can be found in this price range and, if not the equal of the very best, they are likely to be excellent values.

Among the best are:

GOLD SEAL. It costs about $4.95 for the Brut, $5.95 for the Blanc de Blancs, and is a product of Urbana Wine Company.

GREAT WESTERN. It is made by Pleasant Valley Wine Company, now owned by Taylor Wine, whose own champagne is not the equal of Great Western. The price, $4.99.

CHARLES FOURNIER BLANC DE BLANCS. Mr. Fournier is the director of the Urbana Wine Company. This is probably the best of the New York State champagnes, and sells for about $5.95.

A fine example of the lower-priced, "Fermented-in-this-Bottle" wine is:

LAKE GEORGE CHAMPAGNE. It is bottled exclusively for Astor's, in New York, where it can be bought at $2.79. It is not the equal of the best, but is an exceptional buy at the price.

Morrell's in New York has a MORRELL'S OWN BRUT at $2.99. I have not tasted it, but knowing Morrell, I would count on its being good. Many other fine shops are sure to have their own exclusive bottlings in this general price range, from California or New York State.

Sparkling Wines of Other Countries

There is probably no winemaking country that does not make sparkling wine, but only two are important enough to us to be mentioned here.

ITALY

Italy's famous sparkling wine is Asti Spumante, *spumante* meaning "sparkling." Asti is in the north, in the same area that produces Barolo. The wine is always sweet, varying from what might be called semi-dry to the sweetness of a dessert wine. It is, in fact, often described as an accompaniment to desserts.

Most of those shipped here are the least sweet, but they are still sweeter than I prefer. Nonetheless, the sparkle prevents them from being cloying and the wine can serve properly as an aperitif. I think it is best for just drinking. Any way it is drunk, it is one of the world's great sparkling wines and is still inexpensive, the best being only in the high $5 range. Among the best are Gancia, Martini & Rossi, and Cinzano, all at about the same price. All may be bought freely. The best buy by far is Cora, a very fine brand, still at only $3.99, and not of lesser quality because of the lower price.

I recently came across a wine labeled Asti Spumante at $1.79 per bottle. Knowing what we do about tax and duty, we can fairly suppose that the bottle contained only tax and duty. It certainly could not contain Asti Spumante.

GERMANY

Germany's sparkling wine is called Sekt. It can vary from

really awful stuff, fortunately not to be found here, to some as expensive as most French champagnes, but not as good. Most Sekt, interestingly enough, is made of cheap wines imported by tanker from such countries as France, Spain, Italy, and Algeria. A little German wine is added in order to give a "German" flavor. Such wine is very popular in Germany, which also imports a great deal of champagne and other sparkling wine.

Sekt does not approach the quality of German still wines nor is it a match for American champagnes, Vouvray, or Asti Spumante. Still, that is not to say that it is not good, and some enjoyable ones are shipped here. For those who wish to try them (there are many Americans of German origin who have an undying loyalty to German wines) the following might be tried:

HENKELL TROCKEN. The cost, about $5.79.

KREUSCH GOLD EXTRA DRY. Price, about $4.15.

MATHEUS MUELLER, M & M. EXTRA. It sells at about $5.75.

All are quite similar, somewhat lacking in the gay lightness characteristic of most sparkling wines. They are on the sweet side, the last being somewhat drier than the others.

Red Sparkling Wines

The best known name is Sparkling Burgundy. The Burgundy shippers "invented" Sparkling Burgundy as a way of making their poorest, most unpalatable wines salable.

Sparkling red wine is incongruous. The very character of sparkling wine is its lightness and gaiety. No amount of sparkle can impart that to a comparatively big, full-bodied red wine nor, I suspect, to any red wine. Sparkling Burgundy may be an asset to the Burgundian *négociants*, but it has added no new dimension to the world of wine drinking.

America also makes wine called Sparkling Burgundy. I find

it no better than its French counterpart. I would recommend no Sparkling Burgundy from any country.

Italy makes a sparkling red wine called Nebbiolo. It is made of the same Nebbiolo grape that produces such great red wines as Barolo. The sparkling version of the grape is on the sweet side and is no more pleasing than its drier Burgundian counterpart.

Pink Champagne

Pink Champagne is made in France and in the United States by adding a little red wine to the white. It is very attractive in the glass and tastes almost the same as the usual white champagne, but with a slight edge of sharpness that serves to detract from, rather than add to, the flavor.

A name well known to Americans is Cold Duck, which is also a sparkling wine made of a mixture of red and white wines. A little has even been coming in recently from France and other countries. It is largely a fad. According to the California wine industry, sales are falling off and the peak of the fad has apparently been seen.

Whether as Cold Duck or pink champagne, the wine is somewhat less good than ordinary champagne. It serves no purpose for serious wine drinkers and I do not recommend it.

PART VII

Aperitif Wines

AN APERITIF IS, BY DEFINITION, AN ALCOHOLIC DRINK TAKEN BEFORE A meal to stimulate the appetite. Technically, I suppose, a cocktail or scotch-on-the rocks is an aperitif. But in general usage, an aperitif refers to wine, or some reasonable substitute. Aperitif and after-dinner wines both are usually 18 to 20 percent alcohol by volume.

It has been claimed, citing medical authority, that drenching the system rapidly with a high dose of alcohol dulls the appetite and the sense of taste, whereas the gradual absorption of moderate quantities of alcohol stimulates both the appetite and the taste buds. I don't know. I'm not a scientist.

Certainly the fairly rapid downing of two, three, or four cocktails while gorging on quantities of rich and varied hors d'oeuvres is no way to prepare for a meal, that is, not a meal worth eating. I speak as one who knows since, if I don't down the cocktails, I do have an irresistible weakness for delicious tidbits.

The cocktails and the mountains of hors d'oeuvres are an American habit, the latter (if I may wax psychoanalytical) both an overt expression of affluence and a way of keeping up with the Joneses. But how about, for once, being the Joneses?

What's wrong with serving a genuine aperitif accompanied by just enough to munch on to keep the guests' tongues within bounds? It's so much simpler, too, than the preparation of the many appetizers, a mealful of them. And no dips. The only proper use I know of for dehydrated onion-soup mix is to cook it with the requisite quantity of water and serve it as onion soup with a bit of grated cheese. It can be quite good. But not in sour cream.

So try the European way, not because it's European but because it happens to be good and sensible: an aperitif wine with no more than a dish of ripe green olives or the wonderful ripe, black Gaeta olives that can be found here, like the green, in jars; or the Calamata olives of Greece; perhaps, in addition, a can of paté, or a can of smoked oysters or clams or mussels, with a few crackers, perhaps a few Japanese rice-*cum*-seaweed crackers, such as Marukai sesame rice crackers, so good alone that it would be criminal to eat them *with* anything else.

Such a modest appetizer, consumed an hour to a half hour before dinner, instead of up to the moment of staggering into the dining room, bourbon-on-the-rocks glass in hand—iced whiskey and water with a meal!—makes for a keen appetite and a readiness to appreciate the masterpieces about to be served.

Sherry

Sherry is the most famous and, to me, the best of all aperitif wines. The name is a British adaptation of Jeres (or Jerez), the center of the region in southwestern Spain where the wine is produced. Occasionally, it will be found on a label spelled Xeres (or Xerez). No matter. The pronunciation is the same, *Herez*.

There are two basic types of sherry. The Finos are the drier wines, and they are our concern here. The Olorosos are all sweet and will be dealt with in the section devoted to after-dinner wines.

There is also something known as a Solera and you will come across references to it. Simply stated, a Solera is an arrangement, in great length, of three or four tiers of sherry casks in a bodega (a huge shed), in such fashion that the oldest wines are in the bottom tier. All wine is drawn off from the oldest and the casks are replenished from the younger wines above. In this way the oldest wines become constantly diluted by the younger, but always some part of the oldest, very, very intense, is contained in every bottle drawn off. The Solera method has come to be employed in other countries, including the United States, where wines called sherry are made.

The Finos, which are aperitif wines, range from so dry as almost to pucker the mouth, to nutty and slightly sweet. The Manzanillas, so pale they are almost colorless, are the driest. They are too dry for my taste, but perhaps not for yours. Those sold under the designation of Finos are usually not quite so bone-dry.

The glory of the Finos is Amontillado. Do you remember Edgar Allan Poe's gruesome story, "The Cask of Amontillado"? I read it as a very junior teenager. I found it genuinely exciting, quite a good many years later, to drink Amontillado and to find that it is a real wine, not just part of a strange tale.

Amontillado is a Fino that has been aged in oak casks long enough to impart to it a golden-brown color and a nutty flavor. I consider it the best of all sherries and the perfect aperitif, no matter how it is drunk. I keep it in a decanter and just pour it, almost every evening. Some like it chilled, and it is very good that way, though too much trouble for me. Some enjoy it on the rocks. I have no objection, though I hate to dilute so good a wine.

It must be understood that all sherry, in its natural state, is bone-dry, whether Manzanilla or heavy dessert cream sherry. All of it was blended originally to meet the requirements of specific customers, who were most often English wine merchants, and all of the Olorosos, and some others, are sweetened by blending with a wine made of Pedro Ximenez grapes, black, thick, and absolutely too sweet to drink in its natural state. Hence, no two sherries of the same type will taste the same, but each producer will maintain a consistency of taste in what he produces.

The next thing to be remembered is that there just is no such thing as sherry if it does not come from that region in Spain. In some other countries, for example in Australia, almost creditable imitations exist. In the United States, there is a great deal more production (Frank Schoonmaker says three times as much) of so-called sherry than in the sherry-producing area of Spain. Unfortunately, much American "sherry," at least in the past, has been the stuff winos bought for a quick drunk. Nowadays much honest effort goes into making American "sherries" but, if any really resembles sherry, I have not come across it.

For example, I have drunk Taylor's New York State Cocktail Sherry. It tastes most like a light, indifferent port. Widmer's Cocktail Sherry (also New York State) is an adequate aperitif wine, but there is no resemblance to sherry. Paul Masson's Cocktail Sherry (California) is in color halfway between a Fino and an Amontillado, is a perfectly pleasant aperitif wine, but tastes nothing like sherry.

On the other hand, you cannot accept the labeling of a genuine Spanish sherry blindly, either, since they are blended for other people's tastes or supposed tastes. A friend on Long Island has often served me the sherry of A. Soler & Cie., which is carried locally. The wine labeled Amontillado is clearly an Oloroso, a quite pleasant, light dessert wine. The wine labeled Extra Pale Dry Sherry, which I would consider the English description of a Fino, is quite definitely an Amontillado, somewhat thin but a satisfactory buy at a bit more than $2.

This single example is enough to make one understand the importance of starting the sherry habit with one of the fine sherries, even if slightly above our cost limits. The ideal drier sherry with which to start is Amontillado. There will be ample time later to experiment with the taste of the still drier Finos.

HAWKER'S AMONTILLADO. This is the one I consider best. Unhappily, except for New Englanders, it is sold in this country only at Berenson's in Boston and in the stores to which they distribute in the surrounding area. It has increased in cost in the past two years but so has everything else and, at a current price of $3.35, it is an outstanding buy.

HARVEY'S. This is the most famous sherry in the United States because it is so well advertised here. The Amontillado is excellent, can be bought for $4.99, and is also an ideal "starter."

DRY SACK of Williams and Humbert. Costlier than even Harvey's Amontillado, this wine is also better to my taste. It is worth trying at least once, as a taste-fixer. The cost today, $5.39.

PEDRO DOMECQ's Ideal Pale-Medium Dry Sherry. Generally available, this can be an excellent "starter" for a newer wine drinker. It is a bit sweeter than an Amontillado, yet not an Oloroso, and still satisfactory as an aperitif. It has the further advantage of a fairly low price, $3.35.

YORK HOUSE (Macy's house brand). Its Amontillado at $3.80 is actually a typical and excellent Fino, much drier and paler than a true Amontillado, a bit too dry for my taste. It is strongly recommended, but only for those who find they like drier sherries.

There are numerous other makers of Spanish sherry (I do not recommend "sherry" of any other country), some well known, others quite obscure and often appearing on the market for a limited time. Among the well known ones, any of whose sherries may safely be tried, are Pedro Domecq (they practically own the town of Jerez), Sandeman, Duff Gordon, and Gonzales & Byass.

Once you have established for yourself the taste of Amontillado and found it to your liking, it is time to experiment in two directions. One is that of the Finos and, if you find their dryness enjoyable, even the Manzanillas. The other is that of the less well known and also the obscure houses where far better prices will be found. This calls very much for trying and tasting. An excellent group among which to start are the less famous but very fine houses such as Wisdom & Waerter, whose sherries appear under the name of Wisdom's, Avery's of Bristol, and Rolson & Brown.

Madeira

This wine is not nearly as popular as it once was or as it deserves to be. It resembles sherry in general character, but has a burnt taste, very pleasant, peculiar to itself. This is one wine that is rarely imitated elsewhere. Paul Masson does make one but, again, it is an indifferent wine and does not resemble Madeira.

Madeira also comes in a range from dry to sweet. The dry ones, which are superb as aperitifs, are Sercial and Verdelho, the latter being a bit the less dry of the two. A blend of these two is known as Rainwater. Personally, I find Sercial the most pleasing and recommend it as a starter.

Madeira appears to be indestructible. Every good wine shop has a few, both dry and sweet, a century old, and there is no trouble finding vintages going as far back as the 1840s and '30s. They are remarkably inexpensive for such old wines, but they do run in the $40 to $50 range and only a confirmed Madeira lover with a capacious pocketbook should try one, even those a mere sixty or seventy years old and only $20 or so per bottle.

Some Madeiras are, however, within our means although there is much less choice than there would appear to be. Primarily because of the lessened interest in these wines over a long period of time (which also makes them better buys for us), there has been a more or less complete unification of the many shippers, although the old names continue to be used.

In actuality, there are just two or three qualities of each wine, at commensurate prices, and this constitutes practically the entire range of choice. However, there can be a difference in price of wine of the same quality, often of the very same label, between retail dealers. It is worth shopping around.

A Sercial at about $4.50 might well be tried first. The name of the shipper really doesn't matter too much. Still, among those considered best are Blandy, Henriques, and Leacock. If these are not available, buy whichever one is, with no hesitation, especially if recommended by one of the very fine wine shops.

Vermouth

Vermouth is a popular aperitif wine combining two characteristics quite common in such drinks, sweetness and bitterness. The name derives from *Wermuth*, the German word for wormwood, which helps flavor all vermouths. The formula for each vermouth is a jealously guarded secret. All are flavored with spices and herbs. No two, naturally enough, taste exactly alike.

There are two varieties, sweet and dry. The dry is often referred to as French vermouth, the sweet as Italian. Both varieties are bottled by most makers, of whatever country. Both are aperitif wines. The dry is straw-colored and rather sharp but pleasingly so, as well as bitter. The sweet is a deep reddish-brown, fairly sweet but with the same bitterness. The combination of sweetness and bitterness stimulates the appetite remarkably.

Vermouth and, for that matter, all aperitif wines that combine sweetness and bitterness—there are many—is an acquired taste. Someone who has never drunk it before may not care for it at first blush but it is a wonderful aperitif and it is well worth making the effort to learn to like it.

If you have never tried it before, by all means start with the sweet. It is best on the rocks, with a twist of lemon peel or a few drops of lemon juice or a sliver of lemon. Having established a taste for the sweet, next try a mixture two-thirds sweet and one-third dry, and then experiment to find the proportions you like best. Many people prefer the dry undiluted. I prefer it sweetened up a bit, about two-thirds dry and one-third sweet.

Vermouth is perhaps the least expensive of the aperitif wines. It has always come in larger than 24-ounce bottles; the 30-ounce size used to be most common. Now much of it is found in quarts and in liters, while some American vermouths are available in half-gallons as well. A half dozen or so producers, Italian, French, and American, are the best. There are numerous other vermouths on the market, some quite inexpensive.

As usual, start with one of the well known labels. They are not much costlier than others, not really expensive at all, and though no two taste quite the same, they are all authentic and more like than unlike one another. Any one can serve as the taste-setter. Thereafter, experiment with other brands and more obscure, less costly ones. The best are:

CORA (Italy)—$2.19 per liter
CINZANO (Italy)—$3.19 per quart
MARTINI & ROSSI (Italy)—$3.19—30 ounces
NOILLY PRAT (France)—$3.25—30 ounces
BOISSIÈRE (France)—$2.79—30 ounces

Cora is every bit as good as the others, perhaps even better. Why it has not moved up in price with the others is a mystery to me, perhaps because it is less well known here. In Italy it has long had a reputation as one of the finest. Whatever the reason, as long as it remains less expensive it is an outstanding buy.

Stock is a good, possibly not topnotch, Italian brand, less expensive than most of the others, costing $2.49 for 30 ounces.

Tribuno, the widest-selling American vermouth, is less expensive still, at $1.79 for a quart. Both are good but one of the best should be tried first.

Among the numerous other labels found everywhere, many are of well known wine houses, all likely to be good. Some are obscure brands, usually lower in price and worth experimenting with for anyone seeking a rock-bottom price. Many others may not consider them worth the saving, especially in the case of a wine that is not likely to be consumed in huge quantities and the best examples of which are not expensive.

Other Aperitif Wines

There is quite a variety of other aperitif wines, from many countries. A knowledge of some from Italy and France is more than enough. In general, they are all best over ice, with a bit of lemon or lemon peel.

PUNT E MES. This vermouth, flavored with bitters, was both very sweet and very bitter until recently. In an effort to make it more palatable to Americans, many of whom found its flavors just too pronounced, the bitterness was reduced. The result is a smoother, more pleasing, and still surprisingly appetizing drink. The price is $3.56.

ST. RAPHAEL. This wine comes both dark and light. I find the light, which has an amber color, delicious. It is gently sweet, with only a touch of bitterness. The cost, $3.49.

LILLET. One of the most expensive of the French aperitifs, this is also, to me, the best. It is white, delicate, and completely delicious in a large goblet practically filled with ice and with a twist of lemon peel. The cost is $4.19.

DUBONNET. Both red and blond, it is made in France and in California. I have not seen the French Dubonnet for some years. It was infinitely superior to the California, which I don't think is worth the price of $4.49.

There is a whole variety of other French aperitifs, flavored with quinine, or orange, or both, among them Byrrh, Quinquina, Pikina, and La Seine. In general, their cost is in the low-to-mid-$3 range and you can safely try a bottle of any or all, until you find what suits you best.

CAMPARI. This is not really a wine but a bitters, and it makes a remarkable aperitif. It is wine-red in color and much too bitter to drink by itself. In a Campari-and-soda it is delightful. Proportions are a matter of individual taste. One part Campari to at least three parts soda, or, better still, Schweppes Bitter Lemon, should be tried as a starter, over lots of ice in a goblet, and again the lemon or lemon peel. At $5.16 it sounds expensive but a little goes a very long way.

Last, but by no means least, many table wines make perfectly satisfactory aperitifs, especially a white in hot weather. Whatever wine is planned for dinner, if it is white, is an excellent appetite stimulator before the meal. So are the slightly sweet wines, such as Graves, Vouvray, or the less sweet German wines, many of which are best drunk this way. I have occasionally had the red wine intended for dinner served to me as an aperitif. I personally do not find it pleasing. If it is to be done at all, only light reds could sensibly be so used. A big red would not do and a fine one is too good to be drunk before the meal.

The choice of aperitifs is wide indeed. Get into the aperitif habit.

PART VIII

Dessert and After-Dinner Wines

MANY PEOPLE TEND TO THINK OF DESSERT AND AFTER-DINNER WINES as synonymous. Actually, there is a real difference. Each is just what its name implies.

Dessert wines are the naturally sweet white wines, the greatest and best known being French Sauternes, the sweeter German wines, and Hungarian Tokay. I, for one, wine lover though I am, do not care for wine with dessert. If it is fruit, I like it alone. With cake or pie or cookies, I like coffee or tea, like most Americans and contrary to the European habit.

This does not mean that I do not care for such wines. Quite the reverse. The lesser among them are lovely, though not inexpensive, and the better ones, which I have tasted rarely, are wonderful. I just treat them as after-dinner wines, and will do so here.

After-Dinner Wines

In the same way that a meal is usually ended with a sweet dessert, it is pleasant and right also to end it with a sweet wine. It is not a habit that has flourished in this country and is far from universal in Europe for that matter. Even in my home we do not drink after-dinner wine with regularity, though there is always a supply of three or four kinds on hand.

If a good deal of wine has been drunk with dinner, and some before, one is apt to feel he has had enough. There is also competition from liqueurs, of which there is an endless variety. Despite this, there is just no substitute for a glassful of the delicious, honeyed sweetness that an after-dinner wine can be, whether drunk while still gathered around the dinner table or later in the evening in the living room. Even in the TV room it is more enjoyable, and more fitting, especially after a good dinner, than beer and pretzels. It is a civilized habit that we Americans ought to cultivate more, at least for special occasions.

Wine that is merely sweet is common and much of it is low in price. This makes it no bargain. It is cheap stuff, tastes like it, and should be avoided. The wines we are interested in here are never inexpensive and the better ones are far above our means, while the best are priced in the stratosphere. There are still some good ones within our limits and not too much higher. Since after-dinner wines are also, to a degree, "occasion" wines, I will not adhere strictly to our price scale, the more so since they are not to be drunk in as great quantity as table wines and, being sweet, will lose little or no flavor for a week or two after being opened and will last indefinitely without spoiling.

PORT

The best known of the after-dinner wines, port is a product of the region around Oporto in Portugal. It is made by adding brandy about halfway through the fermentation, while much of the sugar still remains in the grapes. The result is sweet and alcoholic, but also harsh. Years of aging in cask are needed to turn this unusual mixture into a real wine.

Vintage port has been aged for only two or three years in

cask, then bottled and allowed to mature for fifteen or twenty years, or much longer. It is expensive, often requires some special handling, and is not our concern here.

Ruby port has been aged much longer in barrel but is still young when bottled, beautifully rich in color, frequently very sweet, and often with a somewhat harsh edge. It should be the least costly, but usually sells here at the same price as tawny port, though it is not as good, at least to my taste.

Tawny port is the most delicious. A good one is aged for as long as ten to fifteen years in barrel. During those many years, the wine loses a bit of body and takes on a lovely brownish tint. What you pour out of the bottle is not nearly so heavy, nor so sweet, as ruby port, and is smooth, almost nutty in flavor. It is an ideal after-dinner wine.

Port is much imitated in the United States, both in California and in New York State, where both ruby and tawny are produced. Most of it is low in cost, only about $2 a bottle, and I am sorry to say that it tastes like it. I would recommend only the true Portuguese product, at least at first. There is always ample time later to risk insulting your palate in the search for less expensive, but still good, ports.

Port is very likely to throw a sediment. It should be checked for this and handled accordingly.

YORK HOUSE. This is one of the finest tawnys I have ever tasted. York House is Macy's own label and can be found only at the various Macy wine shops. It is full-bodied, but not heavy, sweet with an underlying suggestion of dryness, velvety, and in all respects an ideal tawny port. At a cost of $3.50 per bottle, this is an outstanding buy.

DA SILVA FIVE CROWN. A very good example of tawny, it is somewhat less full-bodied than many ports, but nonetheless most enjoyable. The cost, approximately $3.25.

ST. EDMUND'S HALL SENIOR COMMON ROOM TAWNY. For the past several years, St. Edmund's Hall at Oxford University has made available some of the sherries and ports from what must be its very remarkable cellar. This is a very fine example of tawny and an excellent buy at $3.79. St. Edmund's Hall's wines are sold in New York at Sherry-Lehmann's, in Washington, D.C. at Burka's, and in Boston at Berenson's. I do not know whether they are available nationally. If they are sold in your locality, buy them unhesitatingly.

Where these are not available, try one of the standard labels, all good to excellent, as a taste-setter such as:

COCKBURN ALDOURO TAWNY. Price, $4.65.

SANDEMAN THREE STAR TAWNY. Cost, $4.49.

One of the most delightful marriages of taste that I know of is port with hot walnuts. This is a treat for after dinner on a chilly evening while still gathered around the table. (In America's well heated homes it is pleasantly warm indoors when chilly or cold outside, but we still seem to react to cold outdoors with a desire for warmth.) Merely heat the walnuts in a pan in a moderate oven for ten minutes or so, serve, crack, eat, and drink. Just make sure there is plenty of both walnuts and port.

CREAM SHERRY

This forms the sweet (Oloroso) end of the sherry spectrum. Unfortunately it is little understood in the United States. Many of those who buy it at all consider Harvey's Bristol Cream to be the one and only, and more often than not, serve it before dinner as an aperitif. There is no question that Harvey's is one of the finest. There is equally no question that one pays heavily for its reputation, $7.75 a bottle.

Cream sherry is a sweet wine, perfect for killing the appetite, not stimulating it, before dinner, but an excellent after-dinner wine. It ranges from light, delicate, and moderately sweet to so full-bodied as to be almost syrupy, and very sweet. A good one, the only kind that interests us, is never cloying and will always have an undertone of the characteristic, almost nutty, sherry flavor that is so much the mark of Amontillado.

It is widely imitated in the United States but again, with

little success. Many American-made sherries sell at about $2 and are simply no substitute for the genuine wine. For example, Almadén Cream Sherry, $1.99 a bottle, has a noticeably burnt flavor, vaguely reminiscent of Malmsey, but not otherwise resembling it. Nor does it resemble real cream sherry. It lacks the velvet, the rich but not cloying full body. It is merely thick, heavy, and sweet. Christian Brothers Cream Sherry, at $2.10, is considerably better. It has a mere suggestion of a burnt flavor and is palatable, though too sweet and without any compensating subtlety. It does not have the beauty of a genuine cream sherry.

WISDOM'S CREAM SHERRIES. Made by Wisdom & Waerter, these are my favorites. The Golden Cream at $4.49 is closer to deep gold in color than to the deep brown of heavier cream sherries and is lighter, more delicate, and graceful. The Delicate Cream, as its name implies, is literally a more delicate version of the Golden Cream. It is my special favorite, both because of its lightness and its price, $3.25.

HAWKER'S CREAM SHERRY. This is the Oloroso companion of Hawker's Amontillado and is likewise available only at Berenson's in Boston and in surrounding New England shops to which Berenson's, in turn, ships. It is almost indistinguishable from Harvey's Bristol Cream and, at $4.85, is an exceptional buy for those in the area.

ST. EDMUND'S HALL CYRIL'S OWN CREAM. This is hardly a bargain at $5.95 but it is a very fine example of a full-bodied cream sherry and should be tried if available in your area.

Among the well known labels, Gonzales Byass offers a Nectar Crème Sherry at $4.50. Pedro Domecq has a Celebration Cream Sherry at $4.85. Sandeman's Fine Rich Cream Sherry sells at $4.59. They are all very good cream sherries, the prices are not exorbitant, and choices should be made on the basis of availability and cost.

There are numerous other producers whose sherries are usually not widely distributed and often can be found only in a single given shop. Almost invariably their prices will be lower, frequently much lower, than the more standard brands. Some, perhaps many, of these are good and, since sweetness in a wine will partially mask inferiority, the cream sherries of such labels will be more acceptable even where the wine is basically poor. My usual policy is still recommended: First try those known to be of good quality. In fact, even Harvey's Bristol Cream, despite its price, might be tried once as a taste-setter. Its fine quality is undisputed.

MADEIRA

Madeira, like sherry, has its sweet examples, too. These are bual (or boal) and malmsey. Of the two, bual is the lighter, more nearly golden in color, less sweet, but by all means an after-dinner wine. Malmsey is rich, almost syrupy, dark brown, somewhat resembling a cream sherry while retaining the characteristic Madeira flavor. It is a bit less sweet than its sherry counterpart and has a great deal of fragrance. Both bual and malmsey are perfect after-dinner wines and deserve more popularity than they command.

There is not a great deal of choice among brands of Madeira. Blandy has a Duke of Cumberland Bual at $4.64 and a Duke of Clarence Malmsey at the same price. Sandeman sells a malmsey at $3.99. All are delicious and any or all may safely be tried.

MARSALA

Marsala is really an after-dinner wine, although it has for some time been relegated mostly to cooking use only. It resembles both cream sherry and malmsey in taste and is very pleasant indeed after a good meal. It deserves much more popularity than it has. Florio is the most common and is generally available. The White Label and the Golden Cream are equally enjoyable. The enjoyment can only be enhanced by the price, $2.89.

We come now to the white sweet wines, the dessert wines.

Dessert Wines

Wine can be made sweet in a variety of ways. In the case of Sauternes, the sweetest German wines, and Tokay, nature does the job via a fungus that often, but not always, attacks the grapes. In France it is called *pourriture noble*, in Germany *Edelfaul* (both mean "noble rot"), and in Hungary *aszu*. It cracks open the skins and feeds on the juice, thus concentrating the sugar in the grape.

The resulting wines are not strong in alcohol, but intense in sweetness, bouquet, and flavor. They are much lighter and hence easier to drink than the after-dinner wines. They are also generally expensive and their finest examples are among the costliest wines in the world. There are, however, a sufficient number of less expensive ones to make it perfectly possible for people of more limited means to enjoy them.

SAUTERNES AND BARSAC

Sauternes and Barsac adjoin one another in the southern part of the Bordeaux region and their wines often cannot be told apart. The best, starting with the famous Château d'Yquem, are made of grapes laboriously handpicked at the right moment. The wines are very rich and, at the prices at which they sell, they are only for the very rich. At the other end of the spectrum, wines called just Sauternes or Haut Sauternes can be found in the $3 range. They have so much less of the sheer beauty of the fine ones that they are not really worth buying. You might try one or more for yourself after having started with one of the better wines as a taste-setter.

SAUTERNES, CHÂTEAU SUDUIRAUT '67. This is one of the best of the vineyards and '67 was a fine, though not great, year. The combination has produced a wine with a beautiful bouquet, rich, almost honey-sweet but not cloying, just nectar. A delicious, true aftertaste of the wine lies on the tongue for minutes afterward. A wonderful value at $5.90.

Barsac-Sauternes, Château Rounieu Lacoste '70. A G. C. Sumner selection, the wine has a full bouquet, is not as rich as the Sauternes just mentioned, and is somewhat lighter, but sweet and lovely. It would profit from more bottle age for, unlike most white dry wines, the sweet dessert wines will grow for many years in bottle. This wine also leaves a delightful and true aftertaste on the tongue but is hardly an exceptional buy at $5.40.

GERMAN DESSERT WINES

The finest are the Beerenauslese, which start at about $25 and go up into the stratosphere, and the Trockenbeerenauslese, which are among the most expensive wines in the world. Neither is easily obtainable here, especially the latter. In any case, they can have purely academic interest for us. A few Auslese can still be found at approachable prices, but very few.

Piesporter Goldtröpfchen Auslese '71, Leyendecker. It has the typical Moselle character but is simply sweeter and finer than those previously described. It is not as sweet as a Sauternes, yet is clearly a dessert wine, light and lovely. It is a fine value at $4.60.

Niersteiner Auflangen Auslese '71, Senft. It is simply a sweeter, fuller, yet more delicate Rhine wine. On the whole, it is somewhat sweeter than a Moselle Auslese, and more costly. The price, about $6.75. It is worth trying a bottle of it—you will enjoy it greatly—but no person of moderate means can make a steady diet of it, even if prices do not advance further.

TOKAY

Tokay (Tokaj in Hungarian) is as justifiably famous as its French and German rivals. I cannot really describe it, beyond saying that it is very fragrant and as golden on the tongue as it is in the glass.

There are several grades, rather than varieties, of Tokay.

Tokaj Szamorodni is made in the ordinary way, with no special picking of the partially rotten grapes. It is the least costly Tokay and, although both a sweeter and a drier exist, both are aperitif wines.

The sweeter Tokays, those labeled Tokaj Aszu, are made in a somewhat unusual way. The normal grapes are pressed in the ordinary manner while the handpicked, rotten grapes are kept separate in open tubs called *puttonyos*. At the appropriate time, the contents of the puttonyos are added to the ordinary grape juice. The degree of sweetness of the resultant wine depends on the number of puttonyos added to a given quantity of ordinary juice.

Hence you will always see on a Tokaj Aszu label, one or two, or three "putts," which is short for puttonyos. The more putts the sweeter. Also, the more putts, the costlier. I have found three puttonyos to be as sweet as I care for. The maximum is five puttonyos.

Tokay alone among Hungarian wines is shipped in 16-ounce (pint) bottles. This must be borne in mind. The bottle price is deceiving. Tokay is not an inexpensive wine. Tokaj Aszu, three putts, retails at $4.55, which, translated into the more ordinary 24-ounce bottle, would be over $6.80. Nonetheless, the wine is so lovely that I would urge you to try it for a special occasion.

OTHER DESSERT WINES

There are other excellent sweet wines of various countries, many of them somewhat less sweet than those just described, but according to one's taste, qualifying as dessert wines. Here are a few of them:

COTEAU DU LAYON '67, Henri Metraireau. A G. C. Sumner selection, this is an Anjou wine of the Loire Valley. The Anjous, if you will remember, are all on the sweet side. This one is sweeter and, although not rich and somewhat light, it is to me a dessert wine. There is the faintest suggestion of bitter aftertaste, possibly entirely unnoticeable to some. At $3.80 it is a good buy.

An occasional German Spätlese is just about sweet enough to be considered a dessert wine.

ELTVILLER SONNENBERG SPÄTLESE '71, Graf Eltz. To my taste, it is a dessert wine. It is, in any case, a splendid Rhine wine, though hardly a bargain at about $5.10.

TRITTENHEIMER APOTHEKE SPÄTLESE '71, Bischöflisches Priesterseminar. A lovely Moselle, just barely sweet enough to be considered a dessert wine. It has an interesting dry aftertaste. I can see how some might prefer it as an aperitif. The price, $5.99.

CHÂTEAU BEAULIEU '70, Beaulieu Vineyards (California). Made of the Sauvignon Blanc grape, which produces both sweet and dry wines in California, this is round, smooth, and almost approaches a French Sauternes in sweetness. It is quite a lovely light dessert wine at $3.41.

A final comment on how to serve the white dessert wines. All can do with some cooling. It would be a great mistake, though, to chill any of them to the point of inhibiting the slightest bit of the wonderful flavor. Suit your own taste, by all means, but I would recommend an hour in the refrigerator or ten minutes in a wine bucket at the very most.

PART IX

Summing Up

We have reached the end of a rather long but I hope not too exhausting trip among the wines of the entire world. And what have I accomplished? Instead of your having to choose among two or three thousand wines, I have cut it down to perhaps two or three hundred. Well, that is an achievement, but it probably leaves you quite confused, anyway.

No need to be. A fair number of those I have recommended are sparkling, aperitif, and dessert wines, which are more or less "special-occasion" wines, and the sections dealing with them are quite explicit. As for table wines, if I knew your tastes exactly, and knew just which wines could be found in your locality, I could have started you off on your wine life with no more than a dozen or two suggestions. I have tried to make sure that, whatever your tastes and wherever you live, you will be able to find enough of those recommended to satisfy your requirements. So to cut it all down to size—

For Beginners

For the completely uneducated palate, white wines with some sweetness are most enjoyable at first. There is the occasional neophyte who, right off the bat, finds he likes truly dry wines, but he is a rarity. Therefore, start off with a somewhat sweeter, light white, such as a Graves (page 89), a Vouvray (page 113), a Wente Brothers Blanc de Blancs (page 159), a Moselle (page 142), or Rhine (page 140), a Badaczonyi Szürkebarát (page 184), or a Vinho Verde (page 180).

Just be sure to drink the white with a food that calls for whites. Don't just stay with the one sweeter white thereafter. Be prepared to go on to drier whites and reds.

You might well sample a truly dry white next. These are the wines to drink with fish, seafood, egg dishes, or chicken. You should consider a Chablis (page 102), a Muscadet (page 111), a Mâcon white (page 99), an Alsatian Riesling (page 115), a Soave (page 131), a Wente Brothers Pinot Blanc or Sauvignon Blanc or other dry California white (page 159), a Torres Viña Sol (page 173), a Bodegas Bilbainas Viña Paceta (page 173), or a Badaczonyi Kéknyelü (page 185).

Next try, not a sweet red (they exist but are pretty awful), but a light, fruity red, such as a Beaujolais (page 94), a Loire Valley red (page 110), a Zinfandel (page 155), or a Bardolino or Valpolicella (page 131). Again, in fact always, be sure to drink the wine with an appropriate food, in this case a hearty chicken dish or veal or pork, or even a blander beef dish, such as steak.

At this point, on the assumption that you have learned to love the types of wine you have so far tasted, you are ready to branch out into drier, finer, and bigger reds, and the bigger ones should come first. They can also be softer, less subtle, easier on the partially educated palate. The best to start with is Egri Bikavér (page 183) or a Châteauneuf du Pape (page 106), if you feel able to afford it. If unavailable, a good substitute starter would be a California Pinot Noir (page 154) or even one of the better California Burgundies (page 160). Thereafter, it might well be worth trying one of the French Burgundies (page 90), which are more subtle, less easy to enjoy at first taste.

The more delicate reds tend to be very dry and somewhat

subtle. Having, I hope, established a taste for red wine, try a French Bordeaux (page 83), or California Cabernet Sauvignon (page 153), or any one of the several lesser but exceptional Spanish reds (page 176).

Please note that I have said "or," not "and." In each group, try the first that is available in your area and that you think you will like best from the descriptions. Do not go on to any other in the group unless you do not like the first. You are not seeking to create a wine cellar, only to establish some basic likings. The time for spreading out and experimenting comes later.

All this will not be accomplished as easily or quickly as turning from one page to the next. It will occupy weeks or months, depending on how earnestly you pursue your own education. Nor do I really delude myself into thinking that, having found a wine you enjoy, you will resolutely not buy another bottle of it, but will go on to the next tasting. If you like it, of course you will want more of it. Buy more, by all means. If wine drinking is not allowed to give you pleasure it is not worthwhile. Just don't get stuck on it. Do go on to the next step, while enjoying the one before.

Having gone through the procedure I have suggested, however much time it may take, you will no longer be a novice. In fact, you will have learned a good deal more about wine than many a wine drinker who considers himself fairly seasoned. Also, in the process, you will have acquired a knowledge of, and a taste for, a fairly diversified group of wines, suitable for many different kinds of food.

For Everybody

Right at the start, avoid the fatal error of thinking that a real wine drinker must know and have a supply of scores of wines. The wine buff may. I, for example, always have about sixty different wines in my cellar, including aperitif and dessert wines. But then, I don't merely drink wines, I collect them as some people collect coins or stamps.

As few as two table wines, a red and a white, could be enough to make a wine cellar. That is rather extreme. Ideally, eight or nine different wines would be enough to serve for all purposes. A few less would be far from inadequate, a few or many more would add a great deal of enjoyment for those who want to begin to "collect."

Here is what I believe is needed, along with my own favorites, among which you should select for your own use the first you find that you like. Time to branch out later.

REDS

A LIGHT, GRACEFUL WINE.
Zinfandel (page 155); Bourgueil (page 110); Bardolino (page 131). Beaujolais (page 94) would have headed this list only a few months ago but the sharp rise in prices makes them less than best buys. You certainly should try one or two, anyway.

A FULLER-BODIED BUT STILL LIGHT, AND FINE WINE.
French Bordeaux (page 83), particularly Château Rolland and the Johanneton wines; Spanish wines of the lighter variety, such as the Viña Albina of Bodegas Riojanas (page 172); Chianti Classici (page 122); California Cabernet Sauvignon (page 153).

A BIG, MOUTH-FILLING, FULL-BODIED WINE.
Egri Bikavér (page 183); Evel (page 180); Dão (page 178); Torres Sangre de Toro (page 172); Côtes de Rhône (page 108).

A VERY FINE, EVEN GREAT WINE FOR SPECIAL OCCASIONS.
Any of the Spanish Reservas (page 171) (check them through, bodega by bodega); Barolo (page 128); Chianti Classici (page 122); California Cabernet Sauvignon, especially Beaulieu Vineyards (page 154).

WHITES

A LIGHT DRY WINE.

Mâcon white, especially Frank Schoonmaker's Pinot Chardonnay (page 101); Wente Brothers Sauvignon Blanc (page 159); Torres Viña Sol (page 173); Ricasoli Soave (page 131).

A LESS DRY WHITE.

Only if your taste so inclines. Since none of these is a favorite of mine, select by yourself from among the types recommended for beginners.

A BIGGER WHITE.

Viña Paceta of Bodegas Bilbainas (page 173); Badaczonyi Kéknyelü (page 185); Badaczonyi Szürkebarát (page 184); white Dão (page 178). A white Hermitage would have headed this list if they are still generally within the price limits set here.

For the heavier wine drinker one very important category should be added:

EVERYDAY WINES.

La Tarra Burgundy, Claret, and Chablis (page 177); Chianti (page 122); Gomez Cruzado Chablis (page 176); Juan Hernandez Chablis (page 176).

A Wine Cellar

The process is usually referred to as "building" a wine cellar. That sounds so laborious and unenjoyable.

Many writings deal with wine cellars in terms of cost, the $1,000 wine cellar, or in terms of quantity, the fifty-bottle wine cellar. In each case, the conception is buying a given number of wines, at a given cost, at one fell swoop, and laying them down. I don't think that is even much fun. Establishing a cellar is a continuous process, which can be started as you sample various wines and then be pursued literally for the rest of your life, as you branch out and try new wines.

The only limitations should be what space you have available and how much you can afford. If you create a cellar gradually, it will always be easier to afford more. But do go about it, on one level or another. For your own maximum pleasure and for best treatment of the wine, you should have a supply always on hand. How otherwise could you serve wine to the unexpected guest, or on the spur of the moment, on a Sunday, for example, when, in New York State at any rate, all wine shops are closed?

It is really so simple. When you have clearly established your preference for a given wine, just buy at least two bottles, if not more, rather than only one, the next time you buy. If you like it enough and cannot afford to buy a large quantity at one time but can afford to do so a little at a time, buy a bottle of it every time you make any other wine (or liquor) purchase, until you have on hand the quantity you want or have space for.

I would make one exception to this conception of gradualness. In the case of the Spanish Reservas, prices can be expected to go up, perhaps faster than with other wines, because there is so much room for them to "catch up." On top of that, they are older wines, the supply is strictly limited, and the European wine-importing countries have discovered them, too. Therefore, to the extent that you can afford money and space, buy a supply as soon as you can—if not "sight unseen," then "taste untasted." Should you find later that they do not suit your palate (I can't conceive of it), your dealer will take them back with alacrity. He will have no trouble whatsoever in reselling them.

The same really applies to Barolo as well.

PART X

Cooking with Wine

IF YOU ARE EXPECTING A LIST OF RECIPES FOR WONDERFUL DISHES, don't. You will still have to rely on your own cooking ability and cookbooks. All I want to do is to urge and persuade you to use wine in cooking.

Wine adds subtleties of flavor that transform a good dish into a remarkable one. It is also the simplest to use of all cooking ingredients. If you have never tasted food prepared with wine there is much pleasure in store for you.

There has been no occasion for many pages to refer to the wine mystique, but here again it rears its head. Tradition has it that the same wine that will be drunk with the dish should be used in preparing it. Maybe the rich can afford it. You and I cannot. How silly this really is can be best exemplified by the story of the hostess who was so determined to impress her guests and her husband that she raided her husband's wine cellar and cooked up a coq au vin in two bottles of Château Lafite Rothschild! She impressed her guests but also almost lost her husband.

For cooking, what is needed and should be used is a decent and inexpensive wine. There is a concoction labeled "cooking wine" that is sold in stores having no liquor license. This is

234

wine, undoubtedly of minimum quality, undrinkable because it is flavored with herbs and spices (it would probably be equally undrinkable without the flavoring), but presumably just ideal for cooking. Ideal, that is, if you want the manufacturer to flavor your dish for you. Never use such wine.

Any of the less expensive wines recommended here is perfectly satisfactory for cooking. Beef in the Burgundy style is just as good prepared with red Chianti or American "jug" Burgundy as with French Burgundy. Cheese fondue is as good with any other dry white wine as with Swiss wine. And, heresy of heresies, we have long since discovered in my home that a wine whose taste just doesn't suit us for drinking at all is still excellent for cooking.

The same relationship of wine to food that exists for drinking applies to cooking. White wine should be used with fish, veal, and chicken. Red wine goes with hearty dishes, usually of beef, but also with game. As usual, there are exceptions and personal tastes. Some experts suggest sherry with veal or lamb, and some dishes, such as duck, goose, or venison, which can be eaten with sweet sauces, may be cooked with Port.

There are many cookbooks devoted to recipes calling for wine. There are an enormous number of others that feature "gourmet" recipes, many of which call for wine. (Just what "gourmet cooking" is, often puzzles me. Sometimes it seems to me that it means any dish a bit more interesting than a TV dinner or "meat-and-potato" cooking.)

Here are a few suggestions, not recipes, as to how wine may be used in cooking. They are mostly courtesy of my wife, a wonderful cook.

White Wine

BAKED FISH

Any sauce for baked fish will be better if wine is used in its preparation in the proportion of ½ cup of wine for about 1½ to 2 pounds of fish.

CHICKEN IN CASSEROLE

Having browned the chicken with onions, garlic, and whatever else the recipe calls for, remove the chicken, pour in 1 cup of wine to about 3 or 4 pounds of chicken, allow the liquid to boil down a bit, replace the chicken, and go on with the rest of the recipe.

VEAL ALLA PARMIGIANA

After browning the veal, remove it, make the called-for sauce with such ingredients as minced garlic and tomato sauce, add ½ to ¾ cup of wine, boil the liquid down a bit, and then pour over the veal in the baking pan.

ROAST LOIN OF PORK

Simply place the roast in a baking pan, pour over it ¾ cup of wine for a 4- or 5-pound roast, and baste from time to time with the wine and drippings.

CHEESE FONDUE

This is a recipe of Switzerland, consisting entirely of Swiss cheese (Emmenthaler) and Gruyère, or either alone, Kirsch, and white wine. The traditional recipe naturally calls for a Swiss wine only, usually a Fendant. Any dry white wine will do admirably.

STEAMED MUSSELS OR CLAMS

This is so simple that the suggestion is the full recipe. After washing the shellfish thoroughly, place in a pot with a small quantity of wine—1 cup to 5 or 6 dozen clams or 3 or 4 dozen mussels—and a clove or two of minced garlic. Cover and steam just until the shells open. Serve in a soup plate with crisp white bread to sop up the sauce. This recipe is even better, if that is possible, with dry vermouth instead of white wine.

Red Wine

BOEUF À LA BOURGUIGNON

(Beef in the Burgundy style) This is no more than a French version of beef stew but just wine (and a bit of cognac if you like) makes such a difference. Many recipes just call for pouring wine over the browned beef. It comes out better if the beef, after browning, is removed, 1 cup of wine is poured in for 3 or 4 pounds of meat, and it is allowed to boil down a bit before returning the meat to the casserole.

POT ROAST

The wine should be used in the same quantity and manner as for beef stew.

COQ AU VIN

This is the one chicken dish that calls for red wine. It is fairly complicated and well worth the trouble. (I find that delicious, complicated dishes are always worth, to me, the trouble others take in preparing them.) It also calls for more wine than in most recipes, as much as 1 cup per pound of chicken.

MARINADES

Marinating meat can do wonderful things, tenderizing and adding flavor to it. A simple marinade consists primarily of oil (we always use Spanish olive oil), red wine, garlic, and seasoning. White wine should be used in a marinade for chicken and may be used in one for veal.

Sherry

Where sherry is called for, we always use Amontillado. Chinese cooking, in which Americans are developing much interest, often calls for it, sometimes in the cooking, sometimes in a marinade consisting, in addition, mostly of soy sauce and garlic. Even the garlic is optional.

Amontillado can also be wonderful in some soups, such as clear turtle soup, boola (a delicious mixture of turtle broth and green pea soup), if you can find it, and black bean soup. It should not be used in cooking or heating the soup, but should be added just before serving or at the table, in the quantity of 1 to 2 teaspoons per serving. It should not be overused. Too much will spoil, not add to, the flavor.

Sweet Wines for Desserts

The classic dessert made with wine is zabaglione, which consists of no more than beaten egg yolks, sugar, and Marsala—about 1 teaspoon for every 2 egg yolks. Cream sherry is a perfect substitute for Marsala.

Another delicious dessert is peeled whole pears cooked in port wine. Boscs are traditional but Bartletts are equally good and, no doubt, any good eating, not cooking, pear would serve. I don't know how to make it, only how to eat it. Look up a recipe for yourself.

Please use the foregoing only as a general guide. I am not the cook in my family. If, however, I have succeeded in convincing you that food cooked with wine is something special, and that wine is so easy to use that something special can be experienced as often as you like with no trouble at all, then my purpose has been achieved.

Just arm yourself with two or three bottles of wine for cooking (for cooking purposes they will not spoil even if left open indefinitely) and some good recipes. It will probably not take you long thereafter to discover the need for cognac, rum, and even beer in some dishes. Incidentally, the next time you serve a fruit salad for dessert (I mean, of course, a freshly made one, not the canned stuff) try about 1 teaspoon of an orange-based liqueur such as Cointreau or Grand Marnier on each portion. You will then have not a plebeian fruit cup but a lovely dessert, which the French call *macédoine de fruits*, the Italians, *macedonia*.

PART XI

Wine in Restaurants

I WISH I COULD GIVE A DEFINITIVE ANSWER TO THE PROBLEM of drinking wine in restaurants, for a problem it is. I can't. All that I or anybody else can do is explain something of how restaurants handle and price their wine and make a few practical suggestions.

As a general rule, restaurants charge you five times what a bottle of wine costs them. The restaurant's cost is the same as that of the retailer, two thirds of the retail price. Specifically, a wine for which we pay $3 at retail costs the restaurant $2 and is sold for about $10.

That seems pretty steep to me. I know nothing of restaurant economics. I realize that sharp rises in the cost of everything, especially food, have made life far from easy for the restaurateur recently, but then, the five-times formula predates recent price increases. Five times cost still sounds steep to me. One reason, probably the main one, is not hard to find. By and large, the restaurant industry looks upon wine as it does upon liquor, as a high-markup, high-profit item.

Some years ago a man who was then head of one of the largest wine importing and distributing firms in the United States suggested to me that the maximum any restaurant should charge for wine should be two and a half times cost. This would mean $5 for a wine that retails at $3. I'm sure all wine drinkers would like that as well as I would. Unfortunately, far from our trending down to the more reasonable costs that have prevailed in Europe, I read with dismay recently that some of the more expensive restaurants in France have been adopting the five-times-cost ratio.

Naturally, there are some exceptions to the general rule. The prices of the scarce greats have skyrocketed so sharply in the past two years that many a restaurant that is honestly applying the usual markup to its acquisition cost of a few years ago is selling some wines at below their current retail cost. However, that can be of only academic interest to most people.

Some of the more modest restaurants do have more modest markups. I recently had a wonderful Rioja Reserva in an excellent, moderate-priced restaurant, at a cost of $7. The retail price of that wine at the time was $3.79, meaning a cost to the restaurant of about $2.50. The markup was only a bit more than two and a half times cost, a very satisfactory price to the diner and apparent proof that the restaurant can make a decent profit on such a markup. The other wines on their small wine list were all priced similarly.

It is becoming increasingly common for restaurants to serve wine in carafes. Many, especially modest ones whose owners are of European origin, will serve by the glass. Such wine almost always comes out of gallon jugs and is usually California wine although it is sometimes imported, as in the case of a Chianti in an Italian restaurant. The five-times-cost markup is usually maintained but the actual price is low because the wine served is modest in cost and, of course, in quality.

There are also some restaurants that do not serve wine or liquor, sometimes as a matter of policy, sometimes only while awaiting issuance of a license. Such restaurants always allow wine to be brought in and they provide glasses. This is ideal for the wine lover, but is the exception, not the rule.

There is nothing you can do about prices and I know of nobody who is prepared to organize Wine Bibbers Against Restaurant Prices. There is still a good deal, though, that you can do within the prevailing situation.

When planning to visit a given restaurant, do not hesitate to phone and inquire whether they serve wine. If they don't, you will be glad you found out in advance. Bring your own.

Do not allow yourself to be overawed in the restaurant. In most of them, however little you may know about wine, they know even less. Where they really do know they will be polite and helpful and will not condescend.

Where wine is served in carafes, ask for the brand and type. The waiter or waitress may be startled, but will find out and tell you. If you are unfamiliar with the wine and disinclined to risk a full carafe—what's served in some restaurants is virtually undrinkable—try a glassful first.

Elsewhere, always ask for the wine list—and study it, especially the less expensive wines, both imported and domestic. In view of the high cost of restaurant wine, anyone of limited income should have no hesitation in ordering the least expensive wine of satisfactory quality that is available. Drink finer wines at home, where you can better afford them.

If the wine list is of the type that merely lists "Burgundy, Bordeaux, Chablis," and so on, ask about specific brands. The answer will always be forthcoming. Usually, the bottle will be brought and shown to you so that you can see vintage, vintner or shipper, and everything, in fact, that you would check when buying at retail.

Make it a habit to select wine as soon as dinner has been ordered. Thus there will be a little time to give the wine some of the treatment it ought to have. If it is a white, don't assume it will come properly chilled. See to it. If a red, have it brought to the table and opened as soon as possible. If there is any reason to believe there might be sediment, hold it up to the light first. If it is cloudy with sediment, it won't settle for days. Send it back unopened and order a different wine. There is no reason for you to accept a bottle of wine that has been tossed about like an Indian club behind the swinging doors.

Do not allow a red wine to be poured for the initial taste immediately upon opening. You might just smell it to make sure it is not spoiled. Then have it set down on the table to breathe until the food with which you intend to drink it is served. At that point, taste it and have it poured.

Of course, in a really fine restaurant, wine and the details of handling it should be understood. Only where it becomes evident that this is not so should any instruction be given, but it should be given without hesitation if it appears to be needed. And if ever you find yourself in a restaurant that boasts a genuine wine steward, just put yourself in his hands. If he is really a sommelier, he will ask (or should be told) what you wish to spend and will take better care of you than you could yourself. The food and the wine will both be expensive but, if the cost does not sour your taste, you will enjoy it immensely.

Happy
Drinking

Appendix

Bordeaux

Bordeaux consists of a dozen or more districts. The five main ones are Médoc, Graves, St. Émilion, Pomerol, and Sauternes.

Sauternes produces the greatest naturally sweet white wines in the world. They are strictly dessert wines.

The wines of the Médoc were officially classified in 1855, from Premier Crus (First Growths) down to Cinquième Crus (Fifth Growths). Many included in the first classification would surely retain the same place if reclassified today. Some would not. There are Fourth and Fifth Growths that sell today at the price of Second Growths for the good reason that they deserve the price. Price is usually a better index to quality among better wines than is any classification.

MÉDOC

The Médoc breaks down into several subdistricts and communes, each of the latter centering around a village of the same name, and all of them of importance in the world of wine.

Bas Médoc

None of the finer wines derives from here. They will usually carry the designation "Médoc" on the label. Not many such wines will be found in the United States. Where found, they can be perfectly pleasant and excellent values.

Haut Médoc

Many, perhaps most, of the greatest Bordeaux come from this region. "Haut Médoc," rather than just "Médoc," on a label is an indication of superior, sometimes near-great, quality. The characteristics of Haut Médoc are exemplified by those of the wines of its communes. The main ones are:

Pauillac

The most delicate of all Bordeaux but in no sense thin-bodied. If the number of its famous wines is any indication, and it is, Pauillac is probably the greatest of red Bordeaux. It is certainly the only area that boasts three of the giants, Châteaux Lafite Rothschild, Mouton Rothschild, and Latour.

St. Julien

Its wines are delicate and light, yet with body and almost a softness. The better ones are marvelously subtle, as are, for that matter, all of the great Bordeaux. Its greatest exponents are Châteaux Léoville-Las-Cases, Léoville-Poyferré, and Léoville-Barton. The wines of St. Julien are said to have the most consistently good quality of any of the Médocs.

Margaux

It would be more accurate to term its wines somewhat less delicate, rather than more robust, than those of its two predecessors. They, too, exemplify those most engaging characteristics of Bordeaux, delicacy and lightness combined with body. The wine buyer must, however, be careful to distinguish wines labeled "Margaux" from "Château Margaux," which is the great wine of the commune. Ordinary Margaux is usually good to excellent, but it is the wine of the commune, not that of the château.

St. Éstephe

Some call these wines big, but they are not in the sense of bigness in Burgundies or even in St. Émilion. More correctly, they are the least delicate and withal perhaps the warmest of the Médocs and give an impression of exceptional fullness of body. The most famous are Châteaux Montrose and Cos d'Estournel.

There are two or three other, less important communes or regions within the Médoc but it will serve little purpose to include them here.

GRAVES

This district is best known for its white wines. Only the whites, never the reds, are sold under the name of Graves. The reds, which account for about 25 percent of the total production, are always found under château or village names. The greatest is Château Haut Brion. There are almost no ordinary, just good Graves. Perhaps this is because the district includes the city of Bordeaux itself, and real estate surrounding a fairly big city is likely to be too expensive to use for any but the better wines. The wines of the district are quite similar to those of the Médoc, but somewhat less delicate and more powerful.

The wines of Graves were classified quite recently. However, there are no gradations, merely a list of ten specific châteaux that are known as "classified."

ST. ÉMILION

This is the biggest district of Bordeaux, with an enormous wine production. Though often called the Burgundy of Bordeaux, do not suppose that its wines taste like Burgundy. They are most definitely Bordeaux, with its distinctive qualities. They are merely much bigger and less dry (though not remotely sweet) than the Médocs and Graves.

St. Émilions were classified quite recently. There are a small number of Premier Grands Crus Classé (First Great Growths), Grands Crus Classés, and a large number of Grands Crus. The buyer should not be misled by a grand-sounding Grand Cru on the label. It may mean Great Growth but it is only the least of the three gradations. On the other hand, the Grands Crus are certainly very good to excellent.

The St. Émilions are the most popular of all Bordeaux, partly because they are so plentiful, partly, too, because they are early maturing. They are generally quite good, if not fully mature, within four or five years, where a Médoc or Graves of equal quality might need twice as long to reach a similar stage of maturity. The greats of this region are Châteaux Cheval Blanc and Ausone.

There are a number of villages nearby that are permitted to, and do, tag on the St. Émilion name, so that wine will be found labeled Lussac-St. Émilion or Puisseguin-St. Émilion. They are usually good wines, like lesser St. Émilions, correspondingly less expensive, and likely to be good buys.

POMEROL

This is the smallest of the five districts, despite which its wines are almost as popular as those of St. Émilion. They fall somewhere midway between those of the Médoc and of St. Émilion in character. The Pomerols are very soft and gentle and mature the earliest of all the Bordeaux. Most are fully mature in four to five years. The greater ones require longer, particularly the most famous, Château Petrus. Pomerols are classified Premier Grands Crus, Premier Crus, Deuxième Premiers Crus (Second First Growths, if you please), and Deuxième Crus.

SAUTERNES

What many consider the world's greatest naturally sweet wines are made in this district. This is one of the very few areas in the world where, for reasons not perfectly known, the pourniture noble (the "noble rot") will occur. It may sound unpleasant but it is responsible for wines of a honeyed sweetness that cannot be achieved otherwise.

The most famous of the region is the Sauternes of Château d'Yquem, where the wine is almost nursed by hand, grape by grape. I have only tasted the Château d'Yquem of a poor vintage year. Even that was superb.

There are an adequate number of other Sauternes which do not stand at the summit but are still very fine. Some of the wines of the adjoining district of Barsac are indistinguishable from Sauternes and are likely to be better buys.

All of this information may seem formidable, but actually it constitutes a bare-bones description of Bordeaux, a sketchy treatment that will be sheer sacrilege to any traditionalist. If it is to be accepted that the great and near-great French wines will never again be within reach of the ordinary wine drinker, then detailed, almost prayerful descriptions of their various virtues are of only academic interest to some, and of no interest at all to most. It has gotten to be a bit like the fabulous jewel in Cartier's window with the legend: $100,000 TO RICH AND POOR ALIKE. For anyone who wishes, nonetheless, to learn more, I strongly suggest one of the books listed in the Bibliography. My description barely scratches the surface.

Burgundy

THE REDS

CÔTE D' OR

Burgundies are often believed to be big and full-bodied, if not actually heavy. The fact is that Burgundy is the northernmost district in Europe making fine red wines and the lesser sunshine and warmth creates, if anything, the problem of producing adequate alcohol in the wine. This results usually in lighter, rather than big-bodied wines, which are for the most part also remarkably smooth and in all ways delicious. It is just because of the comparative lightness of the wines that the very great Burgundies are so famous for the rich fullness they achieve in a great year. There are many much bigger, heavier wines than those of Burgundy. By comparison with them, Burgundy is far more akin to, rather than different from, Bordeaux.

CÔTE DE NUITS

The wines of the CÔTE DE NUITS, the northern part of the CÔTE D' OR, are bigger and fuller than those of the CÔTE DE BEAUNE and, for that very reason, longer maturing. Moving from north to south, here are the most important ones:

Fixin

Production is tiny. There are only three, the best—Clos de la Perrière, Clos du Chapitre, and Clos Napoléon—which ever seem to find their way to this country. The wine is big, mouth-filling, subtle, and velvety when mature, and long maturing. It used to be a "sleeper," not well known and therefore a bargain in price but, alas, no more.

Gevrey-Chambertin

The famous vineyard is Chambertin, the town is Gevrey, and the hyphenization of the two refers to the wines, from very good to great, other than those of Chambertin itself, whose wine is known as Le Grand Seigneur ("The Great Lord"). It is the fullest of the Burgundies, with great intensity and bouquet.

Chambolle-Musigny

Again the village is attached by hyphen to its greatest vineyard. Musigny itself is somewhat more delicate than

Chambertin. The blended wines of the village partake of the same character and are among the more graceful of the Côte de Nuits.

Clos de Vougeot

A *clos* is a walled-in *climat*, or vineyard, and this is an enormous walled vineyard that actually takes in a number of *climats* and is really in the nature of a village or parish. The wines vary from superb to just good. They are sometimes called the clarets of Burgundy, being on the side of delicacy and dryness. They are nonetheless entirely Burgundian in character.

Vosne-Romanée

Again a village, Vosne, attached to a famous vineyard. This commune encompasses the greatest wines of Burgundy. The very greatest is La Romanée-Conti, all of four and a half acres in size. It is owned by the Domaine de La Romanée-Conti, which also owns all fourteen acres of La Tâche and parts of Richebourg and of Grands Échezaux, the latter not so well known, therefore not quite so expensive as the best known greats, which, in addition to the three just mentioned, are La Romanée and Romanée St. Vivant. The second-grade wines (second to the giants) of Vosne-Romanée are frequently wonderful.

Nuits St. Georges

Most of its wines are blended. None is very great. Many are very good. All are expensive. They are typical Burgundies, soft, fairly big, and mouth-filling.

CÔTE DE BEAUNE

The Côte de Beaune produces a much greater quantity of wine than does the Côte de Nuits, not enough, however, among the reds, to bring prices today down to our levels. The reds are generally lighter, softer, earlier maturing, and also not as great as their neighbors to the north. The most important are listed herewith:

Aloxe-Corton

Once again the village is hyphenated to its great vineyard of Corton, which is the last, on a north-south line, whose wines resemble those of the Côte de Nuits in quality and character.

Beaune

The production is big, the wines varying from good to very fine, the characteristic generally light and somewhat pale in color. The Hospices de Beaune, the local hospital, has had vineyards given to it as endowment ever since the sixteenth century and it owns some of the best *climats* in the Côte de Beaune. The auctions it conducts each November tend to set the price for all of that year's Burgundies. Its wines always sell for more than others of comparable quality, since the prices set at its auctions are partly charitable contributions.

Pommard

Pommard is one of the best known regions of Burgundy, yet its wines are, shall we say, the least good, rather than the poorest. The best have little subtlety and the less than best are somewhat heavy and dull. Because the name is well known, the wine is much overpriced.

Volnay

This is the lightest, the most delicate, and among the loveliest of the Burgundies. While retaining the basic characteristics of Burgundy, it is yet fresh and almost gay. It is way above Pommard in quality although likely to be somewhat lower in price, which still is well beyond our upper limits.

Chassagne-Montrachet

The parish is famous for its whites but it was not well known that about half its wines are red until recently, when everything began to be unearthed in the search for wine to meet exploding demand. The reds are rather big, much like those of the Côte de Nuits, but much softer, with much scent and deep color. This wine, too, was once a "sleeper," but no more.

Santenay

Its wine is much like the Chassagne-Montrachet, but softer and earlier maturing. It is by no means great, but unsubtle, easy to drink, and very satisfying.

THE WHITES

CÔTE DE NUITS

Here and there in the Côte de Nuits some white wine is made. Some is reported to be excellent. It is rarely exported. The bit that is, is outrageously expensive. I have never seen or tasted any.

CÔTE DE BEAUNE

The Côte de Beaune is an entirely different matter. If it cannot equal its northern neighbor in the quality of its reds, it most certainly produces the greatest dry whites in the world. We continue on a north-south trip, mentioning the best known.

Corton and Corton-Charlemagne

The second is the greater, a big wine for a white, with an aftermath of softness. Corton is similar in all respects but somewhat the lesser of the two.

Meursault

It is soft, gentle, mellow, and has a flowery scent. There are no very famous *climats*, and quality is remarkably consistent.

Montrachet

First and foremost, there is the vineyard known as Le Montrachet. It is considered to produce the greatest of all dry white wines. Ecstasies are written about it. I can't, because I've never tasted it (except for a bottle of the '63 vintage, a disaster—the wine was worse than mediocre), because I don't feel I can afford it. It lies in the villages of Chassagne and Puligny both. Its immediate neighbors are Bâtard-Montrachet and Chevalier-Montrachet.

I once owned a case of Bâtard-Montrachet '66. If Le Montrachet is even superior it must indeed be the nectar of the gods. Need I tell you how I felt when I opened the last bottle and found it spoiled, due to a loose cork?

The villages of Chassagne and Puligny have taken full hyphenated advantage of Le Montrachet. The Chassagne-Montrachets and Puligny-Montrachets are village wines, despite the Montrachet connection, and vary from moderately good to most excellent. All, alas, regardless of quality, are by now out of our price class.

WINE INSTITUTE LIBRARY

A Brief Bibliography of
Basic Books

Adams, Leon D. *The Wines of America*. Boston: Houghton Mifflin, 1973.
A definitive historical treatment, including Canada and Mexico.

Grossman, Harold J. *Grossman's Guide to Wines, Spirits, and Beers*. New York: Scribner, 1973.
A comprehensive treatment.

Johnson, Hugh. *Wine*. New York: Simon & Schuster, 1967.
An excellent and most enjoyable discussion of wines of the world.
———. *World Atlas of Wine*. New York: Simon & Schuster,, 1971.
Wonderful photos and maps. The text is not nearly as complete as his earlier book.

Lichine, Alexis. Alexis Lichine's *Encyclopedia of Wiines and Spirits*. New York: Knopf, 1967.
A genuine encyclopedia, chock-full of information.
———. *Wines of France*. 5th ed. New York: Knopf, 1969.
A classic.

Schoonmaker, Frank. *Encyclopedia of Wine*. Rev. ed. New York: Hastings, 1969.

Very comprehensive and detailed.

Simon, André L. *Wines of the World*. Rev. ed. New York: McGraw-Hill, 1972.

Really covers the world.

Index